With warm best ...

Oliver Popplewell is a distinguished retired High Court Judge. He received an MA and LLB from Cambridge University, a BA from Oxford University, an MA from the LSE and a BA from Buckingham University, where he also holds an Honorary Doctorate in Law. He is the author of two autobiographies: *Benchmark: Life, laughter and the law*; and *Hallmark: A Judge's life at Oxford*. He is also the author of the recently published and well-acclaimed book, *The Prime Minister and his Mistress*, the astonishing story of the love affair between Prime Minister Asquith, aged 60 and Venetia Stanley, aged 22, the best friend of his daughter.

"War is always less costly than servitude. Better Verdun than Dachau."
Doutard. J. The Taxis of the Marne (Secker and Warburg, 1957)

Dedicated to the brave Czechs whom the Western allies so shamefully betrayed.

Oliver Popplewell

MUNICH WHY?

AUSTIN MACAULEY PUBLISHERS™

LONDON ★ CAMBRIDGE ★ NEW YORK ★ SHARJAH

A CIP catalogue record for this title is available from the British Library.

ISBN 9781398414846 (Paperback)
ISBN 9781398414853 (ePub e-book)

www.austinmacauley.com

First Published 2022
Austin Macauley Publishers Ltd®
1 Canada Square
Canary Wharf
London
E14 5AA

An acknowledgement to Getty Images in respect of the cover photo showing the England FA XI humiliatingly giving the Nazi salute at the Berlin Olympic Stadium in May 1938 on the orders of the authorities in a match against a German XI.

Table of Contents

Foreword

In *Munich Why?* Sir Oliver Popplewell, a distinguished former High Court Judge, has conducted what is essentially a 'cold case' review of the Munich Agreement of September 1938 by which a British Prime Minister, Neville Chamberlain, masterminded the dismemberment of the democratic State of Czechoslovakia for the benefit of Nazi Germany's territorial expansion in Central and Eastern Europe. Sir Oliver explores the background to the crisis from the foundation of Czechoslovakia in 1918 onward, pointing out that in contravention of President Woodrow Wilson's principle of national self-determination, the new State contained significant non-Czech minority populations – the largest of these being the German speakers (formerly Austrian subjects) of the Sudetenland. He demonstrates that Hitler's motivation in fomenting the crisis with Czechoslovakia in 1938 had little to do with the German-speaking Sudetens and everything to do with undermining Czech independence. He equally shows that Chamberlain never understood this, always believing that Hitler was taking up a genuine Sudeten grievance, which could be 'appeased' by a Czech cession of the territory.

Sir Oliver acutely analyses the factors behind the unwillingness of Britain and France to stand fast against Hitler – a paralysing fear of another Great War and in the case of France, political turmoil, scandal and corruption. He condemns Neville Chamberlain for his vanity and naivety in believing that he, Chamberlain, had earned Hitler's personal respect and therefore the German dictator's word could be trusted. Particularly fascinating is Sir Oliver's account of Chamberlain's deceitful (or self-deceitful) manipulations of his Cabinet and the media in order to win support for his policy of keeping Britain out of war at all cost – meaning at all cost to the Czechs.

In 'Munich Why?' Sir Oliver has delivered a compellingly readable fresh judgment on the most shameful episode of modern British history: the betrayal of a fellow democracy and the opening of Europe's gates to further Nazi aggression.

Correlli Barnett

Introduction

The facts about Munich are not seriously in dispute. It was the final episode in September 1938 which, together with the meetings at Berchtesgaden and Bad Godesberg, settled the fate of Czechoslovakia. We have the official documents from all the major parties concerned. We have Cabinet records, Foreign Office memoranda, the correspondence of politicians and their memoirs. It is, perhaps, the most documented event in history. But that does not mean that we are any nearer to understanding the 'why'.

There were five major players in the Munich affair. They were Germany, Czechoslovakia, France, Great Britain and the Soviet Union. Italy and the United States played a minor role in the events leading up to Munich. The influence of Poland, Hungary and Romania were of lesser importance. Why, then, did each of the major powers behave as they did?

The creation of an independent Czechoslovakia and the terms of the Versailles Peace Treaty are the starting points for any understanding of the events, leading up to Munich. Why at the Peace Conference, in 1919, did the Czechs have to incorporate, within their boundaries, a very substantial minority population? Benes, the Czech spokesman, had wished to improve the frontier with Germany by including a part of the Sudetenland within the borders of the German Reich but the Allied Powers (mainly Britain and France) insisted on the whole area becoming part of Czechoslovakia. Why in the summer of 1938, did the Czechs allow themselves to be bullied by France and Britain? Why did they not call on France, in particular, to fulfil its obligations under the treaties by which it was bound? Why did they not actively seek the help of the Soviet Union with whom they also had a Treaty?

At Versailles, Germany showed little interest in the problems of the Sudeten Germans. The German delegation mentioned them only once, in passing, in its written comments to the peacemakers. The German Foreign Minister made it clear that, while offering sympathy to the Sudeten Germans, Germany would not risk its negotiating position with the Allies by looking out for people, who, after all, had never been part of Germany. Why, therefore, in the summer of 1938, did Germany subsequently find an excuse to occupy Czechoslovakia? Was there a genuine feeling that the Sudetens needed to be protected or was it all part of the long-held view in Germany that to survive, it needed to acquire territories in the south and east (lebensraum)? Why were the German Generals so supine in their loyalty to Hitler and why was the resistance so timid in confronting Hitler's expansionist ideas?

Why did the Governments of Britain and France fail to appreciate that Germany had no intention of adhering to the Treaty of Versailles and every intention of seeking to dominate Europe? German aspirations had been well documented. *Mein Kampf* had clearly set out Hitler's intentions and information came regularly from the German resistance and other sources. Why was nothing done by Britain or France to rearm or to send very clear signals that treaty obligations would be honoured? Why were no steps taken by the French to have meaningful military discussions with the Czech or with the Soviet Union or to react favourably to the overtures from the Soviets in March 1938? Why were the French, after ignoring the occupation of the Rhineland and the Anschluss, so feeble in supporting the integrity of Czechoslovakia? And more importantly, why did they seek to bully the Czechs into giving way?

The Soviet obligation to Czechoslovakia, by reason of the mutual assistance pact of 16 May 1935, depended on the French fulfilling their obligations. But why were the Soviets so Delphic in their dealings with both the Western Powers and Czechoslovakia? If they had wanted to, could they not have overflown Romania or Poland in order to have given aid to the Czechs? Why did they think that invoking the League of Nations, as Litvinoff, the Soviet Foreign Minister, sought to do in September 1938, absolved them from their obligations (moral if not legal)?

All these questions give rise to the 'what if' argument so commonly beloved of historians. If the boundaries of the new Czechoslovakia had been differently drawn in 1919, would it have made any difference to Hitler's plans? If the Western Powers had been more foresighted and more openly supportive of the Czechs, would Hitler still have invaded? If the Soviets had been involved more closely and made their position clear, would Munich have taken place? These are the imponderables of history. We know what happened. Why did it happen?

Part One
The Czechoslovak Perspective

Chapter One:
The Desire for Independence

In order to appreciate the attitude of the Western Powers to Czech aspirations at Versailles, it is necessary to understand something of Czech history. As early as the 9th century, a national, independent state was formed with Bohemia, Moravia, part of Silesia, Western Galicia, Slovakia and Pannonia. But in 1025, the Slovaks were forced under the domination of the Magyars, while the Czechs remained the subjects of the Duke of Bohemia, who in 1198, became the hereditary monarch. In 1355, the Roman Emperor, Charles IV proclaimed the integrity and individuality of the Czech Crown and complete independence from Germany. Bohemia and Moravia became two famous mediaeval states in Central Europe.[1] The Přemyslid and Luxemburg dynasties, initially, ensured independence for the Czechs until after the battle of Mohacs in 1526. In that year, the first of the Hapsburgs, Ferdinand I was elected King of Bohemia. He was already in possession of the hereditary countries of Austria and was to become King of Hungary and King of Croatia. Thus, the four states, Bohemia, two provinces of Austria, Hungary and Croatia were united in the person of the monarch.[2]

In 1619, the Czechs deposed Ferdinand II, but he then persuaded everyone in Europe that he was the champion of the Catholic cause and that the Czechs were part of a Protestant conspiracy. In 1620, the Czechs and Ferdinand's army met at the battle of the White Mountain in which Ferdinand was the victor. Thereafter, with the accession of the House of Hapsburg, the Czech State was practically annihilated and its constitution abolished. In its place, Ferdinand II imposed a new constitution, which remained in force for some two centuries. By

---

[1] Temperley, H. W. V. (1921) *A history of the Peace Conference of Paris*, London: Forgotten Books, Vol. IV, p. 238.

[2] Territorial claims, p. 5.

its term, the King became an absolute ruler, in direct control of the kingdom. Although Bohemia remained as a country, the effect of religious persecution and attacks on the upper classes, ensured that, as an independent nation, it effectively ceased to exist. Under Empress Maria Theresa, it became absorbed into Austria. Throughout the 19th century, the Czechs were subject to Austrian rule, which involved a large influx of German-speaking inhabitants. At the same time, the Slovaks were subject to Hungarian rule under which they were treated as second-class citizens and severely repressed. The legal existence of the Czech State was an historic tradition. The Czechs never ceased, long before the outbreak of the Great War, to proclaim 'we are legally independent'.[3]

Between 1848 and 1867, there were attempts by the Czechs to persuade the authorities to reorganise the Austrian and Hungarian territories and to accept a confederation of free nationalities, sharing the State between them and to eliminate the historic boundaries of Bohemia. The proposals came to nothing.[4] In 1867, the establishment of the dual system, between Austria and Hungary, resulted in Magyar constitutional law and theory, triumphing over its Czech rival. In 1871, the Austrian Emperor promised the reorganisation of Austria-Hungary on federal lines but it was not to be. He was subjected to pressure from Bismarck and with the rise of Prussia, he reneged on his promise. The Czechs did not easily forget. There were spontaneous mass riots from the 1880s until 1914, whenever the Czechs and German speakers came into conflict.

In 1908, during the Bosnian crisis, Czech troops mutinied. In Prague, a state of siege was declared. The Slovaks continued to be subject to a dreary catalogue of injustice and repression. The non-Magyar races were deprived of parliamentary representation and kept in the position of political helots.[5] Over the Czechs, the German speakers maintained a ruthless superiority. In many towns, which had large Czech populations, the local council was entirely German. Selection for public jobs went to those who spoke German. Provision of education greatly favoured the German-speaking population. In Austria, 9 million German speakers had five universities, while 6 million Czechs had one. The number of grammar schools and technical colleges was wholly out of proportion (in the Germans' favour) to the size of the Czech and German

---

[3] Ibid. p. 7.

[4] Temperley, p. 242.

[5] Ibid. p. 247.

population.[6] From 1849–1918, the history of Austria came to centre more and more around the German-Czech quarrel – "Social and economic motives forced the Czech middle class to accentuate still further its national pose and the struggle against centralism and a national bureaucracy were complicated by keen competition for posts of which the State could never provide a sufficient number."[7]

In March 1916, the Austrian authorities issued a memorandum, called the 'Easter Demands', which set out a blueprint for post-war Austria, making German the official language and the use of Czech confined to lower courts. Czech was not to be used in the appellate courts. Bohemia was to be split up into both German and bilingual administrative areas and, in the German area, only German officials were to be employed.

Wherever there existed more favourable provision for the use of the German language, these were to remain in force. Non-German grammar schools, in multilingual areas, were to be kept to a minimum and no new non-German universities were to be built.[8] When the Germans started to complain in the 1930s about the unfair treatment of their Sudeten Germans, it is not unfair to compare the treatment of the Sudetens with the way in which the Czechs were treated before 1918. Thomas Masaryk, often described as the father of the new Czechoslovak State, was painfully aware of the problem of the German minorities in a new and independent Czechoslovakia and of the vital necessity to secure their cooperation for the future benefit of the nation as a whole.

In his New Year message of 1919, he said: "Democracy is also my guideline in the question of minorities. I recognise the national principle and the right to self-determination, but in the given administrative circumstances, there are boundaries, which are the result of interrelationships and which make any straight frontier demarcation impracticable. A union of the German minorities is geographically not feasible, just as it is not feasible to unite all Czech minorities geographically. There is no other way for them, but to remain together… There is moreover an obvious difference in the application of the right to self-determination. With the exception of a few, small, frontier minorities, we,

---

[6] Bruegel, J. W. (1973) *Czechoslovakia before Munich*, Cambridge University Press, p. 9.

[7] Temperley, p. 240.

[8] Ibid. p. 11

Czechs and Slovaks, are a homogeneous nation; our Germans, on the other hand, do not represent their whole nation but only its colonising avantgarde."[9]

The treatment of the Czechs by Austria-Hungary, during the Great War, resulted in massive desertions by Czech soldiers from the Austro-Hungarian army. They had been forced to fight against both the Russians and the Serbs with whom they had ties of kinship. What has been described as little short of a reign of terror was inflicted on the Czech people by the Austrian authorities and a number of distinguished Czech leaders were either imprisoned or sentenced to death.[10] Public meetings were banned. The press was controlled, if not suppressed, though it did not prevent the existence of a nationalist movement, which operated outside the country. This movement was to play a very important part in the emergence of Czechoslovakia as an independent Nation, although the idea, before the war, of breaking up the great and time-honoured Austro-Hungarian Empire, was unimaginable.

In 1900, Masaryk became the leader of the Realist Party. It had one seat in the Parliament in Vienna. He was regarded then as a something of a religious fanatic and belligerently anti-Catholic. He shared the conviction that a Czech State could not exist outside the framework of the Austrian Empire. In his party's official programme, he wrote: "We believe that the previous complete independence of the Bohemian lands is impossible."[11] Another view in 1913 was that "the survival of the dual monarchy was assured – the power of the Hapsburg Dynasty is still the strongest element in the Monarchy; its power is still, to all intents and purposes, absolute."[12] The policy of the Western allies, Britain and France, regarding the reorganisation of Central Europe, did not initially encompass an independent Czechoslovakian state, nor the breakup of the Austro-Hungarian Empire. While efforts were made during the war to separate Austria from Germany, preservation of that empire remained allied policy until near the end of the war. It was thus a long and tortuous process for the Czech negotiators to move the Western Allies from that policy to their supporting the emergence of an independent Czech State. A number of factors altered that situation.

---

[9] Masaryk. T. (1933) *The Path of Democracy*, Vol. 1, Prague, p. 50.

[10] Temperley, Ibid. p. 248

[11] Perman, D. (1962) *The Shaping of the Czechoslovak State*, Leiden: EJ Brill, p. 13.

[12] Steed, H. W. (1913) *The Hapsburg Monarchy*, London: Constable and Company Ltd., p. 295.

By 1914, Masaryk envisaged that the co-existence of the Czechs and the Germans in Bohemia would be achieved if there were a decisive defeat of Germany.[13] At the same time, there were other plans, notably those propounded by Kramar, another Czech politician, who had, for a long time, been an enthusiastic proponent of Slav solidarity and cooperation with Russia. He now favoured a Slav Empire, which would involve the unification of Russia, Poland and Bohemia under the Russian Czar. There would be added Bulgaria, Serbia and Montenegro, making one vast centralised Slavic State, self-governing, but under the protection of the powerful Russian Nation.[14] Masaryk did not believe in the connection with Russia and only Kramar's arrest by the Austrian police prevented a serious dispute between them. Masaryk was thus able to pursue his plans for an independent Bohemia, to which he now added the idea of a system of alliances with other Slav States. He could not envisage a Bohemian State existing in political isolation.[15]

Masaryk was born in 1850. He was the son of a farmer and went to the University of Vienna to study philosophy. In 1915, he had fled to Switzerland and then spent two years at the University of London. He established the Czechoslovak National Committee in Paris. On 14 November 1915, this Committee issued a manifesto which Benes, a leading Czech politician, had brought from Prague, denouncing Austria and Hungary and demanding complete independence for Bohemia.

The Czech manifesto was signed by Masaryk and Durick, a member of Parliament for the Agrarian Party, who had come from Prague as a representative of the Russophiles. It was also signed by representatives of émigré Czech groups in the United States, France, Russia, Britain, and Slovaks in the United States. It read: "All the Czech parties have hitherto demanded independence within the Austro-Hungarian Empire; the fratricidal war (against Russia) and the ruthless repressive measures taken by Vienna force us to seek independence, regardless of Austro-Hungary...our aim is the establishment of an independent Czechoslovak state."[16]

---

[13] Seton-Watson, R. W. (1943) *Masaryk in England*, Cambridge: The University Press, p. 45

[14] Perman, Ibid. p 17.

[15] Masaryk, T. G. (1918) *The New Europe (The Slav Standpoint)*, London: Eyre and Spottiswode, pp. 58–59.

[16] Olivova, (1972) *The Doomed Democracy*, Sidgwick and Jackson, p. 29.

In addition to Masaryk, there were two other important figures who had considerable influence, particularly from the French authorities. One was Benes. He was born in 1873 and had been a lecturer and writer on sociology and economics at the University of Prague. During the war, he cultivated French Foreign Ministry officials and leading intellectuals. They included Denis, a distinguished professor at the Sorbonne and author, who together with Benes had revised the Czech manifesto,[17] and Eisenmann, Benes' former university professor at Dijon. He was an expert on Austro-Hungarian affairs and was in the war ministry. Thomas, shortly to become Minister of Munitions in the French government and Berthololot, who was then political director of the Foreign Office, were also approached. The Czechs gained access to the press through their acquaintance with various journalists, such as Tardieu, Haumant, and Gauvin.[18]

The other important Czech figure was Stefanic. He had been an astronomer in France and an explorer. He became a French citizen, joined the French air force and became an air ace on the Balkan and Italian fronts. He was able, through his extensive social and political contacts to introduce Masaryk and Benes, to influential French politicians, including the French Prime Minister Briand, with whom Masaryk had an audience. An official communiqué was then issued, announcing that France supported the Czech independence movement,[19]

Apart from the skill of their negotiators, there were other factors which had an important bearing on the Czechoslovak position. On 12 December 1916, the Central Powers made a peace offer to the Allies, which the latter turned down. The Allies then set out their own war aims. On 10 January 1917, a note was sent from the Allies to President Wilson, setting out the Allies' demands for the liberation of 'the Czechoslovaks from foreign domination'.[20]

But this did not imply acceptance on the Allies' part of the dismemberment of the Austro-Hungarian Empire or the setting up of an independent Czechoslovakian State. Such an idea was immediately denied by the Czech Union, the official organ of the Czech politicians in Prague. "We declare categorically that, as always in the past, the Czech nation, today and in times to

---

[17] Lias, G. (1940) *Benes of Czechoslovakia*, Allen and Unwin, p. 64.
[18] Wandycz, P. (1962) *France and Her Eastern Allies 1919–1925*, Minnesota Press, p. 10.
[19] Olivova, Ibid. p. 30.
[20] Lias, Ibid. p. 99.

come, sees its future and conditions for its development only under the Hapsburg rule."[21] A negotiated peace, separating Austria from Germany, was at this stage part of Allied (and the United States) policy, in order to preserve the Austro-Hungarian Empire as a Central European power.[22]

On 30 May 1917, the Austrian Parliament was summoned to meet, for the first time in three years. The representatives of the minority Czech groups put forward resolutions setting out their claims for independence. What the Czechs were asking for was nothing less than a single Bohemia State based on historic rights and national self-determination. As a result of a secret meeting between General Smuts (the South African Prime Minister and a member of the British War Cabinet) and Count Mensdorf, the former Austrian Ambassador in London, the phrase 'liberation' used in the note of 10 January 1917, sent by the Allies to Wilson, was replaced, in the language of Lloyd George and President Wilson, by the word 'autonomy'.

At the same time, a Convention of Czech deputies met in Prague, demanding self-determination, a State of their own, within the historic boundaries of Bohemia and participation at a Peace Conference. But it was not all easy going for Masaryk for two reasons. Durick, the Russophile, founded a separate National Council, thus splitting the Czechoslovak movement in two while the French, in 1916, were toying with the idea of peace talks, particularly with Austria. The French proposals were favourably received by the Austrian Emperor and would have forestalled any idea of Czech independence.

It was not only the French who were involved in secret negotiations with Austria. Others did the same. In August 1917, the Pope issued a note urging peace talks and a speedy end to the war with a return to the pre-war political situation. This reflected international concern for the conservative Catholic community, which supported the Catholic dynasty of the Hapsburg Monarchy against the ruling German dynasty,[23] On 5 January 1918, Lloyd George told a trade union meeting that the British Government had no intention of dividing up the territory of the Central Powers, preferring to grant the various nations of

---

[21] Zeman, Z. and Klimeek, A. (1997) *The Life of Edvard Benes 1884–1948,* Oxford: Clarendon Press, p. 28.

[22] Perman, Ibid. p. 28.

[23] Olivova, Ibid. p. 46.

Austro-Hungary their old wish and to give them autonomy based on democratic principles.[24]

In December 1917, Wilson had been of the same view and on 8 January 1918, he published the final version of his fourteen points setting out his peace proposals. They were based, inter alia, on a desire to prevent the spread of revolution from the Soviet Union, particularly in Central and Eastern Europe. Point 10 read: "The Nations of Austria-Hungary, whom we wish to find their rightful place among the Nations, ought to be given the opportunity for an absolutely free, autonomous development." Although the United States had declared war on Germany in early 1917, it was not until some seven months later, on 4 December, that it declared war on Austria. None of this was much comfort to the Czechs, desperately anxious to be accorded an independent status.

In December 1917, the French Government recognised the Czechoslovak army as an autonomous unit and in 1918, the Allies abandoned their policy of seeking a separate peace with Austria. At the beginning of 1918, it became clear that the Hapsburg dynasty was likely to collapse. Grave shortages of food gave rise to countryside strikes. Although, from early in the war, there had been attempts by the Allies to split Austria from Germany, this was not a policy which found favour with Masaryk or Benes because it did not involve the emergence of a separate and independent Czech State. The negotiations between the French and the Austrians were at a high level.

They were started in December 1916 by the mother of Prince Sixtus of Parma, the brother-in-law of Emperor Charles. He had been sent by the Emperor to Switzerland for that purpose. In 1917, negotiations between the French and the Emperor's Officials continued. In March, Prince Sixtus took a letter from the Emperor to give to the French President, Poincaré, in which the Emperor promised to do all in his power to persuade Germany to give up Alsace-Lorraine. At the same time, he demanded that the Hapsburg Monarchy should be preserved within its existing frontiers.

The importance of the negotiations can be judged from the fact that Prince Sixtus saw Poincaré five times and Lloyd George more than once and was received by the King of England.[25] These were not the only negotiations. Count Revertera, a former Austro-Hungarian Embassy Official, was in touch with the

---

[24] Ibid. p. 46.

[25] Masaryk, T. G. (1927) *The Making of a State*, London: George Allen and Unwin Ltd., p. 246–248.

chief of the French intelligence service, Count Armand, as was Benes, and there were discussions between Count Mensdorf and General Smuts. All these negotiations had the approval of the British and French authorities.

The Austrians also sought the support of President Wilson. The Emperor had direct contact with the President through the offices of King Alfonso of Spain and Wilson replied by personally typing his letter to the Emperor. The basis of the exchanges was that a Peace Treaty should be negotiated in which none of the belligerents would annex any foreign Nation. This was designed to prevent French expansion and may explain the reasoning behind Wilson's somewhat Delphic statements in December 1917 and January 1918 about autonomy. But in April 1918, the idea of negotiations came to an end with important consequences for the Czechs. Rebellious Nations in Europe were to be openly supported by the Allies and the creation of an independent Czechoslovakia became one of their war aims.[26]

On 2 April 1918, the Austrian Foreign Minister, Count Czernin, himself a member of the Czech aristocracy, made a speech to a delegation from the municipality of Vienna, which the British author, Compton Mackenzie, described "as notable an example of the destructive power of mere words as may be found in all history." [27] He not only attacked the Czechs for the idea of independence and for sympathising with the Czechoslovak legions fighting on the Allied side but also referred in derogatory terms to Masaryk. "The wretched and miserable Masaryk is not unique in his kind. There are also Masaryks within the borders of the Monarchy." [28]

Czernin also suggested that the French had made secret approaches to Austria, in order to negotiate a separate peace.[29] Publication of one of the Emperor's letters, by the French, however, revealed that both he and the Empress had been engaged in dishonest and treacherous dealings with their German Allies. The Sixtus' letters revealed that the Emperor had agreed to French claims to Alsace Lorraine and that the Empress was in contact with the Allies behind the backs of Austrian Officials and their German Allies. In the result, Count Czernin had to resign. By May 1918, both Britain and the United States had

---

[26] Perman, Ibid. p. 30.

[27] Mackenzie, C. (1946) *Dr Benes*, London: George Harrap and Co. Ltd., p, 95.

[28] FRUS. 1918, Supp. 1. WW, p. 194.

[29] FRUS. 1918, Ibid. p. 191.

changed their minds about the continuation of the Hapsburg dynasty. Wilson's view now was that the Slavs should no longer be subject to Austrian domination.

In the same month, there was a meeting in Rome of a 'Congress of the Oppressed Nationalities of the Austro-Hungarian Empire'. The delegates were exiled leaders of the Poles, Czechs, Slovaks and Yugoslavs. The purpose of the meeting was to show the Allies the military value of the internal national opposition in Austro-Hungary. Clemenceau, the French Premier, not only received a delegation and supported the independent movements which they represented, but also persuaded the British to give their support.[30] The United States too changed its policy. Secretary of State Lansing advised Wilson that there was much to be gained by supporting oppressed Nationalities within the borders of Austro-Hungary. In the same way that Germany had fostered internal dissension in the Soviet Union with great success (Lenin), a similar policy, in regard to Austro Hungary, was now to be adopted.[31] On 29 May, the United States announced that "the proceedings of the 'Congress of Oppressed races of Austro Hungary', which was held in Rome in April, have been followed with great interest by the Government of the United States and that the Nationalistic aspirations of the Czechoslovaks and the Yugoslavs for freedom have the earnest sympathy of this Government".[32] These expressions of sympathy, while welcoming to the Czechs, did not amount to a recognition of the National Council in Paris as the government of an independent Czech State, nor did it start to identify the basis on which the boundaries of such a State were to be drawn. The debate was whether the boundaries were to be historic or to depend on Nationality.

In May and June, there had been further expressions of support from Britain, France, Italy, and the United States. At the end of June, the French Government recognised the National Council as the first step towards a future Government. In August and September, Britain and the United States recognised the National Council to be the future Czechoslovak Government. Attempts thereafter to preserve the Hapsburg Monarchy fell on deaf ears. In June, in the United States, Masaryk had secured the support of various Czech and Slovak organisations at the Pittsburgh Convention. There was an agreement between the Americans, Czechs and Slovaks about the policies which they were prepared to support.

---

[30] Perman, Ibid. pp. 30–31.
[31] FRUS. Lansing Papers. 11, pp. 127–128.
[32] FRUS. 1918. Suppl WW1, p. 809.

There were two significant events which gave rise to this change in Allied policy and the support given, more particularly by the French, to the foundation of an independent Czechoslovakia. They were the Soviet Revolution and the exploits of the Czech Legion. The story of the Czech Legion started in 1914, but it was not until 1917 and 1918 that its influence on Czech affairs manifested itself. The Czech colony in Russia formed its own Legion in 1914 called the Druzina and in October, it left for the front.

The Russians captured a number of the Czechs who had been forced to join the Austro-Hungarian army and who were then absorbed into the Druzina. There were inevitably teething troubles. The Russians wanted the force to be part of the Russian Army, under their control and officered partly by the Russians themselves. Because they were used mainly for propaganda purposes and for some scouting activities, they were widely dispersed and were scarcely a coherent movement. The situation was made more difficult by the rivalry between the Czech factions in Petrograd and Kiev. The 'league' represented the Czech colony in Russia while, in Kiev, a Czech 'association' was set up which attacked the 'league' as being pro-western. But by 1917, Masaryk on his visit to Petrograd found that the two organisations had set aside their differences and were now able to recognise him as the sole representative of the Czech Nation.

The Russians, meanwhile, had been reluctant to allow Czech prisoners to form a unit and for long insisted that they should work in factories. It was only the outbreak of the Revolution in 1917, which now by 'Regulations for the Organisation of the Czechoslovak Army', allowed the Czechs to recruit among their prisoners and to form an army. As a result, General Dukhonin, the Soviet quartermaster-general, ordered that the Czech brigade should be increased to four regiments. In due course, in July 1917, the brigade was to play a distinguished part in the Battle of Zborov, which was part of an offensive against the Germans. It was designed to defend the Revolution and to bolster the morale of the Soviet troops. Although the offensive itself was a failure, it was something of a victory for the Czechs and it was to give them, not only, prestige but also political influence with the Allies.

This influence had not always been apparent. They had been treated as pawns in something of a power struggle by the Allies. In 1916, the French, then in need of manpower, had sought to augment their own forces by negotiating with the Czechoslovak National Council for the transfer of Czech prisoners of war from the Russian front to the west. In December 1916, the French signed an agreement on the formation of an independent Czechoslovak Army and in June 1917, Masaryk agreed with Albert Thomas, the French Minister of Munitions, that prisoners of war should be recruited for the French front and transferred to France. The Legion and prisoners of war now numbered some 80,000. However, it came to nothing because in 1917, France was busily engaged in seeking to enter into negotiations with Austro-Hungarian representatives and only about 200 troops left for France.

Revolution had begun in the Soviet Union in March 1917. By November, the Bolsheviks had started to take control. On 3 December 1917, the Soviets asked for an armistice from Germany and on 3 March 1918, the Peace Treaty of Brest-Litovsk was signed. These events had a significant bearing on the fortunes of the Legion, which was now part of the French Army.

Masaryk agreed with the Bolsheviks that the Legion would maintain neutrality while in the Soviet Union, (the Treaty obliged the Bolsheviks not to allow foreign troops on their territory) and that it should leave for France by way of the Trans-Siberian Railway to Vladivostok. Benes wrote that the earliest departure of the Legion for France was vital and added: "We shall win only on European battlefields, especially in France. If we have 20,000–25,000 troops here, we shall achieve everything in politics we want. In addition, when peace comes, we must be with our army where America and France are."[33] Not for the last time, however, the temptation for the West to interfere with the internal affairs of the Soviet Union proved irresistible. Although some Czechs units succeeded in reaching England from Archangel and Murmansk, the vast majority were stuck in the Soviet Union.

Initially, there were divided opinions among the Western Allies as to the use to which they should be put. Britain's view was that they should remain in various parts of the Soviet Union, to defend Siberia or to join up with the White Russians to fight against the revolutionary forces. Such an intervention was thought to be necessary in order to reconstruct the Eastern Front and prevent German penetration into the Soviet Union and the Far East[34]. Although, the Czechs were urgently needed on the Western Front, the British thought that there was a strong argument for their remaining where they were, instead of transporting them halfway round the world. There were political arguments also involved. The other Allies were anxious about the prospect of French influence

---

[33] Zeman, Ibid. p. 30.
[34] Perman, Ibid. p. 34.

in Central Europe after the war. The French, who commanded the Czech Legions and who were strong supporters of Czech independence, also had their own agenda for wanting the return of the Legions to France.[35]

The Czechs themselves were divided in their own views. Benes gradually realised the political importance and value of the presence of the Legions in the Soviet Union and that the stories of their military successes would be useful bargaining points in the Czech claim for independence The Soviets, also, soon realised the significance of the use to which they were to be put and ordered the Legions to disarm on pain of death. This was to cause constant problems.

The French had also changed their mind. On 2 May, the Supreme War Council decided that the Legions should be used to intervene in the affairs of the Soviet Union. They were to join with American and Japanese troops in the Far East as well as with British and French troops at Murmansk and Archangel. This was not an idea which appealed to the Czech National Council in Paris, which was scarcely consulted about the decision. The Council was anxious that if the Legions were involved in fighting Soviet forces and were destroyed, a vital bargaining factor would be lost in the pursuit of independence.[36] However, on 3 June, at the meeting of the Supreme War Council, with the Germans some forty miles from Paris, Clemenceau now demanded that the Legions be brought back to France as quickly as possible.

The legionnaires themselves were also somewhat divided in their attitude towards the Soviet forces; some were for and some were against. They decided that they would not travel north but go east to Vladivostok. There were a series of successful confrontations with the Soviet forces alongside the Siberian railway. Attempts to disarm them were unsuccessful. At Chelyabinsk, a town in the foothills of the Urals, a serious incident took place on 14 May. Some Hungarian and German prisoners of war, who were on a train, chose to throw a stone at a group of Czech legionnaires, who were standing by their own train, wounding one of them. The Czechs retaliated. They stopped the prisoner of war train, seized the offender and killed him. The local Soviet then took a hand. They arrested ten of the legionnaires and a delegation, who went to seek their release, were also arrested. The legionnaires invaded the town, put it under armed guard, disarmed the Soviet soldiers and secured the release of their colleagues. They then re-joined their train.

---

[35] Olivova, Ibid. p. 62.
[36] Olivova, Ibid. p. 64.

Thereafter, confrontations with the Soviet authorities continued. The Czech Congress, holding its meetings also in Chelyabinsk, decided that the Legions should go on to Vladivostok and should refuse any orders to disarm or to negotiate with the Soviet authorities. There were then a series of armed engagements between the Legions and the Bolshevik forces during which the Czechs occupied the Trans-Siberian Railway, captured Pensa on the Volga and other towns such as Samara and Kazan. At Kazan, they seized the Soviet State gold treasure, said to be worth some 600 million roubles. On 29 June, the Czechs occupied Vladivostok. By August, however, the Czechs started to suffer a series of defeats at the hands of a reorganised Red Army, but their military exploits had had a remarkable impact on world opinion.

"In America" Masaryk observed, "the effect was astonishing and almost incredible – all at once the Czechs and Czechoslovakia were known to everybody."[37] On 22 May, Lord Robert Cecil, on behalf of the British Foreign Office, had recognised the right of the Czechoslovak Nation to complete independence. On 3 June, the British Government declared its readiness to recognise the National Council as the supreme authority of the Czechoslovak movement and the Czechoslovak Legions as a belligerent Allied army.

On 28 June, Lansing announced that America desired that all branches of the Slav race should be completely freed from German and Austrian rule. On 29 June, the French Government recognised the Czechoslovak right to independence and the National Council as the first basis of the future Czechoslovak Government. On 30 June, the French President presented colours to the Czechs of the 21st Regiment. Benes wrote, "I felt that now we had reached an important stage in the struggle, in the victorious struggle."[38]

Balfour, the British Foreign Secretary, summarised the impact of the Czech Legion's exploits when on 9 August, he issued an official declaration. "Since the beginning of the war, the Czechoslovak Nation has resisted the common enemy by every means in its power. The Czechoslovaks have constituted a considerable army, fighting on three different battlefields and attempting, in Russia and Siberia, to arrest the Germanic invasion. In consideration of its efforts to achieve independence, Great Britain regards the Czechoslovaks as an Allied Nation and recognises the unity of the three Czechoslovak armies as an Allied and

---

[37] Masaryk, Ibid. p. 255.

[38] Benes, E. (1928) *War Memoirs*, London: George Allen and Unwin Ltd., p. 353.

belligerent army, waging regular warfare against Austro-Hungary and Germany"[39]

On 2 September, the United States also recognised the National Council as a de facto belligerent Government. On 11 September Lloyd George wrote: "The story of the adventures and triumphs of this small army is, indeed, one of the greatest epics of history – your Nation has rendered inestimable service to Russia and the Allies in their struggle to free the world from despotism; we shall never forget it." [40]

The National Council were apprehensive that the Austrian government would enter into some sort of agreement with other Czech representatives because there was a difference of view between the Czech independence movement in exile and the politicians in Prague. The recognition of the National Council in Paris, as the provisional Czechoslovak government, gave the former considerable credibility but the politicians in Prague were very suspicious of their activities.

In September 1918, a rival group who called themselves 'The Socialist Council' attempted to set up an alternative organisation, which would have resulted in a socialist State. The prestige of the National Committee quickly put an end to this idea. On 14 October 1918, the provisional Czech Government was announced. Masaryk became President, Prime Minister and Finance Minister. Benes became Minister of the Interior and Minister of Foreign Affairs, while Stefanik became Minister of War.

On 18 October 1918, Masaryk issued what became known as the 'Washington Declaration'. In it, he set out as a political manifesto, his programme for the newly independent Czechoslovak state. It read: "The Czechoslovak State will be a republic. Aiming at constant progress, it will guarantee absolute freedom of conscience, religion, science, literature and art, freedom of speech and the press, the assembly and petition."[41] Universal suffrage and the rights of minorities were to be guaranteed and National minorities were to enjoy equal rights. It would be a parliamentary system.

---

[39] The Balfour Declaration of 9 August 1918 Kalvoda J. (1986) *The Genesis of Czechoslovakia*, New York: Columbia University, p. 389.

[40] Ibid. p. 404.

[41] Kalvoda, Ibid. p. 424.

Chapter Two:
Versailles

Thus, the stage was now set for the involvement of Czech representatives at the Peace Conference, where Benes was their leader. A summary of the Czech and Slovak case was prepared by the British Foreign Office. "As regards the claim to the historic frontiers of Bohemia, Moravia and Silesia, the Czechs do not deny that this area includes a very large German minority, roughly 3 1/2 million German (34. %) to 6 1/4 million Czechs (62. %). They base their claim on the fact that this area is (a) a geographical and historical unit and b) an economic unit."

"As to (a) these three countries were originally, in the ninth century, one State (together with the Slovak country), apart from the loss of Prussian Silesia and they have been so ever since. The frontiers are exceptionally clearly defined by three remarkable geographical features namely the Bohmerwald, Erzgebirge and Reisenberge. (b) Economically, the whole area is closely interconnected. The German industrial area is dependent on the Czech agricultural area and vice versa. German Bohemia does not form a compact area attachable to a German Austria. (c) The German population in Bohemia (800,00) is much less than the Austrian statistics state (2 1/2 million). (d) Assured of full cultural rights, they will soon be content to remain an important part of the Czechoslovak state. (e) In Moravia, the populations are completely intermingled."

A further Foreign Office commentary on the Czech proposals read: "For Bohemia and Moravia, the Czech's argument is acceptable, essentially on geographical and economic grounds. German Bohemia cannot form a separate political unit owing to its geographical position, nor can it be allowed what it asks ie union with German-Austria. Economically, the real future of the Germans in Bohemia lies with Bohemia, which is equally dependent on them. It is obvious they must be guaranteed cultural, linguistic and equal political rights."[42] The Foreign Office conclusion on these claims was to accept the historical frontiers of Bohemia, Moravia and Silesia.

On 5 February 1919, the Peace Conference invited Benes, now the Prime Minister of the new Czech State, to appear before it to set out his case. In 1938, Lloyd George wrote: "He presented it with great skill and craft. He either ignored or minimised the fact that he was claiming the incorporation in the Czechoslovak Republic of races, which on the principle of self-determination would have elected to join other States. He was full of professions of moderation, modesty and restraint in the demands he put forward for the new Republic. He larded his speech throughout with phrases that reeked with professions of sympathy for the exalted ideals proclaimed by the Allies and America in their crusade for the international right."[43]

This criticism of Benes, by Lloyd George, some twenty years after the event, does not bear examination. It is clear that at Versailles, he supported Benes' view about the future of Czechoslovakia and even when Benes pointed out that there were some parts of the Sudetenland, which he was happy not to incorporate into the new Czech State, he was overruled by Clemenceau and Lloyd George. Surprisingly, Lloyd George in his book on the Peace Conference makes no mention of these reservations by Benes. Clemenceau told Lloyd George that "we cannot sacrifice unacceptable frontiers out of consideration for Germany…if by giving these young Nations the frontiers, which are necessary for them to live, we are obliged to transfer Germans…to their sovereignty, this is to be regretted and it must be done in moderation, but it cannot be avoided."[44]

Lloyd George quoted Benes: "Czechoslovakia had not fought for territory but the same principles as the Allied Nations. It had risen against a mediaeval dynasty, backed by bureaucracy, militarism, the Roman Catholic Church and to some extent by high finance… All the Nation wanted was to control its own destinies. The Nation after 300 years of servitude and vicissitudes, which had almost led to its extermination, felt that it must be prudent, reasonable and just to its neighbours and that it must avoid provoking jealousy and renewed

---

[42] George, D. L. (1932) *The Truth about the Peace Treaties*, London: Victor Gollancz, Vol. II, pp. 92–929.

[43] George, D. L., Ibid. p. 930.

[44] Néré, J. (1975) the *Foreign Policy of France 1914 to 1945 (Trans)* Routledge & Keegan Paul Ltd., p. 268.

struggles, which might expose it to fresh dangers. It was in this spirit that he wished to explain the territorial problems.

"The first territorial question was that of the four provinces, Bohemia, Moravia, Austrian Silesia and Slovakia...they contain 10 million inhabitants. The first three have been one State from the sixth century... Three times, the Czech people had rebelled, not only against Germany but also against the system of aristocratic and Roman Catholic privilege; three times the Nation has been stifled by the superior number of the German peoples... He must draw attention to the exposed situation of the Czechoslovak Nation. It was the advanced guard of the Slav world and the West and was therefore constantly threatened by German expansion.

"The German mass, now numbering some 80 million, could not push westward because its road was blocked on that side by highly developed Nations. It was, therefore, always seeking outlets to the south and east. In this movement, it found the Poles and Czechs in its path, hence the special importance of the Czechoslovak frontiers in Central Europe. It might be hoped that the Germans would not again attempt forcible invasions, but they had done so in the past so often, that the Czechs had always felt that they had a special mission to resist Teutonic flood. This accounted for the fanatical devotion of the Czechs which had been noticed by all in the war. It was due to the deep feeling of the Czechs that they were the protectors of democracy against Germanism and it was their duty at all times to fight the Germans."

Benes' argument for rejecting the German claim for the division of Bohemia was that "there were some 2 million Germans in Bohemia, according to Austrian official statistics. The presence of these Germans was the result of centuries of infiltration and colonisation. The statistics, however, were only official statistics, drawn up with a deliberate political purpose. It was easy to prove their mendacity... According to the Czech calculations, there are about 1 million Germans in Bohemia. In Bohemia proper, there were 4 million Czechs and in the Bohemian territory, alleged to be German, there was a native Czech population representing about one-third of the whole."

Having mentioned encroachment by Germans after the defeat of the Czech Nation, Benes' argument was based on economic order. "The Czech-German parts of Bohemia contained nearly the whole of the industry of the country. Bohemia as a whole was the most important industrial centre for Austria-Hungary. It possessed 93% of the sugar industry. The whole of the glassworks of Austro-Hungary was on the Czechoslovak territory. It possessed 70% of the textile industry, 70% of the metal industry, 55% of the brewing and 60% of the alcohol production. Nearly all these industries were on the confines of Bohemia in the mixed territory and without those peripheral areas, Bohemia could not live. The centre of the country was agricultural and the two parts were so independent that neither could exist without the other. If the Germans were to be given the outer rim of Bohemia, it would possess the hinterland. In particular, the mining regions attracted large numbers of Czechs. The whole country was really homogenous and must remain united."

"Bohemian Germans fully understood their position. They all realise they must remain in Bohemia... They said, freely, in their Chambers of Commerce, that they would be ruined if they were united with Germany. The competition of the great German industries was such that they could not possibly survive. If they forbore from expressing this feeling openly, it was only because they were terrorised by a small number of pan-German agitators in Vienna. It was not the Germans of Germany proper, who exercised any pressure but only the Germans of Austria, for it had always been a deliberate policy of the Austrians to set German and Czech against one another.

"Benes pledged to give the German Bohemians full minority rights and, in a memorandum, said that the principles applied in the constitution of the Swiss Republic would be adopted. He also pledged proportional representation for minorities under universal suffrage and state-maintained schools for all Nationalities. There would be equal access to all public offices for the various Nationalities and the law courts would be mixed. The Germans would have the right to plead in their language before the highest courts. Local administration would be carried out in the language of the local majority, there would be equal status and freedom for all religions. The official language would be Czech but, in practice, the German language would be the second language of the country."[45]

The question of incorporating German and Magyar majorities was investigated by Smuts. He had been the Boer leader in their war against the British, which ended with the Treaty of Vereeniging on 31 May 1902. He had, subsequently, become a Member of the British War Cabinet and had been tasked by Lloyd George to draft the outlines of British policy at the Peace Conference.

---

[45] George, D. L., Ibid. pp. 931–938.

He had serious doubts as to the wisdom and fairness of the proposals put forward. On 26 March 1919, he wrote to Lloyd George with his trenchant views about the importance of securing German involvement in the future of countries in the position of Czechoslovakia.

"In trying to break Germany in order to create and territorially satisfy these smaller States, we are labouring at a task which is bound to fail. The new States should be founded not in the face of German resistance but with active German help. The fact is that neither Poland nor Bohemia will be politically possible without German goodwill and assistance; without German goodwill, neither Poland nor Bohemia will show any stable vitality. They will become simply problems and burdens for the future politics of Europe."

He wrote about the effect of the sympathetic approach of the British at the Treaty of Vereeniging. "My experience in South Africa has made me a firm believer in political magnanimity and your and Campbell-Bannerman's (the Liberal Leader) great record still remains not only the noblest but also the most successful page in recent British Statesmanship. On the other hand, I fear, I greatly fear, our present panic policy towards Germany will bring failure on this conference and spell ruin for Europe."[46] Lloyd George ignored this advice.

In 1938, Lloyd George added further criticism of Benes: "Of the many misfortunes that befell Austria in the day of her great calamity, one of the worst was that Czechoslovakia was represented at the Peace Conference not by her wise leader, President Masaryk, but by an impulsive, clever but much less sagacious and more short-sighted politician who did not foresee that the more he grasped, the less he could attain." [47] Again, Lloyd George's views do not bear critical examination. Masaryk sensibly left Benes at Versailles to put the Czech case.

Benes realised that it was important to work with the secretaries who prepared the papers for their masters who were often too busy, fully, to digest their briefs. There is no reason to believe that Masaryk's views did not coincide with Benes' or that if he had presented the Czech case himself, his arguments would have been any different from those presented by Benes. Could Lloyd George's view of Benes in 1938, have been influenced by his own sympathy with and Benes' opposition to, the Nazi regime?

---

[46] Smuts Papers, Pretoria: South African Archives, Vol. 4, pp. 83–87.
[47] Ibid. p. 942.

The Sudeten Germans presented a memorandum with a view to proving the injustice by which 3 million German-Austrians would be threatened by being incorporated into Czechoslovakia. They pointed out that it was a breach of the self-determination principle. But they did not deal with the Czech contention that the country, now occupied by the German majority, had always been treated as part of Bohemia and was inside that realm when it had an independent existence.

Nor did they appear to challenge the view that the original inhabitants for this area were almost entirely Czech and that the Germans were a recent importation. Germany itself showed little interest in the problems of the Sudeten Germans. In its written comments to the peacemakers, the German delegation in Versailles mentioned the Sudeten Germans only once, in passing, and the German Foreign Minister made it clear that Germany would not risk its negotiating position with the Allies by looking out for people who had, after all, never been part of Germany.

Otto Bauer, the Austrian Foreign Secretary, nevertheless pointed out, "If the victors had remained bound by the principles it had announced during the war, if the principle had prevailed that no Nation could be transferred from one sovereign to another against its will, if the people of German Bohemia and Sudetenland could be granted the right to decide their own political lot by free choice under neutral control, we should have had no cause to fear the loss of those countries. But the victors no longer considered themselves bound to the democratic principles proclaimed by them before their success."[48]

The Czech Constitution sought to protect the German minorities. It provided that "differences of religion or language do not form an obstacle to any citizen of the Czechoslovak Republic within the general body of the law and in particular do not debar him from admission to the public service or from the practice of any trade or profession. A language law decreed that courts and other administrative tribunals were obliged to accept submissions in the minority language, wherever in the smallest administrative units, more than 20% of the population were minorities."

In 1926, the new Government now included two German ministers, belonging to the Agrarian and Christian Social People's party. In 1929, Dr Czech, the leader of the German Social Democrats became Minister of Social Welfare, a particularly important post at the time of the great depression. Given

---

[48] Ibid. p. 943.

that unemployment was higher in German areas than elsewhere, he was able to make a significant contribution to its alleviation. But Lloyd George's view in 1938 was still critical. "Had the Czech leaders in time and without waiting for the menacing pressure of Germany, redeemed their promise to grant local autonomy to the various places in their Republic, on the lines of the Swiss confederation, the present trouble would have been averted."[49]

Thereafter, the position of German minorities substantially improved, so that, where there was a two-thirds majority of Germans in a particular court district, cases involving Germans were heard entirely in German. But it still meant that Czechs could always use their own language while the Germans were severely restricted. From an early stage, the Czechs recognised that it was essential to incorporate the German minority into the commonweal. In 1918, Benes had had the idea of accepting a German representative as Minister without Portfolio in the new government, but nothing came of the proposal immediately. Masaryk, in 1922, expressed the view that "the Czech-German question is the most important one, in fact, the only one. Our German fellow countrymen have a right to share in the administration; in a democracy that is a matter of course."[50].

There are conflicting views about whether the Czechs lived up to their promises. Lord Runciman, reporting on his visit to Czechoslovakia in 1938, after referring to the negotiations, said: "The responsibility for the final break must rest on Herr Henlein and Herr Frank, (the Sudeten German leaders) and on those of their supporters, inside and outside the country, who were urging them to extreme and unconstitutional action. I have much sympathy, however, with the Sudeten case. It is a hard thing to be ruled by an alien race and I have been left with the impression that Czechoslovak rule in Sudeten areas for the last twenty years, though not actively oppressive and certainly not 'terroristic', has been marked by tactlessness, lack of understanding, petty intolerance and discrimination, to a point where the resentment of the German population was inevitably moving in the direction of revolt.

"The Sudeten Germans felt too, that in the past, they had been given many promises by the Czechoslovak Government, but that little or no action had followed these promises. This experience had induced an attitude of veiled mistrust of the leading Czech statesmen. I cannot say how far this mistrust is merited or unmerited, but it certainly exists with the result that, however

---

[49] George, D. L., Ibid. p. 952.
[50] Bruegel, Ibid. p. 70.

conciliatory their statements, they inspire no confidence in the minds of the Sudeten population.

"Moreover, in the last elections of 1935, the Sudeten German party polled more votes than any other single party and they actually formed the second-largest party in the State Parliament. They then commanded some 44 votes in a total Parliament of 300. With subsequent accessions, they are now the largest party. But they can always be outvoted and consequently, some of them feel that constitutional action is useless for them.

"Local irritations were added to these major grievances. Czech officials and Czech police, speaking little or no German, were appointed in large numbers to purely German districts, Czech agricultural colonists were encouraged to settle on land transferred under the land reform in the middle of German populations, for the children of these Czech invaders, Czech schools were built on a large scale, there is a very general belief that Czech firms were favoured as against German firms in the allocation of state contracts and that the state provided work and relief for Czechs more readily than for the Germans. I believe these complaints to be in the main justified.

"Even as late as the time of my mission, I can find no readiness on the part of the Czechoslovak Government to remedy them on anything like an adequate scale. All these and other grievances were intensified by the reactions of the economic crisis on the Sudeten industries, which formed so important a part of the life of the people. Not unnaturally, the Government was blamed for the resulting impoverishment.

"For many reasons, therefore, including the above, the feeling among the Sudeten Germans, until about three or four years ago, was one of hopelessness. But the rise of Nazi Germany gave them new hope. I regard their turning for help towards their kinsmen and their eventual desire to join the Reich as a natural development in the circumstances. The State police are extremely unpopular among the German inhabitants and have constituted one of their chief grievances for the last three years and this leads me onto the third question, which lay within the scope of my enquiry viz the economic problem. This problem centres on the distress and unemployment in the Sudeten German areas, which has persisted since 1930 and is due to various causes and constitutes, a suitable background for political discontent."[51]

---

[51] CMD 5847 & 5848.

He was not alone in his criticisms. Gosling, the head of the first British diplomatic mission to Prague, expressed the view in 1920, that "some of the worst of the backwoods states in South America were run on more enlightened and less corrupt lines than is Czechoslovakia."[52] Similar views were held in the 1930s by Foreign Office Officials. In November 1936, the situation of the Germans was recognised by the Czech Foreign Minister, Krofta as 'miserable, tragic and lamentable.'[53]. In 1937, Benes accepted that the faults on the Czech side had been very great.[54] In May 1938, Mastny, the Czech minister in Berlin agreed that the Czechs had neglected their duty to the Sudeten Germans for 20 years.[55]

But however, the Czechs treated the German minorities, is it realistic to believe that Hitler would not have sought to use the problem of the Sudeten Germans as an excuse to expand (as Benes had foreseen in 1919) towards the south and east. Whatever the Czechs may or may not have done, the position of the minorities was not (contrary to Lloyd George's view) the reason for Hitler seeking to swallow up Czechoslovakia.

In the summer of 1932, in a private conversation, Hitler expressed the view that "we can never carry through a great policy without a core of power – a core of 80 – 100 million Germans living in a compact area. My first task, therefore, will consist in creating this core, which will not only make us invincible but also, once and for all, ensure our decisive supremacy overall European nations – Bohemia and Moravia belong to this core – today all these regions are inhabited by a majority of foreign tribes. It will be our duty, if we want to lay sound foundations for a Great Reich, to remove these tribes. The Bohemian-Moravian plain and the eastern regions bordering Germany will be resettled with German peasants. We shall transplant the Czechs from Bohemia to Siberia or the Volhynian regions, we shall allocate reservations to them in the new Federal states, the Czechs must get out of Central Europe."[56] If confirmation were needed that this was Hitler's fixed determination, it is to be found in the Hossbach

---

[52] DBFP series 1, Vol. V1, no. 406.

[53] DDF series 2, Tom II, no 505.

[54] DBFP series 2, Vol. XVIII, no 185.

[55] DGFP series D, Vol. II, no 170.

[56] Rauschning, H. (1939) *Hitler Speaks (Trans)*, London: Thornton Butterworth Ltd., pp. 41–43.

Memorandum, which (as will be seen) made it clear that the Sudeten Germans were merely an excuse to expand East.[57]

That the Czechs were anxious at the Peace Conference not to have to incorporate all the Sudeten Germans into Czechoslovakia is clear. A French expert, General Lerond, had indeed proposed this course, which would have excluded some 800,00 Germans who ultimately became Czech citizens. This idea, it would appear, was initially accepted by the British and American experts. But, although Wilson was unhappy about the Eger Karlsbad sector being given to the Czechs, he was eventually persuaded by the historic frontier argument so to do.[58]

On 23 February 1936, Benes had said that "Czechoslovakia had received a small piece of German territory…but he had advocated that in exchange, Germany should receive a far larger portion of Bohemia with a population many times greater than that of the small Hultschin territory." Lloyd George had told him that he was unable to understand this and had frustrated the plan.[59] In October 1937, Benes wrote an article in a similar vein.[60] He seems to have intended to include in the Reich, Eger and Asch as well as two salient in Saxony and Silesia, namely Rumburg, which had 100,000 inhabitants and Friedland. But, in the result, Eger remained in Czech hands. On 14 September 1938, Benes told Newton, the British Minister in Prague, that he, Benes, had been in favour of excluding some of Sudeten Germany from incorporation but that "the suggestion had never been seriously discussed nor had it been agreed to by the other members of the delegation"[61] On 16 September, it appeared to Newton, as if the Czechs were prepared to give up Egerland and other areas, 'as the inclusion of those areas at the Peace Conference had hardly been expected'.[62]

On 18 September, the French drew to the attention of the Czechs the fact that at the Peace Conference, Masaryk and Benes had wished to improve their frontier with Germany by including a part of the Sudetenland within the borders of the Reich, but the Allied Powers had insisted on the whole area becoming part

---

[57] DGFP series D, Vol. I, no 19.

[58] Seymour, C. (1938) *Czechoslovak Frontiers*, Yale Review, Vol. XXVIII, pp. 284–285.

[59] DGFP series C, Vol. IV, no 580.

[60] Prager Presse, 14 October 1937.

[61] DBFP series 3, Vol. II, no 888.

[62] Ibid. no 902.

of Czechoslovakia.[63] Benes told Bruce Lockhart that at the Peace Conference that he and Masaryk had wished to leave at least part of the Eger district to Germany but that the Allied Powers had insisted on including it in the New Republic.[64] On another occasion when Benes was asked whether the historical boundaries of Bohemia, north and west, must be maintained or whether some adjustment would be acceptable, he had to admit that "it should not prove disastrous to trim that line at certain points giving the Eger, Friedland and Schlucknow areas to Germany."[65]

On 2 May 1938, Jan Masaryk, the Czech Minister in London, had seen Lord Halifax, now the British Foreign Secretary, and said that "his father, the old President, had never wished to have the Sudetens in Czechoslovakia but that Lloyd George had insisted on their being incorporated."[66] On 5 October 1938, Harold Nicolson MP spoke in the House of Commons in the Munich debate: "I remember that on that very frontier, which is now in our minds, spending hours of my time with my American opposite number, trying to work out a scheme which we did work out and a very good scheme under which the Eger and Asch areas were given to Germany. We worked that out and we went to our chiefs (ie Lloyd George and Wilson) who both of them said, 'But you are mad. You were going to give Germany territory for having made war against us. It was never German territory. Germany will come out of this war with an acquisition of territory which is Bohemia. And of course, it was impossible to get the plan through.'"[67]

The reason why the Allies insisted on an arrangement which self-evidently, was going to be divisive and which, there was reason to believe, the Czechs did not wholly support was the result of a dispute at Versailles between the Americans and the French. The Americans objected to the whole method of drawing frontier lines on strategic principles and suggested plebiscites in disputed areas. Benes to placate them, offered to give up the territories around

---

[63] Ripka, H. (1939) *Munich: Before and After*, London: Victor Gollancz, p. 86.

[64] Lockhart, R. H. B. (1938) *Guns and Butter*, London: Putnam, p. 305.

[65] Hitchcock, E. B. (1940) *"I Built a Temple for Peace": The Life of Edward Benes*, New York: Harper Bros, p. 180.

[66] Harvey, J. (ed.) (1970) *The Diplomatic Diaries of Oliver Harvey 1937–1940*, London: Collins, p. 135.

[67] House of Commons. Official Report Fifth Series no 339 col 429. 5 October 1938

Friedland and to make concessions in the Eger district. The French refused and were joined by the British and Italians.[68]

The Americans pointed out that by excluding the salients of Rumburg and Eger from Czechoslovakia, Bohemia would enjoy excellent natural frontiers, would suffer no economic inconvenience and would be free of 30,000 persons of German blood whose influence in the Czechoslovak State might lead to grave difficulties. While the delegates were willing to make certain minor rectifications, to which the Czechs themselves agreed, the commission by three to one voted against the idea.

William Bullitt, subsequently, United States Ambassador to France between 1936 and 1940, was one of the members of the United States commission at Versailles. He had pointed out to Wilson that the Treaty, with other flaws, left 3 million Germans under Czech rule. In his resignation letter, he wrote: "But our Government has now consented to deliver the suffering peoples of the world to new oppression, subjection, and dismemberments – a new century of war." He added: "This isn't a Treaty of peace. I can see at least eleven wars in it."[69] But even if the council of four had accepted all the suggestions, over 2 million Germans would still have been included in the new State.[70] And whatever arguments may be raised about the arrangements, which had been made at Versailles, they are all entirely academic since Hitler was interested only in securing the incorporation of Czechoslovakia into the Third Reich.

[68] FRUS Peace Conference IV. pp 543–546.

[69] Brownell, W. and Billings, R. (1987) *So Close to Greatness: A Biography of William C. Bullitt*, New York: Macmillan, p. 94.

[70] Seymour, Ibid. pp. 283–285.

Chapter Three:
The Search for Security

Once the conflict was over there was a search for peace. Nowhere was this desire stronger than in Prague. But first, the effects of the Soviet Revolution had to be dealt with. In May 1919, the Hungarian Soviet Republic invaded and occupied the whole of Eastern Slovakia. In June, a Slovak Soviet Republic was proclaimed in Preslov and later in the same month, a Slovak Revolutionary Soviet government was set up. This gave rise to a political crisis, both internationally and domestically. The fledgling Czech Government was divided. The Communists, strengthened by the return of prisoners of war, who had been serving in the Soviet Union, gradually moved away from the Social Democratic Party and, under Smeral, wanted to adopt a policy of turning Czechoslovakia into a socialist State. However, under the threat of Hungarian sponsored invasion, the Communists remained neutral. Martial law was declared. Wilson and Clemenceau ordered the Hungarians to withdraw. This they did, but Czech relations with Hungary never fully recovered.

The result was to reinforce the power of the 'Castle group' under Masaryk, whose programme was based on political, economic and social democracy. Pilloried, as a bourgeois-democratic movement, it was, for the next twenty years, closely linked with the Versailles system.[71] The events at Munich, therefore, were to provide the Czechs with a real shock. In April 1920, the result of the General Election was a defeat for the right and victory for the Social Democrats. But it was something of a pyrrhic victory for Masaryk.

Left-wing elements in the party demanded a revolutionary policy with the replacement of a bourgeois approach by a socialist republic. But events elsewhere intervened which were to have a profound effect on domestic Czech

---

[71] Olivova, Ibid. p. 117.

politics. In the same month, the Polish Army equipped and commanded by the French, again sought to defeat the Bolshevik Army. They were unsuccessful and the Red Army stood at the gates of Warsaw. From this imbroglio, the Czechs stood aside. But in Slovakia there were problems. The Hungarians in their effort to help the Poles were proposing to march into Slovakia. However. as a result of martial law and the presence of Czech soldiers, the Czech Government was able to stop the Hungarians and put an end to the upsurge of revolutionary movements in Slovakia.

At the same time, as a result of negotiations, normal relations between the Soviet Union and Czechoslovakia were re-established. In September 1920, the Czechs formed a Caretaker Government under the Prime Minister, Czerny, which included a wide political balance and in particular, a strong German element. Initially, the Germans (in exile) had taken up a firm position of opposition to the Czechs but those in Prague were prepared to cooperate. Czech Foreign policy had been spelt out by Benes in a speech made after the signing of the Versailles Treaty. "It so happens that our country will always be at the crossroads of three important influences: Western, German and Russian. We must, of necessity, try and create out of them, a milieu in which we will never become the instrument of any one of them in which we shall be able to maintain our highly important position to create our own political thought, a high culture, and to remain genuinely ourselves. We must be aware of these three influences and our European or perhaps, I should say world situation."

In the quest for security, the Czechs took further steps. In 1920, a trade agreement with the German Social Democratic Government was signed. In 1921, the 'Little Entente' was created by the French. It was an alliance between countries in Eastern Europe consisting of Poland, Czechoslovakia, Romania and Yugoslavia. It was designed by the French to provide some form of protection against aggression in Eastern Europe by way of a defensive alliance. It proved effective once in 1921, when an attempt by Charles to become Emperor of Hungary again, was thwarted by its members. Shortly after the Treaty of St. Germain in September 1919, the Presidents of Austria and Czechoslovakia exchanged visits and in December 1921, they agreed on a pact of friendship involving economic cooperation and compulsory arbitration of any disputes, which could not be settled by diplomatic means. In 1922, a provisional agreement was signed with the Soviet Union, involving de facto recognition of the Soviet Union.

In 1924, the Czechs and the French entered into a Treaty of alliance and friendship. It provided for 'both sides to concert their actions in all matters of foreign policy, which threatened their security or undermined the new order in Europe and to agree on measures to safeguard common interests'. It was thus a somewhat flexible agreement, which bound neither party to do very much. No agreement on how to safeguard common interests was reached except that in another article, it was provided that there should be joint action to prevent the restoration of the Habsburg or Hohenzollern dynasty. It also endorsed the veto on an Austrian Anschluss with Germany. Provision was made for joint consultations over defence and for collaboration of the General Staffs, which merely involved the exchange of military attaches in Prague and Paris.[72] One of the reasons for what happened at Munich can be traced to the failure of this collaboration. Unfortunately, France's borders were nowhere contiguous with those of the members of the Little Entente and, in any case, the French military was bent on a strategic doctrine, which was wholly defensive in character.[73] Further, relations with the Poles (save for a short period after Locarno) and with the Hungarians were never anything but cold.

In the same year, together with France and Greece, the Czechs drew up the Geneva Protocol. This was designed to give force to the policy of collective security but fell afoul of the incoming British Government in 1925 and was rejected. British policy then, and subsequently, was to avoid, at all costs, any involvement with the Eastern European bloc. Austen Chamberlain, then British Foreign Secretary, explained his Government's view when on 4 January 1925, he wrote: "It is one thing to defend the Channel on the eastern frontiers of the Low Countries and France. It is quite another to guarantee the very unstable situation in Eastern Europe which the Peace Treaties 'Balkanised' with a vengeance."[74] Meanwhile, on 16 April 1924, at Rapallo, the Germans and the Soviets signed a Treaty governing diplomatic relations as well as trade and mutual claims. In addition, they concluded a secret Treaty on military cooperation.

Thereafter the four great powers, Germany, France Britain and Italy, bypassing the League of Nations, entered into the Locarno Treaty to which the members of the Little Entente were not party. The British in particular were

---

[72] DBFP series I, Vol. XXVI, no 23.

[73] Zeman, Ibid. p. 77.

[74] DBFP series I, Vol, XXVII, no 180.

critical of the provisions of the Versailles Treaty and were anxious to listen with sympathetic ears to those who pointed out the inconsistencies involved therein and to the claims for revision of the territorial settlements. It was intended that the cooperation of the Great Powers would be the guarantee of peace. For the Czechs, effectively excluded from the discussions and not a party to the agreement, it was something of a bombshell. Germany was now no longer a vanquished nation but, with the resurgence of militarism and relieved by the Dawes plan of some of its reparation obligations, it was to be treated on an equal footing with the Western powers.

In 1926, Germany was admitted to the League of Nations. In order to accommodate the Germans, Benes gave up the permanent seat occupied by the Czechs and opted to share one seat allocated to members of the Little Entente. No one thereafter could have criticised the Czechs for their attitude towards Germany. The Czechs feared not only the economic power of Germany but also its political revival. Locarno changed the political map so that the position of the Czechs was fundamentally altered to their detriment. As Stresemann, the German Foreign Minister, observed in his diary (referring to Locarno): "Messrs Benes and Skrzynski (the Polish Prime Minister) had to sit in the next room until we let them in. Such was the position of countries, hitherto riding high because they had been the servants of others, who dropped them the minute they believed they could reach an understanding with Germany."[75] The main provisions of Locarno were that Germany guaranteed the borders in the West and signed arbitration Treaties. But so far as the East was concerned, though there were arbitration agreements with Poland and Czechoslovakia, any territorial guarantees were noticeably absent.

The Little Entente's attitude towards Germany did not secure universal approval among its members but they all took steps to alleviate the divisive effect of Locarno. For the Czechs, the most important and far-reaching step was to negotiate, in 1925, a Treaty of guarantee with France, whereby the latter undertook 'immediately to lend aid and assistance' in case of unprovoked aggression against Czechoslovakia. It was on this Treaty that the Czechs based their expectation, in 1938, that the French would honour their obligations into which they had so freely entered. Except under the general provisions of the League of Nations Covenant, no other country had such a binding obligation to

---

[75] Stresemann, Gustav. Vermachtnis. (Berlin 1932) ii p. 243.

the Czechs. In 1935, the Czechs entered into a similar treaty with the Soviets, whose support was conditional only on the French first fulfilling its obligations, under their 1925 Treaty.

Benes' view in 1924, had been that peace could only be maintained by reliance both on the League of Nations and more importantly on the Anglo-French Entente. He said in a speech to the foreign affairs committee of the Czechoslovak Parliament on 6 February: "The Anglo-French alliance in the difficult times in which we now live, means peace and quiet in Europe, means that all other countries have to group around this bloc and means the extension of that alliance into an all-European Entente."[76]

The effect of these international agreements was felt domestically. In the elections in November 1925, Masaryk's Social Democrats suffered a serious defeat with most of the votes going to the Agrarian party and the Communists. The Agrarians favoured a closer relationship with the Germans and a retreat from the Little Entente policy. The Communists wanted full recognition of the Soviet Union and 'Soviet friendly' policy. An attempt by the fascists to force a coup was unsuccessful and they ceased to be a serious force in Czech politics until the victory in 1935 of the Sudetendeutsche Partei (SdP).

The new Government accepted German representatives as Ministers and the German Foreign Ministry acknowledged the right of the Czechs to administer the Sudeten German area. Serious attempts were made to accommodate the German minorities into the Czech State as the constitution provided. While rejecting attempts to foster closer ties with the Soviet Union, it sought closer cooperation with Stresemann's Germany. All, however, came to a halt with his death in 1929. The economic crisis which followed caused major divisions between the Sudeten Germans and Czechs, so that by the end of the 1920s, Czech diplomacy came to be seen by the British Foreign Office as incapable of coping with minority issues and especially with the German problem.[77]

The rivalry between the Czechs and the Germans was not a new phenomenon. It stretched back to before the Great War. It was exacerbated by the effects of the Great Depression of 1929–31 in which German industry in Czechoslovakia, particularly, suffered. The National Socialist movement flourished in Austria even before Hitler had started his organisation in Bavaria. In Czechoslovakia, it was known, after 1918, as the Deutsche

---

[76] Lias, Ibid. p. 196.
[77] Zeman. Ibid. p. 94.

Nationalsocialistische Arbeitspartei (DNSAP). Initially, it was essentially a working-class movement with trade union links and without any attachment to the German fatherland, although one of its leaders had, in the latter part of the 1920s, propounded a policy of autonomy for the Sudeten Germans in Czechoslovakia. Its membership rose substantially as a result of the depression from 1932, and, more particularly, with the rise of Nazism in Germany and Hitler's accession to power on 30 January 1933.

However, in October 1933, as a result of the trial in November 1932, of a number of its leaders, as a threat to the State and of the banning of the organisation, the DNSAP ceased to exist as a political party. Many of its leaders fled to Germany. They were replaced by a party which, eventually, came to be known as the Sudetendeutsche Partei (SdP), whose leader was Konrad Henlein.

Elsewhere, events were taking place which were to have serious consequences for the Czechs. In 1930, French troops had substantially withdrawn from German territory. There were further reductions in the amount of reparations to be paid by Germany. In March 1931, Germany and Austria announced a customs union, which was contrary to the terms of the Peace Treaties. In 1933, Germany withdrew from the Disarmament Conference announcing that it would no longer be bound by the Treaty of Versailles and, further, that it was rearming. In the same year, Germany withdrew from the League of Nations. None of these events gave any comfort to the Czechs and Hitler's ever-increasing belligerency merely increased their anxieties.

But Benes, while basing his foreign policy on the League and therefore, on France and Britain, nevertheless was anxious to establish harmonious relations with Germany. He had avoided a military convention with the Soviets, distrusting communism in Czechoslovakia. As the German Ambassador in Prague reported in February 1936: "Benes would make all reasonable and necessary concessions to the grievances of the Sudeten Germans for the sake of relations with Germany and political harmony inside Czechoslovakia."[78] He further reported in November 1937, that "he believed Benes' professions of goodwill towards Germany were genuine for the simple reason that...he must long since have realised that the most important condition for the maintenance of the State which he helped to create must be a permanent good relationship with the Germans, outside and inside the borders of the Czechoslovak State...he

---

[78] DGFP series C, Vol. IV, no 580.

really wishes to improve the position of the minority. He could not afford to dispense with the Soviet and French Alliances – a relaxation of relations between Germans and Czechs inside Czechoslovakia was only possible if the Czechs were confident that we have no wish to touch the Czech Nation and the Czechoslovak frontiers."[79]

One of the questions which remain to be answered is why, with the threat of Nazi Germany becoming more and more apparent, little or nothing was done by the Czechs to enter into serious discussions with the French about military cooperation. Under the Treaties of alliance, it had been agreed that there should be staff talks and joint consultations over the defence. The French guarantee to the Czechs of assistance in case of aggression was of no value if there were no plans prepared to give effect to it. This was particularly important given that France and Czechoslovakia were not contiguous and that assistance in this context, therefore, required very careful planning. Few meetings of staffs seem to have taken place and even in 1938, there were no formal Franco-Czech staff talks.[80] In June of that year, the French urged the Czechs to exercise moderation in military circles.[81] General Faucher, the head of the French military mission in Prague, wrote a personal letter to General Gamelin, the French chief of staff, on 5 September 1938, reminding him that there had been only a provisional reply to General Krejei's (the Czech commander) proposals in June for military co-ordination.[82]

Long before, in January 1933, Weygand, who was vice president of the French War Council and Inspector General of the Army, had set out, in a long note, his current thinking about France's military position. He observed that no action in support of alliances could be exercised without there being a liaison between Allies. While Poland was specifically referred to, there is no mention of the military alliance with Czechoslovakia or how France intended to fulfil its obligations to the Czechs under the Treaties. He recommended a study in depth of how the armed forces should be organised.[83] In January 1936, Gamelin expressed the view that once Germany had built fortifications on its Western

[79] DGFP series D, Vol, II no 18.

[80] Adamthwaite, A. (1977) *France and the Coming of the Second World War*, London: Frank Cass and Company, p. 23.

[81] DBFP series 3, Vol. I, no 428.

[82] French Parliamentary Commission of Inquiry (1948). Evidence of General Faucher.

[83] DDF series 1, Tom. II, no 203.

Frontier, there was nothing to stop them from overrunning the members of the little Entente and that the Soviet Union would be of no assistance.[84] In April 1936, Sarraut, President of the Council, admitted (which was self-evident) that there was nothing useful the French could now do to help their Allies in the East. No suggestions were made about staff talks or liaison with the Czechs.[85] And when the Germans marched into the Rhineland, the French reaction was to tell the Czechs that they should adopt a collective approach to the League of Nations.[86]

In June 1936, a paper presented to the French Permanent Committee of National Defence explained that "at the root of all hypotheses, there was one fundamental fact that France has a defensive philosophy, governed by considerations of ethnological, political and psychological order. France had no intention of attacking and if its frontiers were violated, they had to have the power to defend itself." It went on to refer to the quiet work of the military mission to Czechoslovakia. The only comfort for the Czechs was the recommendation by the Air Minister that a number of aircraft should be provided to the Czechs as the only way to face up to Germany.[87] In July 1936, the French took further stock of their Treaty obligations. In relation to Czechoslovakia, it was to be observed that "the 1924 alliance of amity was not accompanied by a military agreement but by a series of letters which provided an effective form of collaboration and an important French military mission wielded influence in Prague. If Germany attacked, France would put pressure on the Western Front and would hope that eventually, an alliance of the armies of the Little Entente and Italy might occur."[88] Given the state of Franco Italian relations at the time, this idea can only be described as fanciful.

The French military mission, stationed in Prague from 1919, was led, first by General Pelle and then by General Mittelhauser, who became Commander in Chief of the Czech Army. He resigned in 1926. Thereafter, a small mission under Faucher took on a counselling role, partly as a result of the elections in November 1925, when Masaryk's party had suffered a heavy defeat. In 1927, the mission consisted of twenty-two officers and it was assumed that, because of attrition, it

---

[84] DDF series 2, Tom. I, no 83.

[85] DDF series 2, Tom. I, no 83, Tom. II, no. 23.

[86] Ibid. no 372.

[87] Ibid. no 369.

[88] Ibid. no 419.

would be wound up by 1928.[89] Benes however, was keen to keep it, taking the view that it had a political significance as exemplified by the visit of Marshal Petain to Czech manoeuvres, in August 1929 by which he was much impressed. The size and duration of the French mission in Prague helped to lay the foundation for a future Czech army, having methods and mentalities similar to those of the French. [90]

The Czechs themselves seemed somewhat relaxed about the German threat. No military manoeuvres had taken place on the German borders since 1927 and they were unwilling to enter into any sort of arrangement with the Poles. In January 1933, the Czech General, Syrovy, had gone to Paris for talks, which were followed up by a more detailed study in April and May. Germany was now accepted by the Czechs as the principal foe. French planes could for a period be stationed in Czechoslovakia. The Czechs were to increase their bomber force. Because of the problem of using French planes outside its own territory, it was suggested that there should be a collaboration between the two aircraft industries. Provision was made for reconnaissance of German (and other) forces.[91] However, in March 1933, France was described by the British Ambassador in Paris as being discouraged and hesitant and also as having lost confidence in the satellite system as a means of containing Germany.[92]

Nevertheless, there was some rather desultory cooperation between the two countries. From 27 September to 4 October 1933, Weygand visited Prague to improve Czech morale. In 1934, Gamelin and the Czech Staff had talks and in September, Gamelin attended the Czech manoeuvres of five divisions in Moravia and Bohemia. He was impressed by their training and discipline. It was noted that there had been a profound change, during the previous two years, in the Czech attitude to military affairs.[93] Previously the budget had been seriously reduced, there had been an excessive and unhappy reduction in war reserves, the development of the aircraft industry had ceased and large manoeuvres had been

---

[89] Wandycz, P. (1968) *The Twilight of French Eastern Alliances 1926-1936*, New Jersey: Princeton University Press, p. 8.

[90] Alexander, M. S. (1963) *The Republic in Danger*, Cambridge: Cambridge University Press, p. 212.

[91] DDF series 1, Tom. III, no 240.

[92] DBFP series 1, Vol. IV, no 266.

[93] DDF series 1, Tom. VII, no 398.

abandoned.[94] Although the Czechs had now extended military service to two years, Faucher was anxious about French support and General Snejdarek was of the view that France could not give the Czechs security. [95]

Thereafter there was little cooperation between the respective armies, although, in summer 1935, the Czechs came to France again and were treated to a large French exercise. In September 1937, Gamelin accompanied General Syrovy, to manoeuvres in Normandy. Air force cooperation had been more fruitful. It reached the form of an actual Convention, with annexes, which on 1 July 1935 were signed by General Keller.[96]The Convention sought to give effect to the ideas discussed in May 1933, but the French never gave precise information on its mobilisation plans and coordinated planning and a joint command never got beyond theory.

Cooperation with the Soviets was equally limited. The Czechs were afraid that staff talks with them might give the Germans an excuse for aggression and were content to rely on the assurance that, under the Treaties, if Czechoslovakia were attacked, France and the Soviet Union would inevitably come to its assistance.[97] In March 1938, after the Anschluss, the French appreciated that the Czechs were now entirely encircled but it appears that, nevertheless, they were willing to give the Czechs an assurance that they would provide immediate effective aid in accordance with their Treaty obligations, even if Britain were unwilling.[98] Staff talks on 28/29 April 1938, between France and Britain, about how to support the Czechs, seem to have been limited simply to a discussion to determine the arrangements, which would have to be made, in the event of British Forces being sent to France.[99]

Earlier in March, there had been a crisis involving a threatened invasion of Czechoslovakia. This had its origin in a report from a disaffected officer of the Abwehr, Paul Thummel, who was recruited into Czech Intelligence as agent A54. On 12 May, he had informed his handler that the Germans were intending to invade Czechoslovakia using Sudeten German Freikorps, supported by SS

---

[94] DDF series 1, Tom. VI, no 186.

[95] Wandycz, Ibid. p. 379.

[96] DDF series 1, Tom. XI, no 185.

[97] DDF, Ibid. no 44.

[98] DDF series 2, Tom. III, no 432.

[99] DBFP series 3 Vol. I. no 164

troops.[100] The Czechs naturally took the report very seriously, accompanied as it was by other reports of unusual German troop movements near the border. General Krejci, the Czech Chief of Staff, spoke of concentrations of eight to ten divisions. The British Minister in Prague reported that the German 7th and 17th Infantry divisions were advancing in the direction of the frontier.[101] Benes ordered partial, and the immediate, mobilisation of some 180,000 men, principally reservists and technical troops, occupying the fortifications at the frontier and the Sudeten territory.

The result of enquiries by Military Attaches from Britain, from the United States' Consul General in Vienna, from the Vice Consul at Breslau and from others found no sign of any such troop movements. However, the United States Military Attaché in Prague was apparently told that the German Legation there had been expecting a coup over the weekend and were suffering a sense of frustration. This coincided with the French view that some sort of ultimatum was being prepared at the German Legation.[102] But whatever the truth, the view, at the time, of the Western press and their diplomats, was that, as a result of the firmness of the Czechs, Germany had given up the idea of an invasion and had had to climb down.

The sense of jubilation over what was thought to be a humiliation for Hitler had two effects. The Czech mobilisation had allowed them to maintain order in Sudeten areas during local elections and by occupying their fortifications in some strength had apparently prevented the Germans from seizing them by a surprise attack.[103] Secondly, Hitler, in fury, now signed a new directive for 'Operation Green' to complete preparations for an invasion of Czechoslovakia by 1 October. Its preamble read: "It is now my unalterable decision to smash Czechoslovakia by military action in the near future."[104]

It might be thought, therefore, that the West would have learnt the lesson from this episode (even if there had never been a German threat) that strong and public support for the Czechs was vital in dealing with Germany. Sadly, it was

---

[100] Andrew, C. (1985) *Secret Service: The Making of the British Intelligence Community*, London: Heinemann, pp. 392–393.

[101] DBFP series 3, Vol. I, no 244.

[102] DBFP, Ibid. no 283 & 317.

[103] Murray, W. (1984) *The Change in the European Balance of Power*, New Jersey: Princeton University Press, p. 172.

[104] DGFP series D, Vol. II, no 221.

not to be. On the contrary, France and Britain behaved as though the Czechs had committed some mortal sin and needed to be chastised like naughty school children. On 21 May, Sir Eric Phipps, the British Ambassador in Paris reported: "The (French) Minister for Foreign Affairs summoned me to say he has heard Czechs have mobilised two classes without consulting French beforehand. He is, therefore, going to warn Czechoslovak Minister in Paris what serious consequences\this may have and how unfortunate such hasty action is. Minister of Foreign Affairs will tell M. Ousky (the Czech minister in Paris) that Czechs must on no account proceed to any further mobilisation without consulting France and Great Britain.... I felt the Czechoslovak Government had put themselves in the wrong...over the mobilisation of two classes without consulting (the text is uncertain) French Government. I hoped he would speak most severely to M. Ousky and would even warn latter that the Czechoslovak Government had in effect broken their Treaty with the French by thus mobilising two classes." [105]

It is difficult now (or was even then) to see what business it was of the British or French Governments to behave in this way or on what basis it could be said that the Czechs had broken their Treaty obligations. It might be thought that instead of upbraiding the Czechs, the French would now pursue the question of military talks with some urgency. They never did. In May 1938, the French Ambassador in Warsaw went to see Bonnet, the French Foreign Affairs Minister, in Paris, to urge on him the necessity of collaboration between France, the Soviet Union and Czechoslovakia. He recorded: "Is it not normal, even necessary, that before committing all our strength against Germany, the French Government needs to know, not only what military aid the Soviet Union can give Czechoslovakia, but also what it may be able to provide France. It is not enough that military talks should be carried on between Prague and Moscow. They should, without delay, be extended to an examination of ways of coordinating the military activities of the three countries for the defence of Czechoslovakia."[106]

Bonnet suggested that he should submit a paper to Daladier, the Prime Minister, who subsequently saw Bonnet and finally gave his approval to military discussions. Precisely nothing happened. At the beginning of 1938, Faucher from Prague expressed the view to Benes that "the time has now come for us to

[105] DBFP, Ibid. no 256.

[106] Coulondre, R. (1950) *De Staline à Hitler*, Paris: Hachette, p. 141.

consult, as we formerly thought we should, about what attitude we could adopt with regard to the Moscow General Staff and what proposals we could make to them after we, Paris and Prague have jointly concerted our action."

When nothing happened, Faucher wrote a personal letter to General Gamelin on 5 September. "Last night General Krejci showed me a telegram in which M. Ousky gave an account of an interview which he had with the French Premier on the subject of the military measures that the Prague Government has just taken. It appears that the Premier was uneasy at the far-reaching nature of these measures and that he had expressed astonishment at not having been consulted beforehand." [107]

Faucher went on: "May I remind you, General, as regards the agreement that the Prime Minister would have liked, that it seems that some months ago, General Krejci sent you a letter containing proposals for a joint study of appropriate steps for ensuring the coordination of the two Allies' decisions. You passed this letter on to M. Daladier, the Premier. No answer has reached Prague except for yours, which only amounted to a provisional reply or an acknowledgement." [108]

Benes made the same point when he wrote: "After the mobilisation of May 1938, I agreed that the Chief of our General Staff, General Krejci, should enter into direct contact with General Gamelin to settle the steps to be taken to coordinate French and Czechoslovak mobilisation. General Gamelin replied that he had no instructions on the matter. We received no other response and none of our Generals were invited to come to Paris. It was in this way that, a little before the Munich crisis, we reached the conclusion that the French were unwilling or were unable to institute joint preparations... Czechoslovakia and the Soviet Union found that they were completely isolated in the camp among those who were on principle openly and determinedly anti-fascist and anti-Nazi.

"On several occasions, the Soviet Diplomats made serious attempts to organise conferences at which there could have been an exchange of views on the joint defence of Eastern and Western Europe against a fascist attack. We were always ready to take part in conferences of this kind. Yet until the end of September 1938, the Soviet efforts came up against the negative attitude of the

---

[107] French Parliamentary Commission of Enquiry, 1948.

[108] Ibid. and Nogueres, H. (Trans. O'Brian, P.O.) (1965) *Munich or the Phony Peace*, Weidenfeld and Nicolson, p. 394.

French and the English."[109] When in August, the Czechs wanted to introduce a law establishing a three-year military service, they were advised by the French government and by General Gamelin against such a move on the ground that it might be regarded as provocative by the Germans.[110]

On 18 September, Faucher wrote another letter to Gamelin in which he reported that "the German attack may be launched very soon…to comply with the desiderata of the British and French Governments, the army has not taken essential military measures. The army runs the danger of finding itself in a very unfortunate position. This state of affairs cannot go on and the decree for mobilisation will become imperative in twenty-four or, at the latest, forty-eight hours. I beg for an immediate reply."[111] The only reply from the Western Allies was to inform Prague that at the meeting on 18 September, they had agreed that all the Sudeten territories, having a German majority of more than 50%, should be ceded.[112]

The military position of Czechoslovakia in 1938 was by no means negligible. The Soviet air force, for instance, was the most numerous in Europe and the army had 45 motorised divisions on a war footing on its Western borders. Daladier estimated the Czech army to have 34 divisions, well equipped and well officered. Army intelligence estimated that they could resist the Germans for at least a few weeks but not months.[113] Their fortifications based on the design of the Maginot Line had been adapted to take account of the Anschluss and General Faucher, expressed the view that the Czech air force was quite well supplied with fighters and with pilots. Subsequently, during the war, they acquitted themselves with great bravery. Further, the Czechs had Soviet medium bombers, which Faucher described as the best in the world.[114] The evidence from the German side supports this view. At Nuremberg, Field Marshal Keitel, the Chief of the OKW, stated: "We had always considered that our means of attack on the Czech frontier fortifications were insufficient. From a purely military point of view, we did not have the requisite means for launching an attack, which would have allowed us

---

[109] Benes, E. (1954) *Memoirs of Dr Eduard Benes*, London: George Allen and Unwin Ltd., pp. 41–42.

[110] DBFP, Ibid. no 656 & 722.

[111] French Parliamentary Commission.

[112] DBFP, Ibid. no 937.

[113] DBFP 3, series 3, Vol. II, no 11.

[114] Nogueres, Ibid. p 384.

to breach the defences." von Manstein and Jodl also expressed the same view.[115] But Faucher was crying in the wilderness. The French political and military attitude towards the problem was unfortunately different.

Because the names of Masaryk and Benes are the most readily recognised of Czech politicians, there is a tendency to assume that they ruled the country until Munich, without internal political problems and that their policies received universal approval from the Czech people. Nothing could be further from the truth. Apart from having to cope with the threat of Germany and the vacillations of their Western Allies, they were frequently required, as in any democracy, to carry the electorate with ᶦthem and further, to fight off opposition from other political parties.

Benes and Kramar, who was then Prime Minister, had represented Czechoslovakia at Versailles, though the former was the principal delegate. When Masaryk returned from the United States, he became the first constitutional ruler, taking the title of President. He had the power both to appoint and dismiss governments and since all Governments tended to be coalitions, he had the power to appoint his own nominees. Almost his first job was to replace Kramar as Prime Minister. His nationalist views were quite incompatible with Masaryk's vision for the future of the country. Kramar did not believe in a multinational republic but Czech domination. He also looked to the Soviet Union for support while it was to the West that Masaryk turned.

In due course, Benes became Prime Minister as well as Minister for Foreign Affairs. He was the leader of the National Socialist party (unlike its German namesake, it was a liberal organisation) but in the immediate elections, the Agrarians had a majority. They formed a coalition with Benes' party with the moderate Catholic People's party and with the Social Democrats. In 1926, there was a revolt by the right-wing of the Agrarians and they withdrew from the coalition. Thereafter the coalition was formed by the addition of the German Agrarians and it continued to run the country until 1935. The group was known as the 'Castle group' and was broadly liberal and antifascist.

The victory of the SdP in the May 1935 elections was not the first jolt to Benes and Masaryk, though it was, perhaps, the most important. As early as 1925, there had been criticism of Benes for his attachment to France by the Agrarians, the National Democrats and Clerical parties. General Klecanda, a

---

[115] Trial of Major War Criminals Before the International Military Tribunal Nuremberg, 4 April & 9 August 1946, series 3, Vol. 3.

member of the General Staff, had resigned in protest because, with some prescience, he did not think that the French would come to help the Czechs if they were attacked. "The Czechoslovak army will gain six weeks for the French and then the Czechoslovak problem will cease to exist."[116]

In 1935, Benes ceased to be Minister for Foreign Affairs and became President, in succession to Masaryk, who had, in 1934, been elected to that post for the fourth time. The election of Benes, as his successor, was the subject of much intrigue. In 1930, the Social Democrats, even though loyal to Masaryk had refused to support the idea of a Benes' candidature at that time. The National Socialist party was against the idea also. Franke, the Minister for Posts and Telegraph, who was a member of the same party as Benes, in November 1933 suggested that the party should ensure that Benes did not become President and that he should retire from the Foreign Ministry. In the elections in May 1935, the SdP won a majority of votes but, because of the electoral geography and of the way the nationalities in the constituencies were distributed, the Agrarians, a right-wing party became the government with 45 mandates. This was compared with the 44 mandates for the SdP. When the question arose of allowing the SdP to take part in the 1935 elections, Masaryk had to decide on the conflicting views of the Agrarians, who were in favour and the Socialist bloc, who were against. He ruled in favour of the SdP, who enjoyed an electoral success. The opposition itself consisted of separate groups, like the right-wing Agrarians and the Slovak People's party, who favoured cooperation with Austria, Hungary, Italy and Germany and were strongly anti-communist.

In October 1935, the Agrarian party, now under the leadership of Rudolf Beran, wanted to bring about a change in Government policy and to appoint Milan Hodza as Prime Minister. In November, the struggle to succeed Masaryk as President came to a climax. The parties suggested that their supporters should follow the party line and not allow a free vote from which Benes would have benefited. The Agrarians were divided as to whom they should give their support. Hodza told Benes that the Agrarians would not put forward their own candidate but withheld the information that they might support another candidate. Other parties were doing the same, out of dislike of Benes.[117]

The right-wing Agrarians and the SdP announced that they would support Nemec, a distinguished professor, who belonged to the conservative National

---

[116] Zeman, Ibid. pp. 77–78.

[117] Ibid. pp. 106.

Democrats, although Hodza himself and a minority, supported Benes. A combination of support from the Communists, from the Slovaks and the Catholic Church, finally won the day for Benes. In the result, Nemec withdrew from the contest and Benes received 340 votes out of a possible 440.[118] Although it was, in the result, an overwhelming victory, it could not conceal the fact that Benes did not command the wholehearted support of the country.

In 1936, the Agrarian right continued to criticise and was joined by the Slovak People's party. They wanted closer ties with Poland, whose policy of negotiations with Germany they wished to follow. In that year, the Communist party, which had been supportive of the anti-fascist policies of the Castle group, now withdrew that support because they regarded them as too bourgeois and uninterested in the class struggle. Further problems arose when Hodza left the Castle group, supporting a policy based on the Central European concept and distancing itself from the bourgeois-democratic make-up of the State.[119] Czech attempts to reconcile the Sudeten Germans by a nationality statute were thwarted by Henlein as did attempts to make contact with the SdP.

By 1938, however, the Castle group still maintained its position as a coalition anti-fascist bloc without the support of the right-wing Agrarians or People's party. The Communists, though not part of the coalition, continued to support this bloc. Any leader of a democratic nation has always to bear in mind that he has limited powers to impose his own solutions on his constituents. Benes, in the period between 1936 and 1938, faced a number of domestic and international problems. As early as March 1938, the Agrarians had suggested that Benes should resign because an agreement with Germany was impossible if he remained in office.[120]

The dispute between them resurfaced over the question of accepting the Anglo-French plan in September 1938. Nor were the SdP themselves without internal disputes. There had long been friction between Hans Krebs, one of the old Nazi Party and Henlein, who had been Krebs' assistant in 1933. This was not resolved until 1938 when Krebs declared that personal discords within the SdP should be eliminated and that Henlein had the full confidence of the party.[121]

---

[118] Bruegel, Ibid. p. 130.
[119] Olivova, Ibid. p. 210.
[120] Zeman, Ibid. p. 127.
[121] Zeman, Ibid. p. 143.

The Agrarians disliked the policy of association with the Soviet Union and advocated closer cooperation with Poland. A constant theme in the criticism of Benes was that he had neglected accommodation with Poland and persisted in the belief that the Poles would remain neutral. At the time of Munich, General Krejci was voicing a common complaint that the position at Munich would have been different if the Poles had been on the Czech side. In January 1938, Beran had published an article in the party's newspaper. In it, he suggested that proper recognition should now be given to the SdP as a result of the election.

But he went further. Without the knowledge or approval of the President or of the Prime Minister or the Minister for Foreign Affairs, he entered into talks with Eisenlohr, the German minister in Prague, about the future of the Sudeten Germans. He told Eisenlohr that "1,00,00 Sudeten German voters must no longer be ignored in the political life of the country. The atmosphere would have to be created gradually in order to enable the Sudeten German Party to enter the government and take part in the administration of the state." Rudolph Beran, then Leader of the Agrarians, further stated that "the party was opposed to the idea of collective security and advocated a rapprochement with Germany. Hodza observed that the fundamental opposition in Government circles to collaboration with the Sudeten German Party had now been removed. However, it was not a question of bringing the SdP into the Government at once but taking steps with that in view." [122]

Beran further reported that "his party had now taken up the fight for the liquidation of the German Social Democrats as a Government party...in order to facilitate understanding with the SdP, the time was favourable for a fundamental and speedy agreement with the SdP."[123]

Thus, while the British and French thought that the Czechs were totally obstinate in their views about the SdP, it is abundantly clear that if there had been a genuine attempt by the SdP to cooperate, without German interference, there is no reason to believe that they could not have been part of the Government, with a settled peaceful future. It was Hitler's determination to smash Czechoslovakia by force, using the pretext of supposed injustices, which prevented the implementation of the well-intentioned proposals of the Czechs. In March 1938, the German Agrarians decided that they would leave the

---

[122] DGFP series D, Vol. II, no 62.

[123] Ibid. no 105.

Government and join the ranks of the SdP under Henlein. They were speedily followed by the Christian Social Party.

The Germans, however, had decided on a different agenda. The Hossbach memorandum of 5 November 1937 recorded the setting in motion of 'Operation Green'. This involved a surprise German operation against the Czechs in which Czechoslovakia was to be eliminated immediately. It was laid down that the necessary conditions to justify such an action, politically and in the eyes of International Law, must be created beforehand. Thereafter, while the West bullied the Czechs into making more and more concessions, Hitler encouraged the Sudeten Germans to keep making more and more demands. The instructions were: "Always to demand more than could be granted by the other side."[124]

'Operation Green' first commissioned by Field Marshal von Blomberg in June 1937, was regularly updated. Keitel, who had replaced Blomberg, produced a further draft in April 1938. On 28 May, Hitler addressed the heads of the three services and the General Staff. He told them that Czechoslovakia must be wiped off the map. New orders were given for 'Operation Green' to be signed on 30 May. The new directive read: "It is my unalterable decision to smash Czechoslovakia by military means in the near future. It is the business of the political leadership to await or bring about a suitable moment from a political and military point of view."[125]

At hand, ready to bring this about at a suitable moment was the Sudeten German party (subsequently called the SdP), led by Henlein. A National Socialist party had existed in Bohemia for many years before Hitler came to power. In 1918, the German National Socialist Workers Party (DNSAP) had been formed. In 1933, they were dissolved. The German Nationalist party was banned. Thus, the public face of Nazism disappeared to be replaced by Henlein's Sudetendeutsche Heimatfront (Sudeten German Home Front). Henlein had been an official of the German Nationalist Gymnastics League and until then was little known. A further organisation under Henlein, the Comradeship League (Kameradschaftsbund, otherwise known as KB) emerged which ostensibly pledged loyalty to the Czech Government. At the same time as the party was receiving subsidies from Germany, Henlein constantly sought, publicly, to dissociate his party from National Socialism. In the elections in May 1935, Henlein's party, its name now changed to Sudeten German Party (SdP,) topped

---

[124] Ibid. no 369.
[125] Ibid. no 221.

the polls leaving the main Government party in third place. Henlein himself did not stand as a candidate. What the Sudeten Germans were voting for in May 1935 was the party which best represented their radical nationalism.[126]

The German Government continued, thereafter, regularly to supply large sums of money to Henlein, who managed successfully to conceal his party's links with Germany. Sir Robert Vansittart, then Permanent Undersecretary at the Foreign Office, was enormously impressed when he first met Henlein, in July 1936. He described him as 'moderate, honest and clear-sighted, speaking with both frankness and decision that inspired confidence'. He went on to say, "Henlein had no desire for the Sudeten Germans to join Nazi Germany and…I think he is speaking the truth."[127]

Vansittart's views did not change over the years. In May 1938, he was able to record: "I have been on very friendly terms with Herr Henlein for some years past and have seen him frequently during his visits to London… I had, of course, noticed that he had, of late, been no longer ostensibly the moderate Henlein whom I had known and appreciated in previous years… I retained the general impression that I was, as in previous years, speaking to a wise and reasonable man. I found Herr Henlein far more reasonable and amenable than I had dared to hope; he was now going too far and some of his demands exceed the bounds of the possible."[128]

After the meeting in 1936, Henlein had reported that Vansittart had agreed both to take up the problems of the Sudeten Germans at the League of Nations and to give instructions to the British press to do the same. In general, Vansittart had agreed to advise and help the Sudeten Germans. While there was obviously a good deal of exaggeration in Henlein's report, it appears that in August, Vansittart spoke to Hess and other German officials about Henlein's demands. The British public also became more aware of the problems of the Sudeten Germans. [129]

Attempts to negotiate an agreement between Germany and Czechoslovakia in November 1936 came to nothing and the policy, enunciated by the Czechs, known as the 'February 18th agreement', achieved very little in the way of reconciling the Sudeten Germans to their minority status. The idea was to

---

[126] Smelser, R. M. (1975) *The Sudeten Problem 1933–1938*, Folkestone: Dawson, p. 121.

[127] Foreign Office Files (Czechoslovakia) FO 371/ 20374.

[128] DBFP series 3, Vol. I, no 219 & app 11,

[129] Smelser, Ibid. p. 148.

promote all-round ethnic equality, in particular the acceptance of more Germans in the public service, and the allocation of public service contracts. However, the German SS and SD started to take an increased interest in the affairs of the Sudeten Germans. It was not merely an information-gathering exercise, nor solely designed to carry out assignments. They were more positively directed to support the radical elements among the Sudeten Germans in their dispute with the moderates, among whom Henlein was to be counted. Having lost a number of his colleagues and fearing his dismissal from the party, in December 1937, Henlein wrote to Hitler asking him to annex Bohemia, Moravia and Silesia.[130]

In fact, Hitler had already made up his mind, in November 1937, that he was going to smash the Czechs. There were a number of factors which led Hitler to transform the agitation by the Sudeten Germans into a full scale, casus belli. He had in Henlein and his supporters a readymade organisation to stir up trouble and was now able to present to the world, apparently justified German grievances. The radicalisation of the SdP was one element. Another was the accelerating internationalisation of the Sudeten problem. Both in Britain and in France, Governments became increasingly concerned to persuade the Czechs to make concessions to avert the crisis, which Hitler had deliberately created.[131] France, conscious of its Treaty obligations, was anxious to avoid having to fulfil them if only the Czechs would be generous in their treatment of the Sudetens. Britain, for its part, unenthusiastic about the effect of the Versailles Treaty, was only too anxious to remedy its defects and to agree to a settlement of the Czech problems at any price. Thus, with ever-increasing pressure, both Britain and France, bullied the Czechs, while doing nothing to discourage Hitler from pursuing his ambitions towards both Austria and Czechoslovakia.

In January 1938, the British Cabinet Committee on Foreign Policy discussed suggestions for a general settlement with Germany and instructions were then sent to Sir Nevile Henderson, the British Ambassador in Berlin, to tell the German leaders that even colonies would come their way if they behaved.[132] On 3 March, Hitler told Henderson privately that "in Czechoslovakia, the Germans must be granted the autonomy to which they are entitled both culturally and in other respects. This would be the most elementary application of that right to

---

[130] Ibid. p. 206.

[131] Ibid. p. 211.

[132] Cabinet Committee on Foreign Policy, 12 February 1938, F.P. (36) Cab 24/627, no 52.

self-determination of Nations, which figured so largely in Wilson's fourteen points. The present situation could not continue for long, it would lead to an explosion."[133] Anthony Eden, then British Foreign Secretary, had submitted a memorandum to the Committee called 'German contribution to General Appeasement' in which he wrote: "Germany should be asked to conclude with Czechoslovakia an arrangement analogous to the German-Austrian arrangement of July 1936... This had enabled Nazis to have official positions in Austria and had given the Germans an excuse to invade Austria in answer to an alleged call for help from its Chancellor, Seyss-Inquart." [134]

The Anschluss did nothing to dampen the Sudeten Germans' enthusiasm for a similar process in Czechoslovakia. Apart from outflanking parts of the Czech fortifications, it had the effect of increasing Henlein's demands for autonomy from the Government. The Czech Government, therefore, came under sustained pressure both from its so-called Allies and from within. The British sought help from the French to bring pressure to bear on Prague. After a meeting between them, in March 1938, a final draft of their discussions was sent to Paris with the suggestion that a solution should be sought. The phrase 'within the existing boundaries', contained in the original draft, was carefully omitted.[135] No doubt as a result of this pressure, Hodza introduced a 'nationalities statute'. The policy was to give more autonomy to the national minorities.[136]

On 17 March 1938, Henlein asked Ribbentrop to arrange a personal meeting with Hitler and on 28 March, they had a three-hour conversation. The next day, there was a discussion between the SdP delegates and Ribbentrop and other members of his Ministry. Ribbentrop explained that it was essential to keep the meeting a secret. It was agreed that the SdP would not join the Czech Government and that they would make ever-increasing demands on the Czechs, each harder to satisfy than the last. "The aim of the negotiations to be carried out by the Sudeten German Party is finally this: to avoid entry into the Government by the extension and gradual specification of the demands to be made." Meanwhile, the German Government would continue to give maximum support to the SdP without being overtly involved.[137]

---

[133] Documents and Materials, Ibid. no 3.

[134] Ibid. Cab 24/627, no 51.

[135] DBFP series 3, Vol. I, no 107 & 135.

[136] Ibid. no 160.

[137] Documents and Materials, Ibid. no 8.

At the beginning of April, the Czechs, having announced that they would introduce a 'nationality statute', sent a memorandum to London setting out the principles of their policy regarding minorities in which it was pointed out that its ideal had always been the democratic State, guaranteeing justice to all citizens and hence, also, to all nationalities. It added that, while it was recognised that the state was not and could not be racially homogenous, institutions must correspond to ethnic distribution. While the fairer representation of minorities in the administration was promised, a territorial division along racial lines was rejected.[138]

None of this was enough for the SdP and later that month, Henlein put forward his plans, which became the 'Eight Demands of the Karlsbad Program'. He described them as minimum demands. In his speech, he called for a change in foreign policy, for the Czechs to capitulate before German nationalism and to surrender their defences.

'The eight demands' were: "1. Full equality of status for Czechs and Germans. 2. A guarantee of this status through the recognition of the Sudeten Germans as a legal personality. 3. Delimitation and legal recognition of the German areas in the Czechoslovak State. 4. Full self-government for these areas. 5. Legal protection for every citizen living outside his 'national area'. 6. Removal of and reparation for all 'injustices' inflicted since 1918. 7. Recognition of the principle: 'only German officials within German areas' 8. Full freedom to profess membership of the German race (Volkstum) and the German outlook on life (Weltanschauung)."

The latter demand was intended not merely to confirm the right of the Germans to regard themselves as German, which no one was challenging but implicitly to deny freedom to those who thought otherwise. They would include any Germans who supported the Czech Government and racial groups like the Jews.[139] This was a demand way beyond autonomy and one which no Government could possibly accept. But, in this, Henlein was encouraged by Hitler so that, whatever concessions were made by the Czechs, he was always to make further unacceptable demands.

Even though he was unaware of this diktat to Henlein, Sir Basil Newton, the British Minister in Prague, appreciated exactly what Henlein was up to, which was more than the Foreign Office did. In April, Newton had reported to Lord

---

[138] DBFP, Ibid. no 160.
[139] Bruegel, Ibid. p. 206.

Halifax, now Foreign Secretary, that "even so apparently innocent a demand, as that for cultural autonomy for the Sudeten Germans, could, for example, be used, if granted, for the wholesale introduction of *Mein Kampf* as well as a swarm of National Socialist propagandists to influence and organise the Sudeten German population. It is partly on account of this fear that any genuine concession is merely the thin end of the wedge which, apart from a temperamental obstinacy, renders the Czechs so determinedly uncompromising."[140]

Henlein continued to communicate with Vansittart through intermediaries and his protestations about being an apostle of appeasement were passed on to Halifax and accepted by him without demur.[141] A decision to bring further pressure on the Czechs by Britain and France was taken at a meeting in London on April 28/29. [142] It resulted in repeated warnings to the Czechs through the Embassies in Prague. In May, Krofta, the Czech Foreign Minister, was told by Newton to be more conciliatory towards the SdP and that the chances of military assistance were slight.[143]

Later in the month, Halifax sent a message to Newton. "You should, therefore, make immediate representations to the Czechoslovak Government…and make it clear that a definite and concrete proposal on Saturday (May 28) is absolutely indispensable for the prospects of an acceptable and therefore peaceful solution."[144] The French were equally insistent. Bonnet saw the Czech envoy in Paris to demand that the Czechs come to an agreement with the Sudeten Germans, *coûte que coûte*. Ousky was given a memorandum to submit to Prague.[145] Foreign Office files in June and July and Cabinet records for 13 July confirm further pressure from Britain and a reference to Benes' stubborn resistance.[146]

It was at this time that the British conceived the notion of sending a mediator, Lord Runciman, to Czechoslovakia to try to sort out the problems between Benes and Henlein. Very much earlier, on 17 March 1938, the Foreign Office had produced a draft Cabinet paper suggesting that Czechoslovakia should allow an

---

[140] DBFP, Ibid. no 140.

[141] Bruegel, Ibid. p. 218.

[142] DBFP, Ibid. no 164.

[143] DBFP, Ibid. no 195, 200, 223, 226 & 229.

[144] DBFP, Ibid. no 320.

[145] DBFP, Ibid. no 353, 447 & 472.

[146] FO 371, Vols. 21724, 21725 & 21727, CAB 23/94 minute 32(38).

Anglo-French or a purely British Commission of Inquiry to visit Czechoslovakia and report on Sudeten position.[147]

The reason for a mediator now was that British Officials believed that unless a solution was found by the annual Nazi rally at Nuremberg, on 12 September, Hitler himself would act.[148] This was confirmed by Henderson's despatch on 25 August when he wrote: "It may be taken for granted that Herr Hitler at Nuremberg will define Germany's standpoint in Sudeten question... Possible three alternatives at Nuremberg would, therefore, be for Herr Hitler to announce... (c) that the British having failed to bring Benes to reason, Germany claims her inalienable right to secure for herself in her own way the lives and interests of her German brethren across the frontier."[149]

The idea that 12 September was some sort of watershed, further encouraged the British to increase pressure on Benes and it also persuaded Lord Runciman that the situation was urgent. He wrote to Halifax on 24 August: "If accommodation is not reached, I fear an awkward speech at Nuremberg... There is very little time to be lost, barely a fortnight before the Nuremberg oration."[150] On 3 August, Halifax had told Newton that "all intelligence reports indicated that Hitler was committing himself to extreme action at Nuremberg...and that the German Government was determined to find a settlement of the Czechoslovak question in the autumn by force if necessary...and that concessions were necessary."[151]

The appointment of Lord Runciman smacked very much of a Victorian Colonial Office approach to deal with a situation where the natives were proving troublesome. The Czechs were a fiercely independent and democratic nation who had not sought this intervention. Britain had no Treaty obligations to the Czechs. If Mussolini, uninvited, had one day announced that he was going to send an Italian mediator to Britain to sort out the British problems over the unification of Ireland, the British reaction would have been one of fierce condemnation. Lord Runciman's mission, therefore, needed very delicate handling which, unfortunately, it did not receive.

---

[147] Harvey, Ibid. p. 119.
[148] Smelser, Ibid. p. 231.
[149] DBFP, Ibid. no 689.
[150] DBFP, Ibid. no 680.
[151] DBFP, Ibid. no 727.

The idea of appointing some sort of observer or commission of inquiry, was the result of a visit by William Strang, a Foreign Office Official, to HM Missions at Berlin and Prague on 29 May. [152] It was not Halifax's brainchild, but on 16 June, he told the Cabinet Foreign Affairs Committee that he was thinking of appointing an intermediary and Newton was instructed to seek out the views of the Czechs.[153] Lord Runciman was approached and eventually accepted but made it a condition of his appointment that both sides had agreed to receive him.[154]

The French were kept in the dark. On 20 July, Benes was told about Lord Runciman's proposed mission and not unnaturally reacted with considerable vehemence. "It gravely affected the country's sovereignty, would provoke a most serious crisis in the country and might entail the resignation of the Government and even, confidentially, his own."[155] Chamberlain's attitude was fixed, On 22 July, he told the German Ambassador, Dirksen, that it was the policy of the British Government, by intensified and continued pressure on Prague, to bring about a settlement of the Czech crisis. [156]

On 26th July, Chamberlain announced in the House of Commons that Runciman was going to Prague, that he would act in his personal capacity and that he would not be in any sense an arbitrator but rather an investigator and mediator. On this mission, he was to be accompanied by the Head of the Economic Section of the Foreign Office, Ashton-Gwatkin, who was an expert on trade negotiations. Chamberlain added that Runciman was going at the request of the Czech Government, which was simply a lie. Chamberlain concealed from the House that, at that time, contrary to Runciman's condition that he would only go if both parties agreed to receive him, the Czechs had not yet so agreed. Indeed, he appears to have told a similar lie when he said, "He (Runciman) has agreed upon the single condition of being assured of the Sudeten Germans' confidence. I venture to hope that he will obtain it as he has obtained that of the Czechoslovak Government."[157] It was symptomatic of Britain's approach to the whole problem that they chose to treat Benes as though he were

---

[152] DBFP series 3, Vol. I, no 349.

[153] DBFP, Ibid. no 425 & 431.

[154] DBFP, Ibid. no 493.

[155] DBFP, Ibid. no 521.

[156] DGFP series D, Vol. II, no 309.

[157] House of Commons Official Reports, Fifth Series, Vol. 338, Cols 2956–2958.

a primitive chieftain of some small tribe.[158] Eventually, with the threat of making public the Czech's unwillingness to take part, the British bullied them into acceptance.

Runciman's approach to solving the problem was to treat the minority Sudetens on equal terms with the democratically elected Czech Government. His diplomatic skills were confined to persuading the Czechs to make ever more concessions. Further discussions on the nationality statute came to nothing. By the end of August, however, Benes had come up with his 'third plan' which appeared to accept some of the Karlsbad programmes such as language concessions, an increase in the number of German officials and a loan for the relief of distressed areas. It did not involve the surrender of democracy. Henlein was unenthusiastic.[159] Runciman thought it "was covered in bolt holes and qualifications."[160]. It included the division of Bohemia and Moravia – Silesia into Gaue (Cantons) three of which would have had a German majority. Henlein insisted on unconditional acceptance of all the eight parts of the Karlsbad programme.

Further pressure was brought to bear on the Czechs. Runciman told Benes that, faced with a choice between acceptance of the Karlsbad programme or war, he, Benes, should be under no illusions as to what the British choice would be. Newton added that it was vital for Czechoslovakia to accept great sacrifices and even, if necessary, to take considerable risks. [161]

On 31 August, Runciman thought it would help negotiations if he told Halifax to twist Benes' tail.[162] The French were equally keen to exert pressure on the Czechs. At the beginning of September, Bonnet told the German Ambassador in Paris, that he, Daladier and other members of the Cabinet were sincere admirers of the Fuhrer. He added that the only satisfactory solution of the Czech question was the annexation of the Sudeten German regions by the Reich. He pleaded that France should not be forced into a position of having to fulfil its Treaty obligations. After matters were settled, it would then be possible

---

[158] Faber, D. (2008) *Munich: The 1938 Appeasement Crisis*, London: Simon and Schuster, p. 203.

[159] DGFP series D, Vol. II, no 369, 78, 407 & 417.

[160] DBFP series 3, Vol. II, no 723.

[161] DBFP, Ibid. no 753 & 758.

[162] FRUS 1938, Vol. 1, p. 565.

to discuss the question of the German colonies.[163] According to British documents, Bonnet went even further. He declared that if Benes did not accept Runciman's verdict, France would consider itself free from all Treaty commitments to Czechoslovakia.[164]

On 7 September, Benes, in his fourth plan, accepted the whole of the Karlsbad programme. The history of its production was near to farce. On 5 September, Benes had invited Kundt and Sebekowsky, the SdP representatives to visit him in Prague. At the beginning of the meeting, Benes handed over a blank sheet of paper and invited the SdP representatives to set out their full demands, which he was prepared to grant, at once.

When they, perhaps fearful of committing themselves without consultation with their German masters, declined, Benes took the matter into his own hands and invited them to dictate their own terms. This resulted in the SdP achieving every concession which they had sought. But it was to no purpose. Neither Henlein nor the Germans were in the slightest bit interested in negotiations. They simply desired the annexation of Czechoslovakia. 'Operation Green' had already been prepared.

Benes explained why he did it in a letter, which he wrote later. "I was aware that I succumbed in this struggle, against Nazi totalitarianism and for the rescue of Czechoslovak democracy, to the exaggerated and improper pressure of democratic British and French Governments…which striving for the maintenance of peace forced us to concessions, clothed in a mantle of ethnic justice and having as their real aim the destruction of our State and national existence… I wanted to convince the French and British Governments that not even the biggest concessions could satisfy either Berlin or the Sudeten pan-Germans. I saw in it the only and last way, if any existed at all, to bring the Western Powers and the rest of the world onto our side, should an armed conflict break out between us and Germany."[165] But it was to no purpose. The SdP broke off negotiations because of an incident involving a Sudeten German in a street brawl. Only Runciman was left to try and sort it all out.

Runciman's attempts to resolve the problems were doomed to failure. From the start, he gave the impression of paying very much more attention to the views of the SdP than to the views of the Czech Government or the German Social

---

[163] DGFP, Ibid. no 422.
[164] DBFP, Ibid. no 747.
[165] Bruegel, Ibid. p. 248.

Democrats. He was described as 'seeming to have moved very near to the Henlein point of view'.[166] He allowed himself to be entertained by aristocratic supporters of the SdP[167] and to be overwhelmed with documents from the SdP, who incessantly complained about the treatment of the Sudetens by the Czechs. Henlein deliberately kept out of Runciman's way to avoid being involved in any sort of negotiations.

A leader in the *Times*, on 7 September, stated that "it might be worthwhile for the Czechoslovak Government to consider whether they should exclude altogether the project, which has found favour in some quarters,(my emphasis) of making Czechoslovakia a more homogeneous State, by the cession of that fringe of alien populations, who are contiguous to the nation to which they are united by race."[168] It appeared to suggest that the cession of the Sudetenland to Germany was official British Government policy, although it seems that the leader was not sanctioned by the Foreign Office and was denied as representing government policy.

---

[166] Harvey, Ibid. p. 168.
[167] DGFP series D, Vol. II, no 336.
[168] The Times Newspaper, 7 September 1938.

Chapter Four:
The Great Betrayal

On 28 August, Chamberlain decided to intervene personally. He had already conceived the idea of a face-to-face meeting with Hitler at which cession by the Czechs was to be the centre of discussion. All this merely added to the pressures on Benes. It further encouraged the SdP to disengage from any further negotiations, now that the Czechs had accepted the Karlsbad programme. The idea of the cession of territory to the Sudeten Germans became the next political move by Britain and France. It is, perhaps, ironic that the Western Allies, having prevented the Czechs at Versailles from ceding any part of Sudeten Germany to the Germans, now decided to exert maximum pressure on the Czechs to do just that.

Hitler's speech at Nuremberg on 12 September was full of invective against Benes and of complaints about the ill-treatment by the Czechs of the Sudeten Germans. Although the language was violent and abusive, there was no immediate demand for war, but only a threat that Germany would not tolerate any further oppression. The speech triggered an uprising in a number of Sudeten towns involving rioting and the use of rifles, grenades, bombs and machine guns. It resulted in the death of a number of civilians and the death and kidnapping of a number of gendarmes.

The Czech Government declared a state of emergency and proclaimed martial law but, within days, the civil war which Hitler had sought to provoke as an excuse for intervention had petered out. But this was not before the Gestapo had threatened to shoot a corresponding number of Czech citizens living in

Germany if any Sudeten Germans were executed as a result of their involvement in the revolt.[169]

The SdP were to have resumed negotiations with Hodza but Frank, Henlein's deputy, telephoned him with an ultimatum that the SdP would only continue negotiations if martial law were lifted and the State police had withdrawn.[170] When Hodza asked for the SdP delegation to come to Prague, the SdP publicly announced that as the ultimatum had not been accepted, negotiations were at an end. A new situation had arisen and negotiations could only be continued on the basis of self-determination and the introduction of a plebiscite.[171]

In his speech, Hitler, himself, had referred to the necessity for a plebiscite in the Sudeten areas as a solution to the Czech problem. Having issued their communiqué, Henlein and other SdP leaders fled to Germany. The ignominious collapse of the Henleinist putsch, the flight of the leaders of the SdP, the resignation of Party Officials and the disbandment of the party encouraged other Sudeten German democratic organisations to declare their loyalty to the Czech State. On 17 September, the German Social Democrats made a public declaration, announcing the foundation of a 'United German National Council'.

Not all the Sudeten Germans wanted to be linked to Germany and when Henlein announced on 15 September: "We wish to live as a free German people! We desire peace and work in our fatherland! We want to go back to Germany!" his words mostly fell on deaf ears. The picture which emerges of the Czech position at this time is clear. If they had been left alone to sort out the legitimate grievances of the Sudeten Germans, by subscribing to the principles in the 4th Karlsbad plan, to which they had agreed, they would soon have reached a satisfactory solution of the nationality problem. [172] Sadly, they were not to be left alone.

Without a single word to the Czechs, Chamberlain now decided that he would unilaterally sort out the future of Czechoslovakia, along with Hitler. The idea for the visit had its origin in a conversation on 28 August, between

---

[169] Laffan, R. G. D. (1950) *Survey of International Affairs*, Oxford: University Press, Vol. II, p. 312. DGFP series D, Vol. II, no 807. Documents and Materials Ibid. no 17 & 20.

[170] DGFP, Ibid. no 466 & 467.

[171] DGFP, Ibid. no 491–493.

[172] Ripka, Ibid. p 51.

Chamberlain, Halifax, Simon and Henderson.[173] The Cabinet was kept in ignorance until they met on 14 September when Chamberlain revealed for the first time that he was proposing to fly to see Hitler. The central idea was to agree to a plebiscite or cession.[174] The telegram to Hitler, arranging the meeting, gave no hint of Chamberlain's views.

However, the German chargé d'affaires in London reported that a press announcement had been issued which read: "He (Chamberlain) was still prepared to examine far-reaching German proposals, including plebiscites…to take part in carrying them into effect and to advocate them to the public."[175] It might be thought that if he were going to agree that the Czechs, to whom he had no Treaty obligation (and for whom he was acting as some sort of uninvited proxy), should hand over substantial parts of their territory, at the very least, he would have sought their prior agreement for his visit. If that was too much, just to inform them that he was going to make the visit, even without their agreement, would have been an act of courtesy. For him to believe that he, and he alone, could decide to hand over part of the territories of a democratic and independent nation without their agreement, and without any consultation, suggests a degree of arrogance, which, even today, seems breath-taking. Nor were the French, who did have Treaty obligations, invited to take part nor were they even consulted.

On 15 September, Benes had sent a cri de coeur to the French pointing out, once more, that the whole of Europe was interested in preventing a crisis developing, because of the loss of Czech independence to Germany.[176] The best the French could do was to express their profound sympathy to the Czechs.[177] At this stage, it appeared that the French were in favour of a plebiscite, which as Benes politely pointed out would have disastrous consequences for the independence of Czechoslovakia.[178]

On 14 September, Bonnet had again expressed great indignation with the Czechs because it seemed that they meant to mobilise without consulting the French, just as they had previously declared a State of siege, without consulting them. Bonnet, therefore, gave a broad hint to Benes that France might have to

---

[173] Chamberlain Papers N/C 18/1/ 1069.

[174] CAB 23/95/34-41, 49 & 55. Cabinet 38 (38), 14 September 1938.

[175] DGFP series D, Vol. II, no 470.

[176] DDF series 2, Tom. XI, no 150.

[177] DDF, Ibid. no 157.

[178] DDF, Ibid. no 175.

reconsider her obligations towards Czechoslovakia.[179] With friends like France who needed enemies.

Before Chamberlain actually met Hitler, Henlein's demand for annexation had been made public. At the meeting with Chamberlain at Berchtesgaden, on 15 September, Hitler resiled from the idea of a plebiscite and demanded cession. Chamberlain agreed in principle but required to consult with his colleagues and with the French. It seems not to have occurred to him that the Czechs might have views. The Czechs knew that a plebiscite was not going to be based on a free vote because of Nazi intimidation. Runciman also added his weight to the argument against a plebiscite and in favour of cession of territory. He proposed that "those frontier districts between Czechoslovakia and Germany in which a considerable majority of the population is Sudeten German should at once and without delay be given the full right of self-determination…these districts should at once be transferred from Czechoslovakia to Germany."[180] .

The Czech position about any sort of cession is by no means clear. On 15 September, Newton reported "In the course of our conversation, Dr Benes mentioned that some Sudeten Germans lived in areas such as Egerland, which in his opinion could have been excluded from Czechoslovakia without endangering the existence of the State. During the Peace Conference, he personally had suggested in private conversations, or letters, their exclusion, but the suggestion had never been seriously discussed nor had it been agreed to by other members of the delegation.

"Their (ie the Sudeten Germans) exclusion now would, of course, be no adequate solution and would, in any case, be impossible in the present circumstances, as such a precedent could not be admitted."[181] He also reported on 16 September, that he had had a conversation with the Prime Minister, Hodza who had said that "if some territorial secession was absolutely insisted upon, as a sine qua, none of a peaceful solution with Herr Hitler, it might, in the last resort, be feasible to surrender Egerland and other areas…the areas could be drawn to include from 800,000 up to perhaps even 100,000 inhabitants, in the vast majority, Germans. Though, he thought, there would have to be a change of Government before the idea could be put through." [182].

---

[179] DBFP series 3, Vol. II, no 878.

[180] CMD 5847/5448,

[181] DBFP, Ibid. no 888.

[182] DBFP, Ibid. no 902.

A mystery surrounds the activities of a Czech Socialist Minister, Jaromir Nezcas. Benes had, it seems, entrusted him with a piece of paper and a map showing the territorial concessions which he, Benes, was willing to make. They amounted to some 2000 square miles in area (very substantially less than the figures agreed at Munich). Nezcas was to transmit the paper to Blum but on no account to disclose the identity of the author. Daladier's recollection in 1961 was that he was handed a message from Blum, which had come from Nezcas, suggesting the cession of some territory involving a population of some million people. On 27 September, Daladier had told the United States' Ambassador in Paris that Benes had told him that he, Benes, would not object to the surrender of the border territories outside the fortress belt.[183]

At the Anglo-French Conference on 18 September, no reference was made by Bonnet or by anyone else, to any suggestion coming from Prague about ceding territory. The record shows that there was some agreement about cession but nothing was to be done about consultation with the Czechs until the French Cabinet had given its approval. The result of the conference (confirmed by the French Cabinet on 19 September) was twofold—in exchange for a guarantee of the independence of Czechoslovakia by the Western Allies, Czechoslovakia was to cede all the Sudeten territories having a German majority of more than 50% (not Runciman's 'considerable majority') and they were to cancel their Treaties with France and the Soviet Union.

The effect of this decision would have been to destroy the independence of the country and to surrender important industrial areas and fortifications to Germany without a plebiscite. A plebiscite was to take place in other areas which would have unforeseeable consequences. On the same day, the Czechs were now officially informed of what had been agreed on their behalf by Chamberlain. Because Chamberlain was to visit Hitler again within two days, the Czechs were required to give their reply 'at the earliest possible moment'. [184] In the light of previous French threats, the Czechs had not mobilised.

The reaction of the Czechs was unsurprisingly one of dismay. They were presented with an ultimatum. If they did not agree, it would probably result in the French welshing on their Treaty obligations. On the afternoon of 19 September, Newton and Victor de Lacroix (French Minister in Prague) called on Benes and produced the proposed plan. Benes was initially so greatly moved and

---

[183] FRUS 1938 1 1938, p. 687.

[184] DBFP, Ibid. no 928.

agitated that he refused to discuss the matter at all; he was a constitutional President and would need to consult with both his Government and Parliament. Newton explained that there was great urgency because Chamberlain's visit could not be postponed for more than two days. It was also Newton's view that 'Benes was more likely to accept than refuse and that he was very receptive to any reason, which will help him justify acceptance to his people'.[185]

Later that afternoon, Benes met with his Ministers with his Military Advisers and with Leaders of the Coalition Parties. They sat for nearly a day and a half, in almost continuous session. Still, no answer came from Prague on 20 September and the British Government was getting more and more anxious. The French ordered Lacroix to make further urgent representations and to warn Benes that an appeal to arbitration would be folly and lead to war. Lacroix also met Krofta, the Czech Foreign Minister, and urged the same on him.[186] At 7:05 pm Krofta handed a reply to Newton and Lacroix, rejecting the Anglo-French plan by which time, Chamberlain's second visit to Hitler had had to be postponed.

The Czech reply, dated 20 September, read in part: "These proposals were made without previous consultation with the representatives of Czechoslovakia and an attitude hostile to her has been taken up without hearing her case; the Czechoslovak Government has pointed out that they cannot take responsibility for a decision made without their consent (this was the result of a demarche from Masaryk to Halifax on 18 September). It is hence understandable that the proposals mentioned could not be such as to be acceptable to Czechoslovakia."[187]

The reply went on to suggest the application of the Arbitration Treaty of 16 October 1936, which the present German Government had recognised as valid in several pronouncements and by which they themselves were willing to be bound.[188] It finished with the pertinent observation that "at this decisive moment, it is not only a question of the fate of Czechoslovakia but also the fate of other countries and especially France."[189]

The reaction of the British and French Governments was swift and condemnatory. When Krofta, handed the note to the British and French Ministers, the former told him that, if Czechoslovakia persisted in rejecting the

---

[185] DBFP, Ibid. no 961.

[186] 0044BFP Ibid. no 967 & 968.

[187] DBFP, Ibid. no 929.

[188] DBFP, Ibid. no 986.

[189] Documents and Materials, Ibid. no 24.

Anglo-French proposals, the British would wash their hands over the whole affair and the French took the same view. Through the next few hours, both Governments bullied the Czechs with ever-increasing petulance. Phipps suggested that he should deliver an ultimatum to Benes that unless the proposals were accepted without reserve or further delay, Britain would take no further interest in the country.[190]

At 11 pm, Chamberlain, Halifax and Wilson decided to put the screws on the Czechs, and, at 1 am on 21 September, Newton was instructed to tell the Czechs that the result of their rejection of the proposals was likely to lead to a German invasion, that they should take account of realities and that the British Government could take no responsibility for such a situation.[191]

The French were no less belligerent in their attitude to the Czech rejection of their plan and said quite plainly that if the Czechs did not accept the Anglo-French proposals and the Germans invaded, they, the French, would not intervene and would regard their obligations under the Treaty as no longer existing.[192] The British note of 21 September, although couched in diplomatic language, could not be more explicit The final paragraph read: "If the Czechoslovak Government, after reconsideration, would still feel compelled to reject this advice, it must have, of course, freedom for any action which it considers appropriate, in view of the situation which might develop later." [193]

The French claimed that the Czech rejection of the Anglo-French proposals brought their Treaty obligations to an end. One searches in vain in the Treaty itself for some material, which, even by the most generous interpretation based on some spurious Gallic logic, could give the French any sort of legal justification for resiling from their solemn obligation. But one reason for this French decision is now clear. It is to be found in one of their official documents dated 17 September, headed 'Note Juridique'. It is by an author whose identity is not disclosed and suggests that the French could optout from their Treaty obligations for a number of reasons.

The first was that the Treaty of 16 October 1925 preceded the Anschluss, which had the effect of creating a new frontier between Germany and Czechoslovakia. That new fact, it was argued, was sufficient to invalidate the

---

[190] DFBP, Ibid. no 979.

[191] DBFP, Ibid. no 991.

[192] DDF, Ibid. no 249.

[193] Documents and Materials, Ibid. no 25.

Treaty. Secondly, France's obligations were not contained in a treaty of non-aggression but an arbitration agreement. Finally, the events giving rise to the dispute (ie 1919) were in existence before the Treaty was signed and thus, it was argued that France had no present obligation.[194]

It was followed on 20 September, by a lengthy opinion on the subject of neutrality, prepared for the benefit of the Foreign Ministry.[195] The views expressed in the note are said to accord with the pacifist views of the Minister for Foreign Affairs and may also explain his subsequent behaviour. A more tendentious argument about the effect of the Treaty, it would be difficult to find. For over nearly twenty years, admittedly, with various degrees of enthusiasm, the French had assured the Czechs that they would honour their Treaty obligations. What suddenly happened on 17 September to cause them to find some legal excuse? International law would certainly not provide one. Was there not also an expectation, moral or otherwise, that they would fulfil their obligations? It could scarcely be described as France's finest hour.

Surprisingly, the French ultimatum had not even been discussed by the French Cabinet. Unknown to Benes, the decision was taken by Bonnet and by him alone. There is some evidence that Hodza had indicated that the rejection was not the last word and that he regarded the rejection as a concession to the pig-headed elements in the Czech Government. It appears that he told Newton and Lacroix that if Britain and France refused to support the Czechs then his Government would be forced to concede.[196]

Any idea, however, that thereby Czechs were willing supporters of the Anglo-French plan is readily discounted by the contemporary documents. It was further suggested that Hodza had encouraged the French to bring pressure on the Czechs to enable the Czechs to explain its surrender, as force majeure. A much more likely explanation for the whole episode is that the French were keen to make it appear that its failure to fulfil its obligations was at the instigation of the Czech Government.[197]

The British and French Ministers, who had called on Benes at 2 am with their ultimatum, stayed for nearly two hours. The French Minister handed Benes the message of his Government with tears in his eyes. It was the end of a twenty-

---

[194] DDF, Ibid. no 196.

[195] DDF, Ibid. no 243.

[196] DBFP, Ibid. no 979. Faber p. 477.

[197] Bruegel, Ibid. p. 280–281. Laffan, Ibid. 359–362.

year-old policy to which the Czechs had remained faithful. It was a very unhappy confrontation and, unsurprisingly, the two envoys appeared ashamed of the mission, which they had to discharge in the name of their Governments. Benes later met with his own ministers and they agreed they had no alternative but to accept.

This decision was approved by the Cabinet. It was not approved by the Chiefs of Staff or by the opposition parties. No immediate reply was sent to London or Paris while the matter was further debated in Prague. Hodza's secretary phoned Newton at 7 am to convey the private and preliminary information that the reply was to be in the affirmative and that the official reply would be sent as soon as possible.[198] Meanwhile, at noon, the two Ministers saw Benes again. In fact, no reply was sent until 5 pm when Newton and Lacroix were summoned by Krofta and were told that the terms were accepted.[199]

The terms of the Czech note reflected the bitterness of the Czechs toward Britain and France. "Forced by circumstances and by excessive pressure and as a result of communication with French and British Governments of 21 September in which the two Governments express their attitude in regard to assistance to Czechoslovakia, if she refused to accept Franco-British proposals and was, as a result, attacked by Germany, the Czechoslovak Government accepts these conditions of the Franco-British proposals with feelings of grief. They note that these proposals were prepared without prior consultation with the Czechoslovak Government."[200]

The value of the guarantees which the British and French had given in exchange for the Czechs giving up their Treaty rights were always going to be worthless. During the afternoon of 21 September, Benes had asked for written assurance of the verbal promise, given by Newton, that 'if Czechoslovakia accepts the Anglo-French proposals (of a guarantee) and, nonetheless, the German Government attacks Czechoslovakia, then the two Governments will come to their assistance'. He got a sharp reply from Newton that 'it was extremely dangerous to make new conditions for acceptance at the last moment'.[201]

---

[198] DBFP, Ibid. no 993.

[199] Laffan, Ibid. pp. 355–359.

[200] DBFP, Ibid. no 1005.

[201] DBFP series 3, Vol. II, no 998.

The French view of guarantees shows just how devious they were in their dealings with the Czechs. A note, prepared by a legal advisor to the Foreign Ministry observed (on the subject of such guarantees) that 'often they are shown to be ineffective, and that was the point of view of Frederick II, who was close to the truth when he said "all guarantees are like the '*ouvrage* of *filigrane*', more suited to satisfy the eyes than to be of any value'.[202] Chamberlain's view was that the guarantee should be as vague as possible.[203] So much for guarantees. French ideas of the value of Treaties were also no different, as De Gaulle explained some years later: "Treaties were like young girls or roses; they last as long as they last."[204]

The reaction of the Czech people was to mount massive demonstrations coupled with a general strike in Prague throughout the night of 21 September and into the morning of 22 September against the proposed surrender. They demanded the dismissal of the Hodza government and that effective steps should be taken to ensure the defence of the country. At 10 am on 22 September, Hodza resigned and a Government of National Defence was appointed by Benes, to be led by General Syrovy, whose command of the Czech Legion during the Great War was the stuff of legends.

General Obratilek read out a defiant message from Syrovy to the crowd in which he said, "I guarantee that the army stands and will stand on our frontiers to defend our liberty to the last. I may soon call upon you to take an active part in the defence of our country in which we all long to join."[205] At much the same time, Chamberlain was leaving on his second trip to see Hitler at Bad Godesberg. Attempts by the SdP to start a rising by storming public buildings and kidnapping German and Czech democrats were quickly suppressed, although the Sudeten towns of Asch and Eger were occupied for a while by the Freikorps troops from Germany.[206] A Czech general mobilisation was declared for the next day, 23 September.

The talks at Bad Godesberg ended in disagreement and acrimony. Hitler now wanted to enlarge the areas to be ceded, which would have included the main Czech fortifications. He was now prepared to advance the date of the cession

---

[202] DDF, Ibid. no 270.

[203] CAB 23/95 Minutes 40/38.

[204] Fenby, J. (2010) *The General*, London: Simon and Schuster, p. 2.

[205] Gedye, G. E. R. (1939) *Betrayal in Central Europe*, New York, p. 467.

[206] DDF, Ibid. no 279, 305 & 307.

from 26 September to 1 October, which was, in any event, the date when he was proposing to invade Czechoslovakia.

He also added the demands of Hungary and Poland for territorial concessions from the Czechs. The demands were included in a special memorandum drafted by Hitler after the talks. But when news of the Czech mobilisation was reported to Hitler, there was consternation. He declared that he would now have to take military measures against Czechoslovakia, but this did not mean, so Chamberlain understood, an immediate invasion. Hitler agreed to postpone any action until 1 October. [207]

The Czechs were now, in fact, in a better position than after Berchtesgaden. They had successfully mobilised with the eventual approval of the British and French Governments.[208] The Soviet Union declared that if Poland attacked Czechoslovakia, it would regard the Soviet-Polish non-aggression pact as null and void.[209] The Soviet People's Commissar for Defence informed the French General Staff that 30 infantry divisions had been moved to the Western Frontier and that tank unit and the air force were fully alerted.[210] Romania and Yugoslavia also announced that they would be bound to assist the Czechs if the Czechs were invaded by Hungary. On 27 September, Krofta told the Cabinet that the Soviets had said that war was inevitable and that they would do their duty. The Little Entente would also be prepared to go along with France and Britain.[211]

On 25 September, Masaryk had delivered a polemic to the Foreign Office in London, full of pent-up fury caused by his sense of betrayal by France and Britain. He wrote: "His Majesty's and the French Government are very well aware that we agreed under the most severe pressure to the Anglo-French plan for ceding parts of Czechoslovakia. We accepted this plan under extreme duress. We had not even any time to make any representations about many unworkable features. Nevertheless, we accepted it, because we understood it was the end of the demands to be made upon us and because it followed from the Anglo-French pressure that these two powers would accept responsibility for our reduced frontiers and would guarantee their support in the event of our being feloniously attacked."

---

[207] Laffan, Ibid. p. 390.
[208] DBFP, Ibid. no 1035, 1047 & 1049. DDF, Ibid. no 313 & 314.
[209] DDF, Ibid. no 318.
[210] DDF, Ibid. no 380.
[211] Olivova, Ibid. p. 254.

After referring to the new plan, produced after the meeting at Godesberg, Masaryk continued: "My Government has now studied the document and the map. It is a de facto ultimatum of the sort usually presented to a vanquished nation and not a proposition to a sovereign state. The proposals go far beyond what we agreed to, in the so-called Anglo-French plan. They deprive us of every safeguard for our National existence. We are to yield up large portions of our carefully prepared defences. Our National and Economic independence would automatically disappear... My Government wish me to declare in all solemnity that Herr Hitler's demands in their present form are, absolutely and unconditionally, unacceptable to my Government. Against these new and cruel demands, my Government feel bound to make their utmost resistance and we shall do so, God helping. The Nation of St. Wenceslas, John Huk and Thomas Masaryk will not be a Nation of slaves. We rely on the two great western Democracies to stand by us in our hour of trial."[212] Alas, it was no more than a pious hope.

Benes himself, when he learnt of Hitler's demands, was afflicted by the most powerful indignant emotion. Lacroix said that he had never seen him in such a state before. Benes pointed out that "the new map would deprive the Czechs of the majority of their coal mines and all their fortifications. It constituted an 'enormity'." Czechoslovakia would be wiped out as a Nation. If that happened, France and Britain would not only lose their position in Europe but also their honour. France and Britain were willing to allow the destruction of its army of a million and a half million men, who were ready to fight. Neither Czechoslovakia nor the President would submit themselves to a dishonourable death. They would fight, not least, to save their honour.[213]

Chamberlain was not to remain inactive for long. He believed there was still a chance of successfully agreeing to Hitler's terms in spite of the spirited defiance of the Czechs. He, therefore, authorised Wilson, his much-criticised Foreign Affairs Advisor, to visit Hitler to seek to change the Godesberg ultimatum. For the first time, it was suggested that the Czechs themselves should take part in the negotiations about the future of their Nation. Wilson was not successful. Further proposals were sent by the British and French about a timetable for the cession of territory.[214]

---

[212] DBFP, Ibid. no 1092.

[213] DDF, Ibid. no 350.

[214] DBFP, Ibid. no 1138 & 1140.

On 27 September, the British took the important step of mobilising the Fleet in the hope that it might have an effect on Hitler but a note to the Czechs that "there is no possibility that at the end of that conflict, whatever the result, 'Czechoslovakia could be restored to her frontiers of today" was scarcely a clarion call for resistance.[215] When a White Paper containing relevant documents about the crisis was published, this particular note (among others) was deliberately suppressed. On the same day, the Czechs took the precaution of sending instructions to their representatives at Geneva to be ready to hand a note to the General Secretary of the League of Nations, to appeal to the council under Articles 11, 6, and 18 in the event of German aggression.

On the morning of 28 September, Chamberlain sent a last letter to Hitler and a message to Mussolini. No attempt was made to keep the Czechs appraised of Britain's views or to consult them about the future of their country. Nor were the Czechs told that Mussolini was to be involved. Benes' view had not changed since 25 September.[216] When the invitation to the Munich Conference was received in dramatic circumstances by Chamberlain in the House of Commons, it was conditional on neither the Soviet Union nor Czechoslovakia being present or being represented. On 26 September, Benes had told one of his Generals: "We shall defend ourselves to our dying day" and was convinced that if Czechoslovakia could endure the onslaught for three weeks and France and the Soviet Union came in, the war with Hitler would be as good as won.[217]

On 26 September, Chamberlain had suggested to Hitler that Czech representatives should take part in discussions (which the Czechs naturally welcomed).[218] Hitler said that he would agree only if the Czechs accepted the Godesberg terms and allowed the German troops to occupy the Sudeten areas by 1 October. After Chamberlain had told the House of Commons that he accepted Hitler's invitation to the conference in Munich without the Czechs, Masaryk naturally protested that he wanted a Czech presence at the Conference which was to decide the future of his Nation. Who could blame him? He was told forcefully that Hitler had agreed to the conference only on the condition that Czechoslovakia and the Soviet Union were excluded.

---

[215] DBFP, Ibid. no 1138.

[216] DDF, Ibid. no 417.

[217] Zeman, Ibid. p. 130.

[218] CMD paper 5847.

The Soviets were also told that an invitation to them could threaten not only the success of the Conference but its very realisation. [219] Chamberlain expressed the view to Benes that he would have the interests of Czechoslovakia at heart to which Benes replied: "I beg that nothing may be done at Munich without Czechoslovakia being heard."[220] When, during the conference, Chamberlain further suggested that the Czechs should be consulted on a guarantee, to be given on behalf of the Czechs, about the preservation of existing installations, Hitler flew into a rage and the matter was dropped. Daladier expressed the view that the consent of the Czechs was unnecessary observing that 'in England, he had consented, in principle, to the cession of the territory by Czechoslovakia without first enquiring of the Czechoslovak Government, in spite of the existence of the Franco-Czech Pact'. [221]

On 28 September, at Chamberlain's request, two Czech representatives, Mastny, the Minister in Berlin and Dr Masarik, private secretary to the Foreign Minister, arrived in Munich. Their reception at the airport was similar to that accorded to police suspects. They were taken in a police car accompanied by the Gestapo.[222] They were kept virtually under house arrest. They were not allowed to leave their room nor use the telephone. When, during the course of the Conference, they were able to learn of the main lines of the new plan and were given a map on which the areas to be occupied were marked, they raised objections to Wilson, who turned them down summarily. They were further told by Ashton-Gwatkin that if they did not accept, they would have to settle with the Germans absolutely alone and that the French shared the same view.[223]

The terms which were finally agreed, by the British and French, included the occupation by the German army, between 1 October and 10 October, of predominantly German territory, the evacuation which would be guaranteed by Britain, France and Italy, the preservation of existing installations and an International Commission of the Four Powers (with a Czech representative in attendance) to deal with further questions of plebiscites in the Sudeten territory.[224]

---

[219] DBFP, Ibid. no 1221.

[220] DBFP, Ibid. no 1194.

[221] Documents and Materials, Ibid. no 34 & 36.

[222] Documents and Materials, Ibid. no 37.

[223] Gedye, G. (1939) *Fallen Bastions*, London: Victor Gollancz, p. 483.

[224] DBFP, Ibid. no 1224.

The terms were presented to the Czech representatives in the early hours of 29 September, when they were summoned to Chamberlain's private sitting room. They were told in effect that there was nothing further to discuss. The plan, which they were told was to be accepted, "was", said Wilson, "a considerable improvement upon the German memorandum and time was of the essence as the Commission was due to meet at 5 pm that afternoon."[225] This was followed by pressure from Britain, France and Italy on the Czechs, urging a plain acceptance of the terms and pointing out that 'there is no time for argument'.[226]

Chamberlain did not conceal his fatigue, yawned without ceasing and showed no embarrassment. Masaryk's record sums up the position of the Czechs graphically. He wrote: "It had been explained to us in a sufficiently brutal manner and that, by a Frenchman, this was a sentence without right of appeal and without possibility of modification."[227]

The Czech Government then met with the leaders of the political parties, the former Government, the Cabinet and two Generals representing the army. At 12 pm on 29 September, the Czechs announced that they accepted the decisions taken at Munich 'without us and against us', but protested yet again that the decisions taken at Munich were taken unilaterally and without their participation. When the Committee of the Coalition Majority met in the afternoon, they decided that they could do nothing to reverse the decision which had already been accepted.

A French view of the Munich Agreement is contained in the letter of resignation sent to Daladier by Faucher. On 6 October, he wrote: "The Czechoslovak people have enthusiastically welcomed the mobilisation announced on 23 September…it was hoped that France would not delay mobilisation in its turn…the dominant sentiment in Prague is of having been betrayed…people are crying because they feel betrayed by France, which they loved. There are always the same arguments. You have assumed the duties of Hitler's executioners. We have had a humiliation without precedent, in losing our fortifications almost immediately and without a fight…we have been cruelly punished for putting our faith in France. It is said that France will guarantee the new frontiers…but what confidence can there now be that France will keep its word.?"

---

[225] DBFP, Ibid. no 1227.

[226] DBFP, Ibid. no 1225.

[227] Documents and Materials, Ibid. no 37.

Faucher went on to say "I find it difficult to refute these arguments… M. LePresident, I cannot forget that you yourself asked me to give to President Benes an assurance that any attack against Czechoslovakia would immediately involve the French Forces in combat. Memory of that mission has played no little part in my decision to tender my resignation…the resentment of the Czechs is not a passing feeling; it is deep…everyone will always remember the Czech defeat and also inevitably the role played by the French ally, up till then, loved and admired. People say to me that to yield in our present circumstances is cruel but not dishonourable. The essential thing is not the loss of one's honour… In your telegram to me of 28 September, you appealed to me to continue to fulfil my duties as a French General. Among those duties, there is one which I have always been careful to fulfil that of telling you the truth without succumbing to the temptation of embellishing it when I suppose that it may be disagreeable to learn."[228]

On 1 October, German tanks crossed the border. The International Commission set up at the time of the Munich Agreement was dominated by the Germans. Virtually every border fortification fell into German hands. By the time the final settlement was agreed in November, Czechoslovakia had handed over to Germany 1,100 square miles of territory, inhabited by 2,000,000 Sudetens and 800,000 Czechs.

They had also lost up to three-quarters of their industrial production.[229] Benes resigned and fled to England. On 15 March 1939, the Germans occupied the rest of Czechoslovakia. There was no reaction from the Western Allies. The Germans were to remain there for another six years until the Soviets drove them out in May 1945 and the war came to an end. So much for the worth of guarantees.

---

[228] DDF series 2, Tom. XII, no 49.
[229] Faber, Ibid. p. 430.

Chapter Five:
Why and What If?

Three questions remain. Why did the Czechs allow themselves to be bullied by the British and the French? Why did they make no serious effort to ensure, long before the risk of war arose, that they had engaged in sufficient military discussions with France and the Soviet Union so as to present a united front against the Germans? And finally, if they had stood firm, is it possible that they would have been any worse off than they were after Munich?

The first question is most easily answered. The Czechs were a peace-loving Nation with a history forged after centuries of resistance to outsiders. They entered into their Treaties with France and the Soviet Union in the belief that it would provide them with security against any further interference from German-speaking nations. In the same vein, attempts were made to seek peaceful accommodation with Hitler's Germany. Because of their belief in the solemn undertakings into which the French had entered, the Czechs looked to France as their adviser and protector. They may not have known of the old English saying 'he who pays the piper calls the tune' for it was France who had helped to bring the Nation into independence and ensured its future existence.

Notwithstanding the shock of Locarno, the Czechs had no reason to doubt the sincerity of the French until the events of May 1938. Then, perhaps for the first time, the Czechs realised that Britain and France had taken fright and were now themselves anxious to control the Czech political agenda. It was the Czechs' mistaken belief that, if they followed the British and French diktats, they were likely to be better protected. They desperately needed the support of the Western Allies. Sadly, it was not forthcoming.

The answer to the second question is more difficult. The Czechs, like other nations, were slow to appreciate the danger posed by Germany but when they did, they were anxious to ensure that they gave no offence to Germany by way of any perceived threat. There were desultory talks with the French and some more useful cooperation with the Soviets. It is clear that after May 1938, the subject of talks was again raised and was ignored by the French, who must bear primary responsibility for the breakdown. In the light of French indifference, it is difficult to see what more the Czechs could have done to protect themselves.

Finally, what if the Czechs had refused to be bullied and resisted the German invasion? Would they have been worse off? Would the Germans have, in fact, invaded? There is much evidence that a number of prominent German generals were against the idea. It is clear, however, from the manner of Beck's sacking and from the Hossbach memorandum, that Hitler was bent on destroying Czechoslovakia. Hitler was not much given to accepting the views of his Generals as witness his decision in 1941 to invade the Soviet Union against their military advice.

It can, therefore, be taken as given that Hitler was determined on an invasion. What were the prospects? Firstly, there are the contemporary (and conflicting views) of those most closely involved and secondly, there are the views of a number of distinguished historians' writing sometime after the event. The Czech view was communicated to Benes on 29 September by his Military Advisers. They included General Syrovy (who was both Prime Minister and Minister of Defence), General Krejci, chief of the General Staff and General Husarek. There were a number of problems. The Soviet army still did not have transit rights across Poland or Romania and could not arrive for at least six weeks. In any event, the Soviet Union's obligations depended on French intervention or on a resolution by the League of Nations. A number of Czech defence fortifications were still incomplete. Operational plans had been based on the idea of large parts of the German army being deployed on the French frontier, against an attack by French forces, that now seemed unlikely. Further, one effect of the Anschluss had been to expose part of Bohemia and the southern borders of Moravia to a German invasion, which had previously been regarded as comparatively safe.[230]

Both Keitel and von Manstein expressed the view, subsequently, that the invasion would not have succeeded.[231] Field Marshal von Kleist is reported as saying that had the Czech crisis ended in war, the only alternative to catastrophe

---

[230] Zeman, Ibid. p. 135.

[231] Supra.

would have been to arrest the political leadership.[232] General Kluge took the view that the army was quite unprepared for war and the German Military Attaché in Belgrade in December told the British Military Attaché that the war might have dragged on for years.[233]

In August, General von Wietersheim had told Hitler that with the current German forces in the West, Germany could not resist a determined French attack in the West for more than three weeks.[234] At the Nuremberg trials, the German Generals gave evidence that Germany was not prepared for World War if France and Britain had stood firm.[235] The United States' Assistant Military Attaché in Berlin took a different view. He thought that it would have taken the German army not more than two weeks and probably less, to overcome Czech resistance.[236]

On 26 September, there was a report from the Hungarian Minister that Hitler had made some concessions at Godesberg because of the pressure of German 'military spheres', which feared an international conflagration.[237] Beck had resigned in September. There is some evidence too that on 26 and 27 September, a deputation from the General Staff of the army, consisting of Generals Hannerken, von Leeb and Bodenschatz had left a memorandum for Hitler expressing their opposition to a declaration of war.

When Admiral Raeder visited Hitler on 27 September, he, too, supported their view. The memo pointed out that the German population had low morale and was incapable of sustaining the strain of a European war, there was an absence of discipline in the army, parts of the Siegfried line were unsatisfactory; defeat was to be expected in any but a local war, the Czechoslovak army, even if fighting without Allies could hold out for three months, only a part of the German forces could be used as it would be necessary to retain covering forces on the Polish and French frontiers, as well as troops in Austria to prevent a popular uprising.[238] Francois Poncet, the French Ambassador in Berlin also

---

[232] von Hassell, U. (1947) *The von Hassell Diaries 1938–1944*, New York: Garden City, p. 9.

[233] PRO FO 371/21676/132/18.

[234] Wheeler-Bennett, J. (1953) *The Nemesis of Power*, Macmillan and Co., p. 403.

[235] Trial of the Major War Criminals, X 509-510 XV 361 XX 606.

[236] FRUS 1938 1, pp. 735–736.

[237] Documents and Materials, Ibid. no 32.

[238] Ripka, Ibid. p. 212.

reported the conflict between Hitler and his Generals and the financial and economic problems facing Germany.[239]

The state of the German civilian population is well illustrated by an observation of King Boris of Bulgaria, who on a visit to Berlin on 27 September, recorded 'the total lack of enthusiasm, indeed the almost sullen attitude, of the populace when large columns of motorised troops in full field equipment were moving through Berlin towards the eastern frontier for hours'.[240]

The contemporary view of the Czech army is somewhat divided. The British Military Attaché in Berlin reported on 27 September, after visiting Czechoslovakia, that morale was poor and resistance would prove to be feeble.[241] But the Military Attaché in Prague took a contrary view. He reported that morale was good, they (the Czech troops) had confidence in their cause, their leadership and their equipment. "In my view," he wrote, "there is no material reason why they should not put up a really protracted resistance singlehanded. It all depends on their morale. If it holds, it (the war) may drag on for months."[242]

On the previous day, Gamelin told the British Ministers that the Czech army would give a good account of itself, though he seems to have been somewhat Delphic in his views. He gave it as his opinion that the Czechoslovak army (34 divisions) was a good army, good personnel, excellent morale of people fighting for their lives, and with an efficient command. But he added that he was prepared only to say that they could certainly hold out, for a few weeks but perhaps not for a few months.[243]

Gamelin had expressed the view in September that the French army was in a position not only to hold the Maginot line but to carry out successfully a series of offensives into German territory.[244] Any idea that the French would have taken any offensive action can be readily discounted. It is only necessary to look at their behaviour in the winter of 1939–1940.

A more optimistic picture of the Czechs was painted by Gamelin's Chief Staff Officer, Colonel Petitbon, who told the British Military Attaché that the Czech army was well equipped, well trained and efficient in every way. He did

---

[239] DDF series 2, Tom XI, no 21 (n 1) 40 & 54.

[240] DBFP series 3, Vol. III, no 173. Laffan, Ibid. p. 408.

[241] DBFP series 3, Vol. II, no 1143.

[242] DBFP series 3, Vol. II, no 704.

[243] DBFP, Ibid. no 1143.

[244] Faber, Ibid. p. 275.

not think that the Germans would succeed in overrunning the country without hard fighting and great losses, nor did he think it would be done very quickly.[245]

The most realistic conclusion is that of Williamson Murray, who set out his detailed reasoning over a number of pages. "The war would have turned, as it had in the Great War and in the Second World War, on the economic strength and staying power of the opposing sides. In terms of numbers of divisions, economic resources, industrial capacity and naval forces, Germany would have faced overwhelming allied superiority in 1938 whether she faced only Britain and France or an enlarged coalition that included the Soviet Union… Even so, the war against Germany would not have been easy, nor would it have been quickly won. But the results would have led to the eventual collapse of the Nazi regime at considerably less cost than the war that broke out in the following September."[246] It is also necessary to factor the strength of the Czech forces and their fortifications into this conclusion.

There are two other questions which arise. If the Czechs had stood firm, would France have come to their aid? This is a different question from whether they should. Would the Soviet Union have followed? Would Britain have followed? If yes, would it have prevented the destruction of Czechoslovakia in the same way that Poland was destroyed in 1939? There are formidable arguments on both sides from distinguished historians.[247]

One of the most recent while comparing the relative numbers of combatants, serviceable aircraft and production figures wholly fails to take into account French military and political inertia.[248] There is no certain answer to the first question. All the indication from the French Government in the spring and summer of 1938 were that, if the Czechs did not give autonomy to the Sudeten Germans immediately, the French would wash their hands of them.

After Godesberg, the position changed little and after Munich itself, the threats became clearer still. The French had not mobilised. They had not entered into any military talks with the Czechs. They had no plans to invade Germany or to strike at the industrial cities of the Ruhr. They had not invited the Czechs to the Conference. They had simply presented them with a fait accompli. There was no indication, indeed much evidence to the contrary, that neither the French

---

[245] DBFP, Ibid. no 1202.

[246] Murray, Ibid. pp. 217–263.

[247] Murray, Ibid. p. 423.

[248] Bouverie, T. (2019) *Appeasing Hitler*, Bodley Head, pp. 294–297.

Government in the persons of Bonnet and Daladier or the French people were willing to go to war, certainly not without allies.

There are two analogies which can be fairly drawn. In 1914, France had fulfilled its Treaty obligations, but only because the invasion of Belgium was perceived as a direct threat to French territory, the decision was not taken without vacillation. In September 1939, Britain and France, with different degrees of enthusiasm, had felt obliged to honour their guarantee to Poland. The Germans had offered a Conference and made promises about the future independence of Poland. Bonnet was prepared to take part in such a Conference. The British, also, were willing but with the proviso that German troops must first withdraw from Poland. The Germans were unwilling to do this. No doubt, without that proviso, there would have been another Munich.

Hitler invaded Poland on 1 September, but Britain did not declare war until 3 September and France waited until 4 September. In the result, it is difficult to believe, after all the French pressure on the Czechs, that if the Czechs had decided to fight, France would have honoured its Treaty obligations. The British had no such treaty obligations They were certainly not willing to go to war on their own, 'because of a quarrel in a faraway country between people of whom we know nothing'.

Could the Western Allies, have prevented the destruction of Czechoslovakia? What happened after the invasion of Poland, in September 1939 gives the answer. Between September 1939 and May 1940, the French army made no offensive movement against Germany, apart from a few rather desultory patrols into no man's land. Their troops remained safe and sound, in defensive positions, protected by the Maginot line.

Nor was Britain's contribution any greater. In the same period, the Navy, (apart from the action with the Graf Spee) merely sought to enforce a blockade (which in the result had much less impact than was envisaged). The Air Force, for its part, dropped a few bombs on Germany but spent much time and energy dropping leaflets on the Germans. This was in the astonishing belief that the German population was about to rise up against Hitler's regime.

When Poland was invaded, there was mobilisation by the French but they were not committed to taking any offensive action until 16 days thereafter.

Warsaw fell within about ten days. The French army was forbidden to fire on German soldiers, who were happily playing football on the Siegfried line.[249]

France and Britain had a different timetable for declaring war and the French were forbidden to start hostilities until early on 4 September 1939. It is self-evident that Czechoslovakia would have suffered the same fate as Poland and that there was no sensible contribution which the Western Allies could or would have made to its defence. At least, the Czechs could have preserved their honour.

---

[249] FRUS 1937 1, p. 48.

Part Two
The German Perspective

Chapter Six:
Plans for Expansion

No one should have been surprised at the German determination to acquire further land at the expense of its neighbours. In May 1937, Vansittart had observed that "German hegemony meant the conquest of Austria and Czechoslovakia and the reconquest of Danzig and Memel followed by the reduction of the other states (Hungary, Yugoslavia, Romania and Greece) to the condition of satellites, military satellites, when required. This is a quite clear and comprehensible programme, but it is quite incompatible with our interests. We fought the last war largely to prevent this."[250]

At the heart of German imperialism in which it considered that the whole of Central Europe was uniquely within its sphere of influence was the Prussian military machine. A typical British view of Prussia, written in the middle of the Second World War was expressed by Lord Harlech, the High Commissioner in South Africa, in 1943. He wrote to Attlee, then Dominion Secretary: "The Prussian military tradition, ever since Frederick the Great's ghastly father, has been the archenemy of peace and progress in Europe, Germany, east of the Elbe, has been the cancer of Europe for over 200 years."[251]

It is not necessary to go back to 1808 when Scharnhorst and Gneisenau created a new Prussian Officer Corps and the Prussian General Staff. Clausewitz described the officer corps as 'a kind of guild, with its own laws, ordinances and customs. The army was bound to the Emperor. Thus, by the constitution 'all

---

[250] Cadogan, Ibid. p. 15.

[251] Dominion Office Papers DO 121/107. Thomas-Symonds, N. (2010) *Attlee: A Life in Politics*, London: I. B. Tauris, p. 108.

German troops are obliged to obey unconditionally the commands of the Emperor'.[252]

Nor did the relationship change after the abdication of the Kaiser. It was continued by Hitler. On 2 August 1934, the German Armed Forces were forced to swear an oath. "I swear before God to give my unconditional obedience to Adolf Hitler, Fuhrer of the Reich and the German people, Supreme Commander of the Wehrmacht and I pledge my word as a brave soldier to observe this oath always, even at the peril of my life." This oath of personal allegiance was to cause serious issues of conscience among a number of the Officers who opposed Hitler's plans for expansion and also among those who bravely entered into conspiracies against him. In the result, a number of distinguished Army Officers, who distrusted Hitler, decided that they were not prepared to violate their oath by joining these conspiracies.

Prussia's increasingly military capabilities had been reflected in its victories over the French at Leipzig, Waterloo and more recently in the Franco-Prussian War in 1870 at Sedan. Here Germany made a start in its quest for lebensraum, by annexing Alsace Lorraine. Apart from the somewhat unsuccessful search for colonies in Africa, German efforts were directed to an economic strategy, alongside a military one. The German population had, by 1914, increased to some 68 million compared with France's 40 million. Industrially, the Germans were far in advance of the French. They produced four times as much steel and seven times as much coal.

It was no surprise that German policy was described as Weltpolitik or that its imperialistic ambitions were directed to economic expansion. The language of its national anthem '*Deutschland, Deutschland, über Alles*' said it all. As one author wrote: "By this concentration of all its energies, by this unity of direction, economic Germany has become a power, which is at least as formidable as military Germany and of the same order, power of domination and conquest".[253]

Germany had never been afraid to flex its military muscle. When, in 1914, the Austrians sought advice from the Kaiser as to how to deal with Serbia, they were told by the Kaiser, with typical military arrogance, in effect, to go ahead with their threatened action, thus precluding any chance of avoiding a World War. During the War, by the Treaty of Brest Litovsk in 1918, the Germans annexed large areas of the Soviet Union from the Bolsheviks.

---

[252] Wheeler-Bennett, Ibid. p. 11.

[253] Hauser, H. (1915) *Methodes Allemands d'expansion economique*, Paris, p. 214.

But the humiliating defeat in 1918, together with the loss of its colonies and the cession of land to Poland, France, and Belgium, only served to fuel more extravagant German claims to expansion. This loss of the colonies and cessions of land, together with the desire for revenge, gave Germany a *casus belli*, which it was not slow to exploit. The acceptance of the terms of Versailles was a tactical exercise, involving, initially utter defeat of the German army on the Western Front, in order to achieve ultimate victory and success, by providing for the future re-emergence of Germany, as a great and powerful military nation.[254]

There was nothing new about the German claim for expansion. In order to conquer the rest of Europe and, eventually, the rest of the world, it was regarded as necessary by Germany to secure Bohemia and Moravia because of the strategic position which it occupied in Central Europe. Bismarck had pronounced that Bohemia was the citadel of Europe and that he who controlled it was master of Europe. The Kaiser thought that Central Europe, and especially Austro-Hungary, was a natural starting point for German aggression, but he also had his eyes on expansion towards the Near East, Drang nach Osten.[255] "Let the Americans have the plains, the Russians Siberia, the French and Belgians and British, various malaria ridden lands in Africa, Germany would build her own economic empire in the very cradle of western civilisation."[256]

In September 1914, Bethmann-Hollweg, the Foreign Minister, had expressed the view that the concept of Mitteleuropa was part of German war aims – a Central Europe in which Germany would be the hegemonic power. German industrialists had the same view.[257]

In 1925/1926, Hitler had written, in *Mein Kampf,* about the problems facing Germany: "What form must the life of the German Nation assume in the tangible future and how can this development be provided with the necessary foundation and the required security within the framework of general European relation of forces? A clear examination of the premises for foreign activity, on the part of German statecraft, inevitably led to the following conviction: Germany has an annual increase in the population of nearly 900,000 souls. The difficulty of

---

[254] Wheeler-Bennett, Ibid. p. 59.

[255] McMeekin, S. (2010) *The Berlin-Baghdad Express: The Ottoman Empire and Germany's Bid for World Power* London: Allen Lane, passim.

[256] McMeekin, Ibid. p. 2.

[257] Gagan, K. and Kvacek, R. (1965) *Germany and Czechoslovakia 1918–1945* Prague: Orbis, pp. 9, 10 & 44.

feeding this army of new citizens must grow greater from year to year and ultimately end in catastrophe unless ways and means are found to forestall the danger of starvation and misery in time.

"There were four ways of avoiding so terrible a development for the future…either new soil could be acquired and the superfluous millions (of people) sent off each year, thus keeping the Nation on a self-sustaining basis or we could produce for foreign needs, through industry and commerce and defray the cost of living from the proceeds. In other words, either a territorial policy or a colonial and commercial policy. The acquisition of new soil, for the settlement of the excess population, possesses an infinite number of advantages, particularly if we turn from the present to the future…it must be said that such a territorial policy cannot be fulfilled in the Cameroons but today almost exclusively in Europe.

"We must now coolly and objectively adopt the standpoint that it can certainly not be the intention of heaven to give one people 50 times as much land and soil in this world as another. In this case, we must not let political boundaries obscure for us the boundaries of eternal justice. If this earth really has room for all to live in, let us be given the soil we need for our livelihood… For Germany, consequently, the only possibility of carrying out a healthy territorial policy lay in the acquisition of new land in Europe itself."[258] France was to be regarded as Germany's immortal enemy. No one, thereafter, could complain that Hitler had not made abundantly clear his intention to expand Germany in Europe.

In January 1933, Hitler became German Chancellor. In the same year, Germany withdrew from the League of Nations and the Disarmament Conference. It denounced the provisions of the Versailles Treaty. In 1934, it began re-arming. On 16 March 1935, Hitler issued a decree giving public effect to a rearmament programme, which was warmly welcomed by the military.

In November 1930, Hitler had written: "It is impossible to build up an army and give it a sense of worth if the object of its existence is not the preparation for battle. Armies for the preparation of peace do not exist; they exist for triumphant exertion in war."[259] For Hitler, the last remaining shackle of Versailles was the demilitarisation of the Rhineland. In 1936, in order to justify the reoccupation, Hitler announced that he regarded the Franco-Soviet Treaty as a breach of the Locarno Agreement. At the Olympic games, in the same year, Ribbentrop told

---

[258] Hitler, A. (1969) *Mein Kampf. (Trans. Manheim, R.)*, Hutchinson, pp. 120–128.
[259] Wheeler-Bennett, Ibid. p. 290.

Vansittart that "if England did not give us the possibility to live, there would eventually be a war between them and one of them would be annihilated."[260]

On 5 November 1937, Hitler held a secret conference in the Reich Chancellery with his senior Military Commanders and others. Colonel Hossbach, Hitler's adjutant, made notes, which are usually referred to as the 'Hossbach Memorandum'.[261] Present were the German War Minister, Field Marshal von Blomberg, together with the Commander-in-Chief of the Army, Colonel-General von Fritsch, the Commander-in-Chief of the Navy, Admiral Raeder, the Commander-in-Chief of the Air Force, Herman Goering, and the German Foreign Minister, von Neurath. Hitler said, "The aim of German policy was to make secure and to preserve the racial community and to enlarge it. It was, therefore, a question of space... Germany's future was wholly conditional upon the solving of the need for space."

Hitler repeated that Germany could never be more than partially self-sufficient in raw materials and with an ever-increasing population, there would never be sufficient food from her own resources. Germany's future could only be safeguarded by acquiring additional land. The desire for lebensraum and *grossraumwirtschaft* (sphere of economic dominance) were at the very forefront of German motivation.

Such living space was to be sought, not overseas but in Europe and it could be found only at the risk of conflict. "The history of all ages," he said, "the Roman Empire and the British Empire had proved that expansion could only be carried out by breaking down resistance and taking risks; setbacks were inevitable... The question for Germany was how it could achieve the greatest gain at the lowest cost."

Thus, Germany's problem could only be solved by means of force. There remained to be answered the question 'when?' and 'how?' Although 1943/1945 was the suggested deadline for action against Austria and Czechoslovakia, it was envisaged that the events in Europe might enable Germany to act before then. The Hossbach Memorandum makes no mention of rescuing German fellow Nationals (the Sudeten Germans), said to be living as second class citizens, from foreign tyranny. The assault on Czechoslovakia was to be carried at lightning speed and on a manufactured pretext It was simply an excuse to further Germany's politico-military ambitions.

---

[260] Colvin, I. (1965) *Vansittart in Office*, London: Victor Gollancz, p. 108.
[261] DGFP series D, Vol. I, no 19.

What was envisaged for the Czechs? Hitler's view was that 'even though the population concerned, especially of Czechoslovakia, was not sparse, the annexation of Czechoslovakia and Austria would be an acquisition of foodstuffs for 5 to 6 million people, on the assumption that the compulsory emigration of 2 million people from Czechoslovakia and 1 million people from Austria was practicable'.[262]

That this was not some ill-thought idea of the moment, can be shown from what Hitler is reported as saying in 1932. "We shall never be able to make grand politics without a firm, steel-hard power centre, a centre of 80 or 100 million Germans, living in an enclosed area. My first duty, therefore, will be to create this centre which will not only make us invincible but ensure, once and for all, the decisive ascendancy over all European nations.

"Part of this centre is Austria. That is a matter of course. Bohemia and Moravia, however, also belong to it. In all these areas there is today a large majority of alien tribes and if we want to put our great power on a permanent basis, it will be our duty to remove these tribes. There is no reason why we should not do so."[263]

What then was to happen to the 'tribes' of Czechoslovakia? Hitler's view was simple. "The technical possibilities of our time will enable us to carry out these resettlement plans comparatively easily… The Bohemian-Moravian basin and the Eastern territories bordering on Germany will be colonised by German farmers. The Czechs will be settled in Siberia or Wolhyinia, we shall allocate reservations to them in the new federal states…the Czechs must be expelled from Central Europe."[264] That Siberia was part of the USSR and Wolhynia, a marshy part of Poland does not seem to given Hitler any cause for concern. 'Ethnic cleansing' had not yet found its way into everyday language.

The Hossbach Memorandum continued: "The first objective must be to overrun Czechoslovakia and Austria and so secure Germany's Eastern and Southern flanks." Hitler believed that Britain, almost certainly, and France, probably, had already tacitly written off the Czechs and were reconciled to the fact that this question would be cleared up in due course by Germany. Once Austria and Czechoslovakia had been overrun, this would greatly increase Germany's economic resources and add 12 divisions to her army. Any attack on

---

[262] DGFP, Ibid. no 19.

[263] Rauschning, Ibid. p. 46.

[264] Ibid. p. 46.

Czechoslovakia would have to be effected with the speed of lightning, but it was not inconceivable that the annexation of Austria and the subjugation of the Czechoslovak might be brought about by peaceful means. The occupation of the Rhineland in 1936 was a good precedent.

On 24 June 1937, Blomberg issued a top-secret directive, which bore the code name 'Operation Green'. It proposed the occupation and elimination of Czechoslovakia. On 21 December, he issued a further directive amending 'Operation Green', the purpose of which 'was to carry out an offensive war so that the solution of the German problem of living space can be carried out to a victorious end'. On 21 April 1938, Keitel was summoned to discuss 'Operation Green' where Hitler favoured lightning action based on an incident (for example the murder of a German Minister in the course of an anti-German demonstration).[265]

Keitel sent Hitler the final draft for 'Operation Green' on 20 May and the official directive was signed by Hitler on 30 May. It ordered an attack on 1 October. It made no mention of the Sudeten Germans or their grievances. Its purpose was explained by Hitler at a meeting on 28 May at the Reich's Chancery. "It is my unshakable will that Czechoslovakia shall be wiped off the map."[266]

Hitler's view that the British Government would quietly acquiesce in his plans for expansion in Europe was amply confirmed by the visit in 1937 of Lord Halifax, then Lord President of the Council, to Germany at the invitation of Goering to go to a hunting exhibition. He met Hitler on 17 November. The tenor of the conversations can be gathered from Schmidt, (the German interpreter's) record. "Lord Halifax spoke of possible alterations in the European Scheme, which might be destined to come about with the passage of time. Among these questions were Danzig, Austria and Czechoslovakia".[267]

A flavour of how easily Halifax had been deceived about German intentions is contained in his report to the Cabinet on 24 November. "Lord Halifax's general conclusion, therefore, was that the Germans had no policy of immediate adventure. They were still too busy building up their country…he would expect a beaverlike persistence in pressing their claims in Central Europe but not in a

---

[265] DGFP series D, Vol. II, no 133.

[266] DGFP series D, Vol. II, no 221.

[267] DGFP series D, Vol. II, no 31. Documents and Materials, Vol. 1, no 1.

form to give others cause to interfere."[268] Within four months of this optimistic assessment, the Germans had marched into the Rhineland.

---

[268] CAB 23/90a/165–167. Cabinet 43(37), 24 November 1937.

Chapter Seven:
Military Affairs

The meeting on 5 November 1937, giving rise to the 'Hossbach Memorandum' was to have a profound effect on the future of those present and the world at large. In particular, it encouraged conspirators to do everything possible to prevent a European war and to take steps, if possible, to overthrow the regime. At the meeting, it is clear that objection was taken not only by Neurath but by Blomberg and Fritsch. The latter two in particular were concerned about the military problems involved, not only in having France as an enemy but also about the strength of the Czechoslovak defences.

Neurath found himself replaced shortly by Ribbentrop. Blomberg and Fritsch were also subsequently removed on trumped-up grounds. Blomberg was regarded by Hitler as much too independent and had objected to Hitler's policies. Hitler clearly thought that it was for the political leader and not for the Commander-in-Chief to take the necessary decisions and that those who raised not only military but also political objections to his proposals, were failing in their duty to the State.

In December 1937, Blomberg asked Hitler for permission to marry. In January 1938, he and Erna Gruhn were married with Hitler and Goering as witnesses. It turned out that Erna Gruhn had been a prostitute and had posed for pornographic photographs. Hitler, therefore, seized the opportunity to dismiss Blomberg. At the same time, Hitler was able to rid himself of Fritsch by the use of false evidence that he was a homosexual. In those circumstances, Hitler could not possibly contemplate his succeeding Blomberg as War Minster nor as remaining as Commander-in-Chief of the Army. Hitler himself took over command of the entire Wehrmacht, nominating von Brauchitsch as Commander-in-Chief of the Army.

His decree of 4 February 1938 read: "From henceforth, I exercise personally the immediate command over the whole armed forces. The former Wehrmacht office in the War Ministry becomes the High Command of the Armed Forces (OKW) and comes immediately under my command as my military staff."[269] Eventually, in June 1938, Hitler publicly expressed regret at the mistake which had been made about Fritsch but took no steps to reinstate him. Hitler had thus succeeded in taking charge of the army and with the successful Anschluss in March 1938 now occupied a position where any resistance by the Officer Corps was marginalised. They soon forgot the unhappy business of the Fritsch affair.

What is, perhaps, remarkable about all of Hitler's plans was the supine acquiescence in them by most of his Generals. While they frequently criticised his plans on the grounds that they would not succeed or that it would result in a war for which Germany was not ready, they never sought to question the morality of his ambition to rule the whole of Europe. Nor did they regard it as in any way, unthinkable, for a so-called civilised country like Germany, to seek to enslave another independent Nation.

It is true that the decision to reoccupy the demilitarised Rhineland zone had caused consternation among the Generals. That was because it was inconceivable to them that neither the British nor the French would regard such action, in defiance of the Treaty of Versailles and in breach of the Locarno Pact, as an occasion, at least, to impose some sanction if not to declare war. How, they asked themselves, could the French possibly acquiesce in the presence of German forces on their frontier or with the City of Strasbourg at the mercy of German guns? Fritsch, Blomberg and Beck each in their separate ways sought to deflect Hitler from his plans.

There were various suggestions. One was that the reoccupation should be accompanied by a declaration that Germany would not fortify the area west of the Rhine. Another was that the German forces should withdraw if the French also withdrew a more substantial number of their troops from the frontier. These suggestions fell on deaf ears. So did their idea of withdrawing some of the troops in the event of the French manning the Maginot line. Hitler's successful gamble gained him immense prestige. It represented a major victory in his battle with the Generals.

---

[269] Faber, p. 74.

The reaction of the Generals to the Hossbach Memorandum was no different. They pointed out that it was foolish to embark on war unless the odds were in favour of success and, in their view, they were not. There was not a word about the immorality involved, nor any criticism, as such of unprovoked aggression. The nearest there was to any criticism, was contained in a letter which Field Marshal Ludwig Beck, the Army Chief of Staff, wrote about the 'memorandum'.

Having cited Hitler's "renewed endangering of the unity of the German people, his wishful thinking and his outstanding lack of solid foundation," he went on, "the enormity of French and British opposition to any extension of German living space or German power is beyond question. But is it out of place to label this opposition as irrevocable or insurmountable? Politics is the art of the possible. It would, therefore, be far better first, to exhaust all possibilities in trying to arrange some settlement, especially in view of the mutual power relationships. Moreover, such a policy would be more intelligent, even should it come to some future confrontation." [270]

Mutiny and revolution are words not normally to be found in a German Officer's dictionary. Nevertheless, Beck, as Chief of Staff wrote on a number of occasions, (the first on 5 May 1938) suggesting that for military reasons the invasion of Czechoslovakia was to be avoided. Hitler rejected his views. On 28 May, Hitler announced his unalterable decision to destroy Czechoslovakia by military action within a foreseeable time. On 30 May, Beck read a new memorandum to Brauchitsch. In it, he observed that Germany was not very strong and as regards to finance, foodstuffs and raw materials, the position was worse even than that in 1917/1918. He added that the Wehrmacht was inferior in personnel, equipment and morale compared to the 1914 army.

He, therefore, concluded that, although Germany would win the Czech campaign, against a coalition of Czechoslovakia, France, Britain and the United States, Germany would lose the war. Beck thought that Hitler lacked realistic advice and that, if the situation persisted, the fate of the Wehrmacht and therefore the fate of Germany could only be painted in the blackest colours.[271]

On the same day as this memorandum, Hitler instructed his Service Chiefs to be prepared to carry out the decision to invade Czechoslovakia by the end of

---

[270] Heineman, J. (1979) *Hitler's First Foreign Minister, Constantin Freiherr von Neurath*, Los Angeles: University of California Press, p. 163. Hoffman, P. (1988) *German Resistance to Hitler*, Mass: Harvard University Press, p. 76.
[271] Hoffman, Ibid. p. 80.

September, so that action could be taken at any time thereafter. Beck's next memorandum pointed out that Hitler's directive had been issued without prior consultation with the Chief of Staff of the Army and that an invasion of Czechoslovakia could only lead to disaster. The Army General Staff, he wrote, must refuse to take any responsibility for measures based on these principles. [272]

In another memorandum, dated 16 July, Beck pointed out the dangers of a general European and, probably, worldwide war. He did not now believe that there was any prospect of success in an invasion of Czechoslovakia because France and Britain would intervene and the result would be the defeat of Germany. In his discussions with Brauchitsch, Beck proposed that Senior Commanders should force Hitler to halt his war preparations and that, in the alternative, they should all resign. [273]

Beck was acutely conscious that the army had sworn a personal oath to Hitler as a Supreme Commander, but believed that if the Commander-in-Chief of the Army together with its most Senior Generals, resigned from their posts, it would precipitate an internal crisis, which would almost certainly result in some sort of coup. To this end, the plotters set out their ideas.

"It will thereafter be necessary for the Army to be prepared not only for a possible war but also for upheaval at home, which it should be possible to confine to Berlin. Issue orders accordingly. Get Witzleben together with Helldorf." (The former commanded the 111 Army Corps and Berlin Military District, while the latter was Police President of Berlin.) In addition, Brockdorff-Ahlefeldt, the Area Commander of Potsdam was also to join the conspiracy. [274]

Beck continued to seek to persuade Brauchitsch to warn Hitler of the follies of his plans but Brauchitsch would have none of it. Thus thwarted, Beck sent another memorandum to him restating the view that he and his fellow Generals were opposed to a policy, which would involve Germany in an aggressive war against France or Czechoslovakia because Germany was not prepared for war against the great powers. In addition to his memorandum, he proposed to Brauchitsch that the Leading Generals should make a formal joint declaration to Hitler to stop his invasion plans. If they were unsuccessful, they should resign en masse.

---

[272] Hoffman, Ibid. pp. 79–80.
[273] Hoffman, Ibid. p. 80.
[274] Hoffman, Ibid. pp. 79–84.

Now, for the first time, he raised the moral issue. "The Generals were to protest not only against the war which they could not win but also against the abuses of the regime; the rule of terror, the persecution of the churches, the suppression of free speech and expression, the corruption and extravagance among the Bonsokratie. They must demand from the Fuhrer a return to the rule of law in the Reich and the principle of 'Prussian cleanliness and simplicity'."[275] Beck continued to press Brauchitsch but without effect.

On 29 July, Beck exercised his right as Chief of Staff to call a meeting of his Generals, so as to be able to present his views to the High Command. The idea was that Brauchitsch would preside, Beck would state his views, get the approval of the other Generals and Brauchitsch would sum up in a speech, prepared by Beck. The matter would then be reported to Hitler. On 4 August, the meeting duly took place. Of the 20 present, only two dissented from Beck's views But, when Brauchitsch summed up, there was no call by him for action. No decision was taken. Brauchitsch simply forwarded Beck's memorandum of 16 July to Hitler.[276]

Hitler did not remain quiet for long. On 10 August, Senior Army and Luftwaffe Staff Officers were summoned to a meeting. After a three-hour monologue on the subject of his political views, Hitler gave them a dire warning about defeatism and loss of morale. They left in some disarray. On 15 August, he repeated his intention of invading Czechoslovakia. He followed this up on 18 August at a gathering of Generals at Juteborg when he reminded them of Stalin's widespread military purges. "I too would not recoil from destroying 10,000 officers if they opposed themselves to my will. What is that in a Nation of 80 million? I do not want men of intelligence. I want men of brutality." He then issued an order that interference by the Army in political affairs was categorically forbidden and demanding unconditional obedience from his Officers. This was too much for Beck and he resigned. He allowed news of his resignation to be withheld and it made no impact. He was succeeded by General Halder, who continued with the plans for a coup.

---

[275] Foerster, W. (1953) *Generaloberst Ludwig Beck*, Munich: Isar Verlag, pp. 98–106.
[276] Hoffman, Ibid. pp. 83–84.

Chapter Eight:
Conspiracies

The difficulty facing the conspirators was that they were anxious to avoid any form of civil war or bloodshed. They appeared to think that the best course was to wait and see whether the invasion of Czechoslovakia was actually going to take place. The critical moment for the coup was to be the period between the issuing of the orders to invade and the beginning of the war. The behaviour of the Western Allies was central to the success of any coup. Unless it were clear that the Allies would be prepared to stand up to Hitler over Czechoslovakia, any internal coup was doomed to failure. The events of 20 May had encouraged the conspirators to believe that there might be a united stand by the Allies over Czechoslovakia, but as the summer went on, the signals from Paris and London showed a considerable weakening in the support of Prague.

A large number of groups were involved in the various conspiracies. Inevitably, they had separate objectives, separate plans and separate tactics. Was Hitler to be taken alive or was he to be assassinated? When should they make their move? Was Hitler to be declared insane? What form of Government was then to take charge? What policies were to be adopted? Brauchitsch, who was one of the key figures, was reluctant to give the order for the coup to take place until he was completely satisfied that the decision for war had been taken. In the result, the Runciman mission and the visits by Chamberlain to Hitler had a disastrous effect on the spirit of the conspirators. After the four-power meeting in Munich, the order for the coup was never given. There was no point, thereafter, in the resistance taking any action.

The reason that there never was a successful putsch, according to Halder, was the absence of clear and resolute leadership and an inability to choose the right moment to act. The conspirators made the excuse that Hitler had remained at the Berghof, while the putsch was planned to take place in Berlin. Initially, it seemed that Chamberlain might stand up to Hitler as a result of their warnings. But when Chamberlain announced that he was going to Munich, the whole purpose of the exercise was frustrated, although it may have been Chamberlain's first visit to Hitler, which caused the conspirators to hold back.[277] In any event, the very idea of Chamberlain actually negotiating with Hitler was quite sufficient to dampen the idea of a putsch.

Could the conspirators not have struck much earlier? They had known the details and timetable of 'Operation Green' that September 30 was the last possible day of peace and that if they were to succeed in their purpose, they must carry out their plans before then. The questions which cry out to be answered are not only whether the proposed coup was realistic but also whether the Western Powers should have taken German resistance seriously and given proper encouragement to the conspirators.

During the '30s, there were a large number of visits by Germans to London in an attempt to persuade the British and French Governments of the warlike intention of the German Government and to encourage the former, in particular, to give support to the resistance movements in Germany. Prominent among these was the former mayor of Leipzig, Carl Goerdeler, one of the leaders of the opposition to Hitler. He first visited London in June 1937 where he met Vansittart, who recorded that "Goerdeler was an impressive person, wise and weighty, a man of great intelligence and courage and a sincere patriot."[278] One problem was that Goerdeler had an all too optimistic faith in Goering and took the view that the positions of Austria, the Sudetenland and the Polish corridor needed revision. These nationalistic views undoubtedly diminished his influence with the British.

In March 1938, Goerdeler visited Paris. There he met Pierre Bertaux, who was Chef de Cabinet in the French Ministry of Culture. He had a number of meetings with the Secretary-General of the French Foreign Ministry, Alexis Leger, but when Goerdeler urged the French to adopt a firm attitude on the Czech question, he received no assurance or support. This was partly due also to French suspicions of Goerdeler's connection with Goering and partly because the French realised that Goerdeler's proposals might mean war.[279] The fall of the

---

[277] Wheeler-Bennett, Ibid. pp. 420–423.

[278] FO 371/20733/ C 5933/165/18.

[279] von Klemperer, K. (1933) *German Resistance Against Hitler*, Oxford: Clarendon Press, pp. 95–96.

Blum Government ended his attempts to influence the French. Nor, when he visited London again, in March 1938, did he have much more success.

The attitude of the British Government was summed up in a Foreign Office memo: "I don't see how these Germans can ask us to make their revolution for them".[280] While some of the emissaries were well regarded by Vansittart, their views that the Sudetenland should be ceded to Germany did not seem to form a firm basis for replacing the Hitler regime with some other unknown Government. There was even talk of a monarchy, which must have sounded very unrealistic. It was not thought by the British, that an alternative German Government would be any less enthusiastic about lebensraum or the revision of the Versailles Treaty. Further, their anxiety about the risk of a Government, run on a military basis or even the possibility of a communist regime, was a matter of concern. These were all problems which confronted the Western Allies in deciding how seriously they should treat the conspirators.

Throughout the spring and summer of 1938, Vansittart received a vast amount of intelligence from inside Germany. In addition, there were many visits to London and Paris by members of the opposition, warning the French and British Governments of Hitler's intentions and seeking support for the resistance.[281] But one of the problems confronting the British Government was that they were being asked to support a whole lot of unknown conspirators against the legitimate Government of another nation. Contrary to their policies of appeasement, they might run the risk of finding themselves involved in a world war.

The attitude of the British Government was well summed up in a letter written by Chamberlain to Halifax on 19 August, after the visit to London by von Kleist-Schmenzin, another of the conspirators. "I take it that von Kleist is violently anti-Hitler and is extremely anxious to stir up his friends in Germany to make an attempt at his overthrow. He reminds me of the Jacobites in the Court of France, in King William's time and I think we must discount a good deal of what he says."[282]

There can be no doubt but that the conspirators made it very clear, to both the British and French Governments, of Hitler's intention to invade

[280] Nicosia, F. and Stokes, L. (ed.) (1990) *Germans Against Nazism*, Oxford, Berg Publishers, p. 313.
[281] von Klemperer, Ibid. pp. 86–103.
[282] DBFP series 3 Vol. II. no 686–687.

Czechoslovakia and urged upon them the policy of issuing an open warning to Germany in the hope that Hitler would be deterred from such an exercise. It was, however, the view of the two Governments that in the words of Canning 'a menace not intended to be executed is an engine which Great Britain could never condescend to employ'. In September 1938, Chamberlain wrote in his diary an extract from Professor Temperley's '*Foreign Policy of Canning*'.[283] "Again and again, Canning lays it down that you should never menace unless you are in a position to carry out your threats".[284]

In June 1938, the German Attaché, in Paris, told his British counterpart that the German military wholeheartedly opposed the war.[285] In August 1938, von Koerber, who was a journalist, visited the British Military Attaché in Berlin, Colonel Mason McFarlane, on a number of occasions, to alert him about Hitler's war plans against Czechoslovakia. He spoke about the necessity of supporting the opposition in Germany in order to overthrow the regime.

However, in his case, an enthusiasm for the restoration of the monarchy did nothing to increase his credibility, in the same way, that Goerdeler's support for the monarchy, the Sudeten Germans and the Polish corridor had lessened his. In the same month, the acting head of the Attaché group in the German High Command informed the British Military Attaché that "the Army was now being called on to undertake much that the General Staff considered undesirable or unwise, but that it was obligated to do so unless the Army cooperated sufficiently with the Government. There was always the possibility that control of the army might be taken out of the Army's hands."[286]

Earlier in March 1938, Kleist had approached Ian Colvin, then the *News Chronicle* correspondent for Central Europe, and explained to him about Hitler's plans for Czechoslovakia. It was important, he said, for Britain to prevent this by issuing a firmly worded 'no', which would have the effect of providing the Army General Staff with 'a sheet anchor' in order to restrain Hitler. This message was passed on to Sir George Ogilvy Forbes, counsellor and chargé d'affaires at the British Embassy, from where it was forwarded to the Foreign Office.

---

[283] Temperley, H. W. V. (1966) *The Foreign Policy of Canning*, London: Frank Cass & Co. Ltd.

[284] The Chamberlain Papers, University of Birmingham, NC 18/1/982.

[285] PRO FO 371/21675.

[286] DBFP series 3. Vol. II. no 714.

Meanwhile, at the end of July and the beginning of August 1938, Colvin reported to Lord Lloyd, the Chairman of the British Council, that he had received some information from a General in the German High Command. He, in turn, communicated the information to Vansittart. This was Kleist. On 18 August, with the blessing of Henderson, Kleist arrived in London. He had been instructed by Beck: "Bring me certain proof that Britain will fight if Czechoslovakia is attacked and I will make an end of this regime."[287] What was required was a public declaration of support.

Kleist met Vansittart and Winston Churchill. Kleist reminded Vansittart that the British Government already knew, from previous warnings, that 28 September was the final date for the attack on Czechoslovakia. Churchill sent a letter of appreciation to Kleist of the risks he was running to preserve the peace of Europe and assured him that the Nazi aggression would inevitably lead to war. But Kleist's insistence on bringing up the question of the Polish corridor did not commend itself to Churchill, who was able to offer Kleist very little.

The attitude of the British Government towards the Czech problem had been set out by Chamberlain on 24 March when the French had sought from the British a declaration of support for France. He said that 'British vital interests were not involved like those of other countries, bound by Treaty obligations. While Britain would fulfil its obligations under the covenant, it was not willing to give a guarantee to be automatically brought into force where the discretion of the British Government would be removed.'[288]

This statement was repeated by Simon in a speech at Lanark on 27 August. It fell very far short of a firm commitment to go to war on behalf of Czechoslovakia. The only step taken by the Government, apart from Simon's speech, was the recall of Henderson from Berlin for consultation. The view of the latter was that any firm declaration was likely to irritate Hitler and have an adverse effect. Kleist concluded, after his visit, that there was no one in London who was prepared to wage a preventative war.

A minute by Sir Ivo Mallet of the Foreign Office, on 22 August 1938, after Kleist's visit, (like Chamberlain's letter to Halifax on 19 August) fully sets out the views of the British Government about the various conspirators. It reads: "We have had similar visits from other emissaries such as Doctor Goerdeler, but those for whom the emissaries claim to speak have never given us any reason to

[287] Hoffman, Ibid. p. 85.

[288] House of Commons Official Reports. Fifth Series. Vol 333. Col 1405. 24 March 1938.

suppose that they would be able or willing to take action such as would lead the overthrow of the regime. The events of June 1934 and February 1938, do not lead one to attach much hope to energetic action by the army against the regime."[289]

Another emissary to be sent to England was Lieutenant-Colonel Hans Bohm-Tettelbach. He went at the instigation of Halder. Their intention was to urge the British to stand firm in the face of further demands by Hitler. He failed to meet anyone in any sort of authority. He did give warnings to Julian Piggott, a businessman, whom he had met when he was Inter-Allied High Commissioner in Cologne in the 1920s. Whether the message ever reached the Cabinet is doubtful and, in any event, it is quite clear that it was not likely to have any effect in changing British policy.

In September, there were further attempts to engage with the British Government. This involved a visit by the Kordt brothers at the instigation of the German State Secretary, von Weizacker. Erich Kordt was the Chief of the Ministerial Bureau and his brother, Theo, was the Councillor at the German Embassy in London. Erich had already been on a mission to Brauchitsch, the Commander-in-chief of the Army. He told the General that Germany was isolated and that the idea that France and Britain would not intervene if Germany invaded Czechoslovakia, was a mistaken one. Thus, the responsibility now lay with the General. Although he received a polite hearing, Kordt did not persuade the General to take a more active role. Weizacker had a further line of approach.

On 1 September, Professor Burckhardt, the League of Nations High Commissioner for Danzig, visited Weizacker in Berlin and was told of the proposal to send the Kordt brothers to England. Burckhardt was asked to stop in Berne and to convey to the British Legation there the urgent message that in order to deter Hitler, unambiguous language needed to be used. Burckhardt's retrospective view was that 'Weizsacker was conspiring with a potential enemy for the purpose of securing peace'.[290] Burckhardt drove to Berne where he saw the British Minister, Sir George Warner. He spoke to Halifax's Parliamentary Private Secretary on the telephone. A few days later, he spoke to Sir Ralph Stevenson, the League of Nations expert in the Foreign Office, who in turn passed on the information to Sir William Strang. [291]

---

[289] FO 371/1/21732/C8520/1941/18.

[290] Klemperer, Ibid. p. 101.

[291] DBFP series 3. Vol. II. App IV. (iv) pp. 689–692.

Weizacker's idea was that a letter from Chamberlain should be handed directly to Hitler so that he understood the true position. It was important that it should reach him before the end of the Nuremberg Party rally, which was due to begin on 5 September. Burckhardt further told Stevenson that members of the German Government and Senior Army Officers, to whom he had spoken, were opposed to a war against Czechoslovakia and that any failure would lead to the collapse of the regime. It is clear that if this information ever reached the Cabinet, it was not acted upon.

Throughout this period, it was Henderson's advice against giving an open warning to Hitler, which carried the day. The reason for this was two-fold. Henderson made it clear during his period of office that he thought that Germany had a good argument in relation to the Sudeten Germans and therefore, the whole matter could be settled peacefully and without threats. Secondly, by the end of August, he knew that Chamberlain was intending to fly to Germany, in the immediate future, to negotiate with Hitler.

On 23 August, Theo Kordt had met Wilson, Chamberlain's Political Adviser. He urged Wilson to encourage Chamberlain to take a firm line to prevent an outbreak of war.[292] In September, the British Government were again being urged by the Kordt brothers to use strong language to call Hitler's bluff. Erich announced that if the British Government were to make a firm declaration, he was authorised to reveal to them that the Military, under Beck, would be able to prevent an outbreak of war in which case there would be no more Hitler.

He then composed a letter to his brother, which called for a firm stand on the part of Britain as this would allow the opposition 'to deploy its forces'.[293] On 6 September, Kordt got in touch with Wilson again. On 7 September, he had a meeting with Halifax at 10 Downing St. Cadogan's diary on 6 September records that 'Horace Wilson came over and told me that he had been visited by Herr X (it was, in fact, Herr Kordt), who had said that he put conscience before loyalty and told him that Hitler was preparing to 'march in' on 19th or 20th'.[294] Cadogan's diaries continue on 7 September: "Herr X wants us to broadcast to the German Nation. I said that fatal and the suggestion almost makes me suspect Herr X."[295]

---

[292] DGFP series D. Vol. II. no 382.

[293] Klemperer, Ibid. p. 102.

[294] Cadogan, Ibid. pp. 94/95.

[295] Ibid. p. 95.

On 8 September, Cadogan's diaries record that Chamberlain did not think the warning was a good idea and wanted to visit Hitler.[296]In fact, on 9 September, a warning was sent to the British Embassy in Berlin with instructions for it to be passed immediately to Nuremberg where a Nazi rally was taking place. Henderson was also instructed to have an audience with Ribbentrop. He was to make it clear that if force were used to settle the Sudeten question and if France in the fulfilment of its Treaty obligations came to the assistance of Czechoslovakia, there would be a general conflict from which Great Britain would not stand aloof. The message was to be passed immediately to Hitler.[297]

Henderson's attitude throughout had been against the idea of issuing a warning to Hitler on the ground that it would not restrain him but would have the effect of driving him into further activities. He, therefore, advised Halifax against this idea on the ground that he had already made similar representations on 11 September. No such warning was therefore given. The most that was done was that Chamberlain issued an unofficial statement to the press referring to his somewhat Delphic speech of 24 March and to Simon's speech at Lanark on 27 August.

Erich Kordt, however, continued his efforts and made contact with a French journalist, Pierre Maillaud. He also engaged von Herwarth, then the Second Secretary at the Moscow Embassy, to pass on secret information to the diplomatic community. In addition, Kordt talked to members of the French Embassy and to the Third Secretary at the British Embassy in Berlin about the necessity of standing up to Hitler. Other warnings continued to be received. Von Kessel, who had been Private Secretary to Weizacker, warned the Second Secretary at the British Embassy in Berlin, who passed on the warning to his Ambassador, of the necessity of ceasing to appease Hitler. Von Selzam, one of the junior officers at the German embassy, talked with Group Captain Christie, one of Vansittart's agents. He also had an interview with the American Ambassador, Joseph P. Kennedy, to try to persuade President Roosevelt to threaten intervention if Germany attacked Czechoslovakia.[298]

One of the more remarkable warnings from an emissary resulted from a visit by Beck to Basle in mid-September. Dr Manfred Simon was a German refugee from Nuremberg and entered the French secret service. He was appointed press

---

[296] Ibid. p. 95.
[297] DBFP series 3. Vol. II. no 811 & 815.
[298] von Klemperer, Ibid. p. 104.

attaché at the French Embassy in Berne, where he established contact with the German opposition and exiles. He was told that a major figure opposing Hitler would meet him in a hotel room in Basle. It was Beck. The General encouraged the French to remain firm because if it were made clear to the German army and to the German people that an attack on Czechoslovakia would mean a world war, Hitler would be overthrown. The army might accomplish that even in a totalitarian State because of Kleist's position. Dr Simon sent the information off to the Secretary-General of the French Foreign Ministry, Alexis Leger. Nothing seems to have happened thereafter.

One further warning came, this time to the United States. Jacob Beam, who was stationed at the American Embassy in Berlin, was invited to a party given by Edwin Respondi, formerly the Whip of the Catholic Centre Party in the Reichstag. Beam was informed about the existence of a group of conspirators who, under Halder, were going to assassinate Hitler and, in the event of war, overthrow the regime. This information was apparently forwarded to the State Department but, again, to no effect.

It is clear that the German resistance, in various forms and at no little risk to themselves, consistently made it plain to the British and French Governments that the policy of appeasement was unwise and that the only way to stop Hitler was to issue unequivocal warnings that if Germany went to war with Czechoslovakia, Britain and France would inevitably intervene. This the Western Allies were unwilling to do. While they had some sympathy with the Sudeten Germans, they were also conscious of Canning's aphorism that they should not take up a position, which, if their bluff were called, they would be unable to sustain. Nor did they have much faith in the effectiveness of the conspirators whose various proposals for the future of Germany, after a coup, were regarded as totally unreal. So much then for the conspirators.

Germany's responsibility for the events in Austria and Czechoslovakia is self-evident and indefensible. It has to be remembered that on no fewer than five occasions, in little more than one generation, Germany had launched an unprovoked attack on its neighbours. (France in 1870, France, Belgium and Luxembourg in 1914, Czechoslovakia and Poland in 1939, France, Belgium, Holland, Luxembourg, Denmark, and Norway in 1940, and Greece, Yugoslavia and the Soviet Union in 1941.) The damage and suffering the Germans caused was immeasurable and on a horrific scale.

Nor was Hitler's appetite satisfied by the acquisition of Czechoslovakia. In August 1939, he said, "Everything I undertake is directed against Russia. If those in the West are too stupid and too blind to understand this, then I shall be forced to come to an understanding with the Russians to beat the West and then after its defeat, turn with all my concerted force against the Soviet Union."[299]

It is clear that the so-called grievances of the Sudeten Germans played no part in Hitler's determination to seize Czechoslovakia. While the Sudeten Germans had, like any other minority, some reason to feel that they were being treated as second class citizens by the Czech majority, as Runciman pointed out in his report, this was totally unrelated to Hitler's reason for invading Czechoslovakia. This act of aggression was all part of the German idea of being the commanding power of Mitteleuropa. Hitler in *Mein Kampf* had set out the problems of a Germany with limited space and an increasing population made worse by the loss of its colonies. He could, with some justification, contend that it did not lie in the mouth of the French or of the British, who had spent most of the nineteenth century acquiring an Empire in Africa and elsewhere, to criticise Germany, which had been slow to enter the colonial race and which was now deprived of what little it had, by the Treaty of Versailles.

It could be argued that a more robust approach by the Western Allies to Hitler's plans might have resulted in stopping him in his tracks. But the success of Hitler in taking on the military, with his sacking of Blomberg and Fritsch and his insistence on a personal oath of obedience, allowed him to castrate their power and negate their influence. It is, perhaps, difficult to understand why the Military, with few exceptions, were prepared to criticise details of his plans, they were not willing, to raise any objections on moral grounds. Some, it is true, joined the conspiracy but this was late in the day and their motives were decidedly unclear.

The conspirators, undoubtedly, did their best to alert the British and French to the danger of Hitler's plans. They ran a great risk in so doing. The all-powerful SS posed a constant threat. But, in the final result, the conspirators failed with dreadful consequences for all concerned. For the British and French Governments, there was the natural caution of one Government when asked to support a conspiracy against another lawful Government. This played a major part in their failure to take the conspirators very seriously. In any event, given

---

[299] Kershaw, I. (2007) *Fateful Choices: Ten Decisions that changed the World 1940– 1941*, London: Allen Lane, pp. 63, 496 & 497, note 29.

that their whole policy was based on a determination to avoid war at all costs, it is not surprising that they adopted this attitude.

Unlike the Kaiser, it was not Hitler's desire to seek lebensraum other than in Europe. He made it clear that the return of the colonies was not an option worth a moment's consideration. It was the 'tribes' of Czechoslovakia who were to be removed from their lands. It seems not to have occurred to the Germans that Czechoslovakia represented an independent, democratic and thoroughly civilised Nation. There is not a single redeeming feature about German behaviour. It simply epitomised the worst features of the Prussian military psyche. Germany must take the major responsibility for the events leading up to Munich (and indeed, thereafter).

Part Three
The French Perspective

Chapter Nine:
The Background

There is a very strong argument that the French were equally the villains of the piece, though for different reasons. While the Germans were fiercely aggressive, the French were consistently feeble. France had been primarily responsible for the establishment of the Czech Republic. They had encouraged Masaryk and Benes to seek independence and had recognised the emerging nationalist movement as the legitimate Government of Czechoslovakia. France followed that up by being the leading supporter of the Czech aspirations at Versailles. While the French gave no thought to the problems which 'self-determination' might cause in the future, it was their abject failure, subsequently, to support the Czechs, which is at the very heart of complaints about France.

In 1921, France sponsored alliances with Czechoslovakia, Romania and Yugoslavia. In January 1924 and October 1925, France and Czechoslovakia signed two treaties in which, in the event of a threat to their common interest, they agreed to consult and assist each other. In 1924, the two governments exchanged letters, providing for cooperation between the General Staffs, though it appears that no more than one staff meeting ever took place. The 1925 treaty placed an obligation on France to go to the aid of Czechoslovakia in the event of it being invaded.

In May 1935, the French and the Soviets entered in an alliance and the Czechs and the Soviets entered into an accord. They were Treaties of mutual assistance and both pacts were interdependent. The Treaty of assistance between Czechoslovakia and the Soviet Union was conditional on the operation of the Franco-Czechoslovak alliance.

It is quite clear that for a number of reasons, by 1938, France had little intention of fulfilling its obligations under the Treaties. As late as 20 July, France had made it plain to the Czechs that neither France nor Britain would go to war over the Sudetenland and that, while publicly the French would continue to assert their solidarity with the Czechs, it was up to the Czechs themselves to find a peaceful solution.[300] This was not a sudden decision but a policy which had gradually evolved during the 1930s. It culminated in Munich. Daladier summarised the dilemma facing France when he spoke to a gathering of ex-servicemen in November 1938. He said that "there could be no greater tragedy than to see one's country, through a falling birth rate, the slowing down of production, disordered finances and the undermining of its currency, running the risk of sinking to second class power."[301] In general, the problem of France's own security and of its attitude to the Czechs cannot be separated from the internal problems which afflicted France. These were many and various including economic, social and political.

More detailed explanations (they can scarcely be described as excuses) for France's behaviour are easy to find. There was a declining population. The economy was generally in a poor state. Particularly after the Stavisky scandal, politics and politicians were regarded as corrupt. There were constant changes of Government, which were mostly incompetent. By 1935, Italy was of greater concern to France than Germany. In 1936, the Spanish Civil War and France's attitude thereto, split the country politically and nearly gave rise to civil disobedience. Its countryside had been devastated in the Great War from the Channel to Switzerland. There was a determination that it must never happen again. Fear of Bolshevism caused the right-wing to prefer Germany to the Soviet Union.

There were no serious staff talks between France and Czechoslovakia, nor any exchange of intelligence. France did not believe that England would be a staunch ally. The state of the armed forces, with good reason, gave rise to considerable anxiety. There was further concern about whether the Soviet Union would or could fulfil its obligations under its Treaty with France and little was done by way of military cooperation between them.

In an age of conscript armies, the real test of great power was the number of men it could put into the field. During the Great War, 25% of Frenchmen, under 30, had been killed. In total, France had lost a million and a half men and some 700,000 had been wounded. Although, shortly after the end of the war, the birth rate revived, thereafter there was a fall. The number of French soldiers eligible

---

[300] DDF series 2. Tom. X. no 238.

[301] Daladier, E. (1939) *Defence du Pays*, Paris, pp. 108–109.

for military service was, for this reason, limited. Particularly, in the years 1935–1940, there was to be a real problem. In 1937, Herriott, President of the Chamber of Deputies, said that "France with only 40 million inhabitants could no longer regard herself as a great power of sufficient military strength or human resources, to maintain her position in Central and Eastern Europe and to bring effective support to her allies."[302]

In 1850, France was the most populous country in Europe. In 1880, it had nearly 16% of the European population. By 1900, it was under 10%. Ever since 1871, the German population had increased more rapidly. Thus, between 1880 and 1910, the increase in the French population was some 5%, while that of Germany was 43%. By 1940, although Germany had lost territories from the Peace Treaty, it still had a population of over 60 million. France's population was now no more than 42 million. One explanation for this German preponderance was that their losses during the First World War, in absolute terms, were not much greater than those of France, while in relative terms, they were lower.[303]

French intellectuals were among the hardest hit. Over 40% of the alumni of the elite Ecole Normale Superieure were killed. Additionally, as a result of their losses in the war, the French population was now older. One consequence was that, in 1940, France would be able to mobilise fewer men than in 1914. In 1919, Clemenceau presciently had observed: "The Treaty means nothing if France does not agree to have more children…if France renounces large families, we will have taken all the guns from Germany for nothing."[304]

During the war, the areas of France occupied by Germany included the manufacturing and heavy industries. Some 50% of the coal industry and over 60% of the iron and steel and cotton production were in German hands. The territory, occupied, accounted for one-fifth of the country's wheat supply.[305] When the Germans left, they flooded the coal mines and carried off large quantities of industrial plant.

During the war, loans from the United States and Britain had prevented the French Government from becoming bankrupt, but it was still in debt to the tune

---

[302] DDF series 2. Tom. I. no 82.

[303] Adamthwaite, A. (1977) *France and the Coming of the Second World War*, London: Frank Cass, p. 4.

[304] Ibid. p. 8.

[305] Ibid. p. 4.

of some 30 billion francs. By 1919, these loans had ceased and the French had to apply to the Americans to lend them ships in order to be able to supply their own colonies. Britain provided a large proportion of the coal needed by France, but the high cost of British coal and the reduction in France's own exports produced a severe coal crisis in 1919–1920.

The occupation of the Saar and the Ruhr by the French did something to alleviate this problem but at a high cost in political prestige. The enormous French debt meant that France spent the whole of the 1920s seeking to extract reparations from Germany and to persuade the other Allied Powers to cancel the French debts, or to link them to the payment of reparations. The phenomenon of inflation was exacerbated by the reluctance of the French to impose a simple system of direct taxation. They sought to rely on borrowing as a way of paying for essential measures. Of the estimated 55 milliards spent on the war, less than 10% had been raised by taxes.

When, in 1920, the French did belatedly introduce income tax, it was not universally applied. In 1921 and for some years thereafter, there was industrial expansion. By 1924, the industrial production equalled 1913 figures. In 1930–31, the economy was at its most prosperous and industrial output reached record levels. The devaluation of the franc in June 1928 had helped to halt the fall of the franc and gold reserves rose to a level in 1932, four times as high as in 1925–27.[306] It did not continue. Because France had a peasant economy, there was under-industrialisation and protectionist tariffs did nothing to help the economy. Whereas in the 1930s, industrial production increased in both Great Britain and Germany by some 15–20%, in France it fell by some 24%. French wheat yields were among the lowest in Europe. In 1940, a French farmer was feeding four of his fellow countrymen, while an American was feeding twenty.[307]

The result of this fiscal policy was that the economy remained static and from 1930 onwards, the budget deficit showed an increase every year. The French determination to have a balanced economy meant that the resources of the country were equally divided between town and country. This was due to the policy of supporting the dogma of a peasant economy. In the 1930s, one half of the population were rural. The effect was to encourage protection of the farming community, while at the same time ignoring the concept of industrialisation.

---

[306] Ibid. p. 8.
[307] Ibid. p. 13.

Financial instability had been a feature of the French economy almost since the end of the World War. One unintended result of the ill-fated decision to invade the Ruhr was to enable Germany to stabilise its currency at the expense of the franc. By the end of 1922, the franc was showing a loss of some 30%.[308] Over the next few years, the value of the franc continued to fall and the Government was forced to borrow heavily from the Bank of France. By the end of 1925, the Government was close to bankruptcy. Bank advances now amounted to some 36 million francs. The depression in 1929 did not affect France until towards the end of 1931, which was later than in other countries. However, it lasted longer, effectively until after Munich.

One result was to widen the gap between French and German industrial output. Whereas in 1933, Germany produced the same amount of steel as the French, by 1938, the Germans were producing three times the French output. Manufacturing output for Germany in 1937/1938 were, as a percentage of the figures for 1913 and 1928/1929, respectively 144 and 122. The comparable figures for France were respectively 119 and 88. Between 1936 and 1938, the French Government had ordered 761 planes, (a month's production in Germany in 1938), but by September, only 83 had been delivered.[309]

In 1938, France produced 47 million tons of coal while Germany produced 351 million tons. It was not until October 1938 that industrial production returned for the first time to the level of 1928. The depression undoubtedly enfeebled France and contributed to the collapse in 1940. [310] On 8 January 1936, the Treasury warned the French Government that it could no longer borrow on the home market and was teetering on the brink of bankruptcy[311] This was only two months before the Germans marched into the Rhineland. It is difficult not to see some connection between the two events.

The effect of this economic malaise was widespread. It necessarily affected the ability to finance the armed forces so as to be able to resist German aggression or equally to invade Germany in support of Czechoslovakia. It restricted any foreign policy which ran the risk of having to go to war. It was

---

[308] Adamthwaite, A. (1995) *Grandeur and Misery*, London: Arnold, p. 101.

[309] Eubank, K. (1963) *Munich*, Oklahoma: Norman: University of Oklahoma Press, p. 282.

[310] Adamthwaite, Ibid. p. 141.

[311] Ibid. p. 201

thus quite impossible for the French to provide a properly equipped army or air force. A comparison between the military expenditure in France and Germany shows that between 1935 and 1938, the Germans spent on average nearly twice as much as a percentage of their GNP and national income as the French.[312] The anxiety about the relevant state of the two rival armed forces was a vital element in French policymaking. Rearmament had to be carefully controlled because a wholesale increase in weapons was regarded as financially impossible. In 1937, the rearmament programme, which had been agreed the previous year, was reduced by something over 20%.

The financial situation also had an effect on the social budget because it affected domestic cohesion and gave rise to much internal strife. One example, of which there are many, was the withdrawal in 1939 of old-age pensions by the Government, although it had been approved by Parliament, some few months before. In January 1937, in order to finance the national railways, the French Government had to seek a loan of some £250 million from Great Britain. Although France had promised Poland and Romania to supply arms, provided that the orders were given to the French industry, it couldn't supply the former and only supplied the latter after long delays.

During the 1930s, the weakness of the franc was not assisted by the devaluation of the United States dollar which had occurred in April 1933. The French were determined to preserve the policy of clinging to the gold standard, while most other countries were then devaluing. The effect was that the franc was overvalued and exports were uncompetitive. However, eventually, in September 1936, the franc was devalued. A policy of exchange controls was rejected for political reasons. By 1937, the gold reserves in the Bank of France stood at about half of what they had been in 1934. In 1937, the budget deficit was some 21 milliards of francs. The economy showed no upturn until 1938. The franc was in constant trouble with investors exporting gold.

In early 1937, the French had intercepted telephone calls from the British Embassy in Paris. In one conversation with the London partner of Lazard Brothers, it was predicted that in March 1937, a tremendous financial crash in France was inevitable.[313] In June 1937, the franc was again devalued. In May

---

[312] Sauvy, A. (1972) *Histoire Economique de la France entre les deux guerres*, Paris, Vol. 1, p. 277, Vol. 11 pp. 319, 576–7. Adamthwaite, A. (1977) *France and the Coming of the Second World War*, Frank Cass and Co. p. 164.
[313] FRUS 1938 11, p. 256.

1938, it was now devalued for the third time.[314] These financial crises in France inevitably encouraged those in Germany, advocating war.[315]

Political scandals and the incompetence of Governments went hand in hand. Riots were part and parcel of French political life. Those which followed the Stavisky scandal in 1934 and the scandal itself were symptomatic of the malaise at the heart of the French Nation. Alexandre Stavisky was a shady financier from Ukraine. He was involved with politicians who controlled Bayonne and more particularly with the city's bank. He had sold 200 million francs' worth of phoney bonds from the municipal pawnshop he owned, the security for which was some jewellery belonging to the former Empress of Germany. The jewellery and the bonds were both worthless.

His manager was arrested and the trail led to Stavisky, who fled with his mistress to Chamonix. He had been on bail for similar crimes since 1926 and his trial had been postponed 19 times. When the police broke into his chalet, they found him dead.[316] The radical socialist Government of Daladier was accused by the right of having had Stavisky murdered. It was claimed that if he had been brought to trial, the evidence might have revealed the fact that left-wing politicians were involved in Stavisky's financial dealings.

Daladier's predecessor, Camille Chautemps, the radical Prime Minister, had refused right-wing demands for an investigation. From this, it was thought that he was seeking to protect his brother-in-law, Pressard, the Public Prosecutor, who, it was alleged, had been responsible for the many postponements of Stavisky's trial. This it was claimed had enabled Stavisky to flee and thus avoid justice. Chautemps was forced to resign in January 1934. Georges Bonnet, who became Foreign Minister in 1936, was also accused of having lunched with Stavisky in July 1932 at the Lausanne Conference and having employed one of Stavisky's lawyers. Both allegations were shown to be untrue. Daladier lasted as Prime Minister, on this occasion, for only a few weeks.

There were massive demonstrations in January 1934. On 6 February, the right-wing mounted a demonstration to protest against the corruption in the Government. When the mob tried to cross the Seine to reach the National Assembly, the demonstration turned into a riot, lasting some six hours. Buses were set on fire and Daladier ordered the police to shoot. This resulted in some

---

[314] Adamthwaite, A. (1995) Grandeur and Misery, London: Arnold, p. 210.

[315] DDF series 2. Tom. X. no 370.

[316] Sowerwine, C. (2001) *France since 1970*, Basingstoke, Hampshire: Palgrave, p. 144.

17 people being killed and over 2,000 seriously injured. The radical leader, Herriot, narrowly escaped being thrown into the Seine. Both the left and the right believed that the other was conspiring against the State. It was but one example of different factions resorting to violence and seeking to undermine the fabric of Government.

In 1936, the prospect of Leon Blum's Popular Front securing victory at the following General Election, aroused enormous passion, involving the assassination of members of the militant royalist group and acts of violence against Blum himself.[317] In March 1937, there were riots at Clichy, which resulted in seven dead and several hundred injured. In November 1937, there was a warning by the General Staff of a communist putsch. In the same month, there was an attempted coup by the Cagoulards, a right-wing, anti-communist, secret organisation. This resulted in their leaders being tried and imprisoned.

There were constant changes in the personnel of successive French Governments. There was widespread incompetence among the politicians. Between February 1930 and September 1938, there were no fewer than twenty-one Prime Ministers, though, some, like Daladier, were Prime Minister on more than one occasion. He was also Defence Minister in four Governments. In the same period, there were twelve Foreign Ministers, some more than once. In a number of cases, members of the old Government simply occupied places in the new Government but with different portfolios. It was not unlike a game of musical chairs. Unfortunately, no Government was much of an improvement on its predecessor.

Between 1934 and November 1938, there were some seven separate Governments. The effect of these constant changes had a serious debilitating effect on any sort of settled policy. The French Prime Minister had none of the control over his Cabinet as the Prime Minister in Britain. Ministers in Britain were required to follow Cabinet policy, a situation unknown in France where Ministers frequently acted autonomously, without reference to the Head of Government.

At two important moments of crisis, France was either without a Government or had been so, immediately, before the crisis. On 7 March 1936, when the Germans marched into the Rhineland, France had been without a Government between the 15 and 18 of January because Laval had resigned as Prime Minister.

---

[317] Duroselle, J-B. (1979) *La Decadence 1932–1939*, Paris: Imprimerie Nationale, p. 201.

Sarraut now became Prime Minister of a caretaker Government, awaiting the results of the forthcoming elections, which, it was widely anticipated, would result in victory for the Popular Front.

Blum became Prime Minister from June 1936 until 22 June 1937. Chautemps then became Prime Minister until 14 January 1938 when the administration fell. On 18 January, he formed a 'Government of Transition' until he resigned on 10 March 1938. On 17 January, Corbin, the French Ambassador in London had reported that 'the persistence of our internal quarrels was discouraging British opinion.'[318]The Government found itself paralysed in every way. It contained both opponents and supporters of the Popular Front. It was fated not to last long, to do nothing and to avoid making decisions.[319] Pierre Flandin was the Foreign Minister from January 1936 until he resigned in June 1936. He was succeeded by Yvon Delbos until, he too, resigned in March 1938.

Thus, at another important moment of crisis in French political history, when German troops marched into Austria on 12 March 1938, the French Government was rudderless. The French Government of Chautemps had resigned on 10 March and the Government of Blum did not take office until 13 March. It only lasted until 8 April. Delbos' successor after March 1938, as Foreign Minister, was Joseph Paul-Boncour, who held the office for only three weeks. The French made no objection to the Anschluss.

For the Czechs, however, it was important because part of their defences was now outflanked by Germany. Nor were they much encouraged by German promises. The night before the invasion, Goering had taken Mastny, the Czechoslovak Ambassador, aside at a reception and assured him that 'Germany has no unfriendly intentions towards Czechoslovakia and that on the contrary, after the completion of the Anschluss, it expects an improvement in the relations with it, as long as you don't mobilise'. Goering gave his word of honour and for good measure, Hitler's as well.[320] Given Hitler's views in 1932, the plans for Operation Green in June 1937 and the contents of the Hossbach Memorandum, to which Goering had been a party, this was economical with the truth.

On 4 April 1938, Cadogan observed that France not only had no Government but that "Paul-Boncour was not a Foreign Minister who, at so serious a moment,

---

[318] DDF series 2. Tom. VIII. no 1.

[319] Duroselle, Ibid. p. 154.

[320] Caquet, P. E. (2018) *The Bell of Treason*, People Books Ltd., p. 22.

could be a worthy partner in a discussion of the European crisis."[321] In April 1936, Lord Cecil had written to Churchill: "Whatever may be said of the British Government, it is nothing to the perfidy of men like Laval and Flandin... I know Flandin and have always had a very bad opinion of him. I am sure he hates this country and that all his pretended love for it is mere bunkum...please do not underrate the very strong anti-French feeling that is raging in this country."[322]

Laval was Prime Minister in 1931 and in 1935/1936. He had been Foreign Minister in 1934. Of him, Sir Samuel Hoare, the British Foreign Secretary said: "He was like a French peasant who was always thinking of getting the better of someone over the price of a chicken."[323] He was also believed by Baldwin to have been bribed by Mussolini over Abyssinia.[324]

When Blum succeeded Chautemps as Prime Minister in March 1938, there was a general view that if the parties could not agree on forming a National Government, how would they be in a position to take important decisions in Foreign Affairs. Herriot, then President of the Chamber of Deputies, was told that there was no point in having meetings with the British Government until the days of transitory French Governments were over. [325]

The litany of constant changes of personnel would, if it had not had such disastrous consequences for the world, have been worthy of a Feydeau farce. Chamberlain set out the contemporary British view of French Governments. On 16 January 1938, he wrote to Mrs Fanny Morton Prince (a cousin of his stepmother): "Unhappily, France keeps pulling her own house down about her ears... France's weakness is a public danger. Just when she ought to be a source of strength and confidence, and as a friend, she has two faults which destroy half her value. She can never keep a secret for more than half an hour, nor a Government for more than nine months."[326]

---

[321] Documents and Materials, Vol 1, no 9.

[322] Cecil, R. The Papers of Viscount Cecil, British Museum. Add. MSS 51073.

[323] Adamthwaite, Ibid. p. 195.

[324] Middlemas, K. and Barnes, J. (1969) *Baldwin*, London: Weidenfeld and Nicolson, p. 887. House of Commons Official Reports. Fifth Series. Vol. 307. Col 856. 10 December 1935.

[325] FO 371/21590.

[326] Massachusetts Historical Society. Feiling, K. (1946) *Life of Neville Chamberlain*, London: Macmillan and Co. Ltd., p. 323.

Paul-Boncour was succeeded in April 1938 as Foreign Minister by Bonnet. On 1 May, Chamberlain wrote: "Bonnet, I have known since 1932. He is clever but ambitious as an intriguer. The French are not very fortunate in their Foreign Secretaries."[327] When they had met at the London Economic Conference in 1933, Chamberlain found him 'cagey and lacking in frankness'.[328] Churchill described him as the quintessence of defeatism. Paul Mandel, who was Minister for Posts and then Minister for Colonies, said of him that 'his long nose sniffs danger and responsibility from afar. He will hide under any flat stone to avoid it'.

Oliver Harvey (private secretary to the Foreign Secretary), subsequently wrote: "I do not trust him a yard…he was a public danger to his own country and to ours".[329] Gamelin wrote that he was without morality. Vansittart wrote: "If I ever had to play cards with M. Bonnet, I would always run through the pack first, just to make sure that the joker had been duly removed."[330]

Others describe him as being incapable of following any line save that of least resistance and that, when under attack or in a tight corner, he would lie automatically to extricate himself. Bonnet's deviousness was a common theme.[331] French opinion of their British colleagues was equally scathing. Daladier's view in January 1939, was that "he considered Chamberlain a desiccated stick, the King, a moron and the Queen, an excessively ambitious woman, who would be ready to sacrifice every other country in the world, in order that she might remain Queen Elizabeth of England. He considered Eden a young idiot and did not know, for discussion, one single Englishman for whose intellectual equipment and character he had respect. He felt that England had become so feeble and senile that the British would give away every possession of their friends rather than stand up to Germany or Italy." [332]

The policies which Daladier and Bonnet, in particular, followed were to avoid, at all costs, being involved in a war over Czechoslovakia. To that end, it was necessary to force the Czechs to make significant concessions to the Sudeten Germans. The French could not publicly renounce their obligations to the

---

[327] Chamberlain Papers NC 18/1/1069.

[328] Eubank, Ibid. p. 40.

[329] Harvey, Ibid. pp. 226 & 233.

[330] Adamthwaite, A. (1977) *France and the Coming of the Second World War*, London: Frank Cass, p. 266.

[331] Nogueres, Ibid. p. 44–45 per Gamelin, Benes & Churchill.

[332] Bullitt, W. C. (1973) *For the President, Personal and Secret*, London: Deutch, p. 310.

Czechs. But, as Lord Strang wrote: "While the declared policy of France was to stand by her obligations, a very different impression was given by what French Ministers said behind the scenes, whether in social gatherings or to foreign representatives."[333]

It was, therefore, politic for France to allow Britain to take the major initiatives with regard to the Czechs and thereby escape the implications of and responsibility for failing to fulfil its Treaty obligations. On 20 July 1938, without consultation with Daladier or his Cabinet colleagues, Bonnet told Ousky, the Czech Ambassador, that 'the Czechoslovak Government should have a clear understanding of our position. France will not go to war over the Sudeten affair…in no case should the Czechoslovak Government believe that if war breaks out, we will be at its side as in this affair our diplomatic isolation is almost total'.[334] On 16 September, he repeated the same advice to Ousky.

Bonnet's behaviour, when the crisis broke in September, speaks volumes about his character. On 10 September, he had called Phipps to the Foreign Ministry to enquire of him as a friend, rather than as the Ambassador, what the reaction of Britain would be if Germany invaded Czechoslovakia and France mobilised. If France marched, would Britain do the same? Bonnet repeated the question, adding that it was very important and very private. Phipps made a non-committal reply and reported to Halifax. He, in his turn, sent a telegram to Phipps declining, in effect, to answer a hypothetical question. When this was reported to Bonnet, he became somewhat hysterical and summoned Phipps again. Phipps described him as 'being in a state of collapse, in a panic and very upset'. Phipps thought that Bonnet's collapse was so sudden and so extraordinary that he sought an immediate interview with Daladier.[335]

Bonnet's appointment has given rise to a certain amount of speculation, as to whether the British Government played any and, if so, what part in it. It appeared that Daladier was intending to keep Paul-Boncour, a well-known supporter of collective security, in post. However, Phipps with the approval of Halifax let Daladier know that it would be most unfortunate if Paul-Boncour did remain. Phipps reported that 'we were nearly cursed by having Paul-Boncour again at the Quai d'Orsay. We, therefore, had Daladier and Reynaud informed, indirectly, that it would be most unfortunate if Paul-Boncour were to remain.

---

[333] Strang, L. W. (1956) *Home and Abroad*, London: Andre Deutsch, p. 134.
[334] DDF series 2. Tom. X 10 no 238.
[335] DBFP, Ibid. no 855.

Daladier was in full agreement. Finally, after an interview of over an hour with Paul-Boncour, he did the right thing. I felt it was my duty to take a certain risk, though it was a very small one as my messages were quite indirect and I can always disavow them'.[336] As a result, Bonnet, well known for his support of appeasement, was appointed in his stead.

Bonnet was described by the German Ambassador in Paris as 'having gone through fire and water to win recognition for, in his opinion, justified claims to the Sudeten German territory'.[337] It was said that he was 'even keener than Daladier in steering clear of France's obligations'.[338] Nor could Daladier be described, at this time, as a statesman maintaining a firm resolve. On 8 September, he had declared that 'if German troops cross the Czechoslovak frontier, the French will march to a man'.[339] But by 13 September, this had become 'at all costs Germany must be prevented from invading Czechoslovakia because in that case, France would be faced with her obligations'.[340]

Daladier had been at the heart of French politics for decades. He had first been elected a deputy in 1919. He held Cabinet rank from 1924 onwards. He was Prime Minister three times, Defence Minister four times and Foreign Minister three times. His rise to power was halted as a result of his actions in the Stavisky riots. He had been regarded, then, as a man who would take vigorous action to restore the prestige of the State. When, in 1938, he became Prime Minister again, he was expected to be the strong man, who would restore order and authority.[341] It was not to be. Critics suggested that he did not give proper consideration to the papers which he had to read. [342]

Indecision was a feature of his character. He might well be compared to Lord Derby of whom it was once said that he was like a pillow who bore the imprint of the last person who had sat on him. Strength of purpose was not how he or the French Government were viewed by the British. Indeed, contemporary diaries paint a quite different picture of Daladier. Harold Nicolson recorded in April 1937, that 'compared to our own ministers, he (Daladier) looked like an Iberian

---

[336] FO 800/311/ 27.

[337] Documents and Materials, Ibid. Vol. II. App. II. no 2.

[338] DGFP series. D. Vol. II. no 147.

[339] DBFP series 3. Vol. XI. no 807.

[340] DBFP, Ibid. no 852 & 857.

[341] Adamthwaite, Ibid. p. 92.

[342] FRUS 1938 Vol. II. p. 294.

merchant visiting the Roman senate'.[343] Harvey's view was that 'neither Halifax nor Chamberlain had such an abhorrence of dictatorship as to overcome their innate mistrust of French democracy and its supposed inefficiency'.[344]

Daladier was described by one observer as *'ce n'est pas le Taureau de Vaucluse, c'est la vache hesitation'*.[345] At the meeting with the British on 28/29 April in London, Cadogan had recorded: "Daladier made an impassioned appeal which was very beautiful but awful rubbish."[346] On 17 September, Phipps reported to Halifax that "Veracity is not, I regret to say, the strongest point of the average French politician".[347] About the meeting in London on 18 September, Cadogan wrote: "Daladier and Bonnet and the circus arrived, listened to Daladier with his voice trembling, talking of French honour and obligations, we brought him back to earth."[348] Later in November, Cadogan recorded that "Daladier looked as if he was drinking heavily and was much the worse for wear." [349] Benes thought Daladier had surrounded himself with frivolous, immoral and politically corrupt associates, ever ready for a compromise, to whom any means was good enough if it helped to get him what he wanted.[350] Another observer wrote: "I am always a little doubtful of Daladier's decision if he was in a tight corner, remembering his complete collapse in the February 4th riots."[351]

The French attitude to the Czech problem was admirably summarised in a despatch from Bullitt in Paris, to Washington on 15 September 1938. "The conviction that the Treaty of Versailles is one of the stupidest documents ever penned by the hand of man is general... Both (Daladier and Bonnet) are convinced that the Treaty must be revised...and regard an alteration as a necessary revision in the Czechoslovak State... Daladier said he did not intend

---

[343] Nicolson, N. (ed) (1966) *Harold Nicolson: Diaries and Letters 1930–1939*, Collins, p. 298.

[344] Harvey, Ibid. p. 124.

[345] Coulandre, Ibid. p. 143.

[346] Cadogan, Ibid. p. 73.

[347] Phipps Papers (Churchill College, Cambridge), PHPP 1 1/20/86.

[348] Ibid. p. 100.

[349] Ibid. p. 126.

[350] Benes, Ibid. p 39.

[351] Harvey, Ibid. p 142.

to sacrifice the entire youth of France merely to whitewash the criminal errors committed...during the conference which produced the Treaty of Versailles."[352]

In June 1938, Daladier had armed himself with the power to govern by decree. He then sent the Members of the Chamber of Deputies and Senators on an extended holiday, so they were not in session from June until October. By this time, the Munich Agreement had already been signed. During 1938, there was only one debate in the Chamber on the subject of foreign affairs. This had been held in February. In the critical days of September, the French had no diplomatic communication with the Germans. The French Ambassador had not visited the German Foreign Office for nearly a fortnight and was getting his information from another source.[353] It is not surprising, therefore, that French policy appeared to lack any central or cohesive direction.

---

[352] FRUS 1938 Vol. I p 601.

[353] Documents and Materials, Ibid. no 33.

Chapter Ten:
Pressing Problems

France's preoccupation with the problem of Italy and Abyssinia meant that it failed to pay sufficient attention to Germany's aggressive stance in Central Europe. It seems very unlikely that Germany would have walked into the Rhineland if the French had not been so willing to accommodate the Italians in Abyssinia. Laval's suggestion of a 'freehand' to Mussolini was the clearest possible indication of France's determination to avoid any sort of conflict. The different attitudes of the British and French Governments on the question of sanctions did nothing to improve relations between them and led the British Government to have a distinctly distrustful attitude towards French Foreign policy. In defence of French policy, it is said that by seeking a political alliance with Italy, as they did in January 1935, they were seeking to detach Italy from Germany and to form a pact, which might have the effect of deterring German aggression. Whatever its purpose was, it was a hopeless failure.

The background to Italy's disenchantment with France can be traced back to Italy's invasion of Abyssinia and France's attitude to the involvement of Italy in the civil war in Spain. In 1931/1932, France and Italy had discussed the fate of Abyssinia, the acquisition of which had been, for some fifty years, an important part of Italian ambitions. In January 1935, the relationship between France and Italy was cemented by the Rome agreements. By then, France and Italy were to consult together, not only in case of a threat by Germany against Austrian independence but also if Germany unilaterally modified its obligations in respect of armaments. The quid pro quo for the French alliance with Italy against any German threat was the provision that Abyssinia would hand over its economic interests to Italy. It was in this context that Laval offered Mussolini a 'freehand', (France's non-intervention in Abyssinia). This Mussolini took to be a green light for his proposed invasion. Letters exchanged between Laval and Mussolini, during December 1935 and January 1936, make it clear that a 'freehand' was, in fact, discussed, although, subsequently, different interpretations were sought to be put on the phrase.[354]

At Stresa, in April 1935, France, Britain, and Italy had reaffirmed their obligations under the Locarno agreements and expressed their determination to 'oppose by all practicable means any unilateral repudiation of treaties which may endanger the peace of Europe'. A few days later, Germany reintroduced conscription. Stresa had been aimed at preserving Austrian independence while at the same time effectively conceding the right of Mussolini to invade Abyssinia. In June, the Italian and French Chiefs of Staff signed a Military Convention, which was designed to ensure joint action in the event of a threat to Austria. Thus, by mid-1935, Franco-Italian relations were at their most cordial. By October 1936, however, Italy had joined the Axis and in March 1938, when the Anschluss occurred, Italy was firmly in the German camp. Something had gone sadly awry.

During 1935, various attempts were made by Britain and France to find a compromise in the dispute between Italy and Abyssinia. Britain tried to persuade the Abyssinians to accept some land in Somaliland in exchange for their yielding various concessions to the Italians. All attempts at a compromise were rejected by the Italians and on 3 October 1935, they invaded Abyssinia. By November, economic sanctions under clause 16 of the League of Nations Covenant were authorised. But crucially, while it contained an embargo in respect of arms and essential war materials, it did not initially, at any rate, cover oil, coal or metallurgical products. This created something of a dilemma for the French who recognised the importance of consolidating its position in Central Europe of which the entente with Italy was an essential element.

At the suggestion of the League of Nations, Laval and Hoare were tasked with the responsibility of finding a peaceful solution. On 8 December, they agreed on a plan by which two-thirds of Abyssinia would be ceded to Italy, while a strip of land, giving access to the sea, would be retained by the Abyssinians. When the details were leaked, there was a political storm in Paris and London, and both Ministers were forced to resign.

But it was the effect on Italo-Franco relations that the episode most strongly impinged. France was in a difficult position. If it upheld the Covenant of the

---

[354] Documents and Materials Ibid. no33

League of Nations and proceeded with sanctions, clearly Stresa would go. If, on the other hand, the League were abandoned, where did Collective Security and the Little Entente stand to say nothing of France's relations with Britain? In April 1936, however, it now appeared that Italy wanted to restore the Stresa front.[355] At the same time, Mussolini was expressing the view that Italy had no intention of yielding to German force. He added that although they had no obligation in respect of Czechoslovakia, except under the Covenant of the League of Nations, as soon as Italy was secure in Africa, Italy would defend those stipulations.[356]

There were strong divisions of view among the French politicians, among the press and among the public about relations with Italy. The fascist groups vied both with the communists, the socialists and the radicals of the Popular Front. The former supported Italy as a Locarno guarantor of Austrian independence and a makeweight against Germany, while the latter called for sanctions to uphold the League of Nations. Strong support for sanctions would have upset the right and would have destroyed the Government's base, where the Cabinet had only a slender majority. Abandonment of the League would have enraged the radicals. These divisions resulted in a half-hearted approach to the question of sanctions with the result that by June, with sanctions still being in force, Mussolini decided to seek an arrangement with the Germans over Austria.

French policy over the Spanish Civil War, if it can be so described, was nothing if not confused.[357] Attempts to limit the intervention of foreign arms and troops (mainly German and Italian) fell initially on deaf ears and did nothing to persuade the Italians to continue an alliance with France. By November 1936, Mussolini was referring publicly to the Rome-Berlin Axis.[358] When, in March 1938, the Anschluss took place, there was no condemnation by Italy.

Part of the fallout from the attempt to turn a blind eye to the Italian takeover of Abyssinia was the entry by German troops into the demilitarised zone of the Rhine on 7 May 1936. By Articles 42 and 43 of the Versailles Treaty, Germany was forbidden to maintain any military establishment whatever, however, transiently (which covered manoeuvres), on the left bank of the Rhine or within fifty kilometres of the right bank. Its purpose was to enable France or Belgium to enter Germany without opposition, so as to enforce the provisions of the

---

[355] DDF series 2. Tom. II. no 46.

[356] DDF, Ibid. no 17 & 18.

[357] DDF, Ibid. no 16.

[358] Murray, Ibid. p. 133.

Treaty. This they had done in 1923 by invading the Ruhr to secure reparations due to them. Under the Treaty of Locarno, the sanction for a breach of the Treaty was for the League Council to recommend to the other signatories to take appropriate military action.

Nothing better illustrates the sheer lack of French resolve or will than the behaviour of the French Politicians and their Military Advisers over the Rhineland issue. It led the Axis leaders to believe that France was a paper tiger. Further, it caused immense consternation among France's allies in Central Europe. From this event, it is possible to trace a pattern which, like some Greek tragedy, led inexorably to the melancholy events at Munich. It can fairly be described as a defining moment in the history of international relations in Europe.

The entry of German troops into the demilitarised Rhineland, in March 1936, was in breach of the Treaties of Versailles and Locarno. The ostensible excuse was the signing of the Franco-Soviet Treaty on 2 May 1935 and its ratification.[359] Although Sarraut announced that 'Strasbourg would not be left under German guns', no action was, in fact, taken by the French to resist.[360] Nor had any precautions been taken by the French, in advance, against the possibility of such an event. Were the French taken by surprise? What if anything could they have done either to prevent it happening before it did or after the event to take urgent steps to remedy the situation?

One explanation for the failure of the French was the political situation at the time. Laval's government had fallen on 18 January. The main reasons for this were his surprising acquiescence in the Italian aggression in Abyssinia and the ineffectual applications of sanctions. Nor did the Laval/Hoare Pact do anything to enhance the Government's reputation. Laval's indulgence towards the fascist threat in France and his economic policy of deflation also played their part. The Treasury warned the Government on 8 January that it could no longer borrow on the home market and was on the brink of bankruptcy.[361] The Government of Sarraut, which replaced Laval's, found itself paralysed in every way, while the prospect of the Popular Front victory, under Blum, aroused enormous passion.

---

[359] DGFP series C. Vol. V. no 3.

[360] Adamthwaite, Ibid. p. 37.

[361] Adamthwaite, A. (1995) *Grandeur and Misery*, London: Arnold, p. 201.

A German move into the Rhineland had been forecast as early as the summer of 1935, without a specific date being indicated.[362] In January and February 1936, the French Consul General in Cologne gave several warnings about the proposed reoccupation, as did the Consul General in Dusseldorf. Again, no certain date was known to the French.[363] Surprisingly, the French Ambassador in Berlin seemed wholly unaware of German intentions and indeed, right up to 6 March was optimistic.[364] Almost no steps were taken by the French before 7 March.

On 14 January, the Foreign Ministry had discussed a policy document about the prospects of a Germans reoccupation. There was a reference to the obligations of the signatories to the Locarno Pact and to the remedies available at the League of Nations. Before taking any firm steps, however, it was decided that the British must be consulted. [365] On 18 January, the French General Staff prepared a memo for the Military High Committee. In it, they stressed the imbalance between the French and German military forces, which was made worse by the fact that because of the Abyssinian war, France had to provide fourteen divisions in the Alps and Tunisia.[366]

It was reported that Eden did not think that there was an immediate problem and that in any event, there was nothing effective that Britain could do.[367] This was unsurprising in view of the advice from the British Chiefs of Staff on 18 March that 'any question of war with Germany, while we are at present heavily committed to hostilities in the Mediterranean, would be thoroughly dangerous'.[368] Eden gave an assurance that Britain would honour its obligations under the Locarno Treaty but that the British did not think that the use of force was justified.[369] On 13 February, he indicated that he did not intend to commit himself as to what British policy would be in the hypothetical case of violation of the demilitarised zone.[370] The British Foreign Office took the view that the

[362] DDF series 2. Tom. I no 638 & 350.

[363] DDF, Ibid. no 75, 96, 126, 188 & 189.

[364] DDF, Ibid. no 49, 242, 286 & 294.

[365] DDF, Ibid. no 53.

[366] DDF, Ibid. no 82.

[367] DDF, Ibid. no 112.

[368] CAB 53/27 COS 442.

[369] DDF, Ibid. no 184.

[370] DBFP series 2, Vol. XV, no 517.

maintenance of the zone, over anything but a restricted future, was quite impractical.[371]

Having eventually discovered that the British could not, or rather would not, help, the French continued to remain passive. At a meeting on 7 February, the War Minister was asked what countermeasures could be taken against a re-occupation. There is no record of an immediate reply.[372] However, in a memorandum from the War Minister, dated 12 February, he stated: "I propose reducing to a minimum the number of precautionary measures to be taken in the event of a sudden attack, so as to avoid giving any legitimate excuse for conflict. Calling up of reservists and requisitioning transport was to await a Government decision."[373]

On 14 February, the Foreign Minister, before going to discuss the matter with the British, needed to be able to tell them what steps France was going to take and on 17 February, the War Minister finally set out his point of view. It envisaged both a military and political plan. Apart from suggesting that the French should not themselves occupy the demilitarised zone but should put troops at the frontier on the alert, it was short of any practical suggestions to deter the Germans.[374]

On 24 February, the Foreign Minister pointed out that the War Minister was not answering the questions which were being asked and observed, rather waspishly, that 'the War Minister sees the reoccupation of the Rhineland by the Reich as a favourable opportunity to obtain new credits'. The Foreign Minister went on to ask what precautionary measures were to be taken and whether any positive action, by way of reprisal, was envisaged. Again, he pointed out that the War Minister's letter said nothing about the initiatives which France could take to intimidate the enemy or make him retreat.[375] Nor did the Air Ministry show any greater resolve. On 2 March, the Air Minister expressed the view that the reoccupation of the Rhineland did not constitute an immediate and sudden attack, adding that taking preventative measures would be regarded by the Germans as a provocation.[376]

---

[371] DBFP, Ibid. no 455.

[372] DDF, Ibid. no 155.

[373] DDF, Ibid. no 17.

[374] DDF, Ibid. no 196.

[375] DDF, Ibid. no 223.

[376] DDF, Ibid. no 269.

Thus, there was no mobilisation of the reservists. There was no warning given to the Germans about the consequences of their reoccupation or any threat of reprisals or of sanctions. In effect, the French did nothing except that, on 8 March, they referred the issue to the League of Nations which, on 14 March, took no action. Thus, nothing at all was done to secure the removal of the German forces.

The French took the view that the army could not act without the authorisation of the League of Nations and that in any event, a general mobilisation would be required to expel the German troops. This necessarily ruled out any immediate action.[377] The French were still wedded to the citizen-soldier concept of 1792. No division could be brought up to strength without the recall of reservists. There were five stages, leading up to full mobilisation: 'the alert', 'reinforced alert', 'security', 'general cover' and 'general mobilisation'. This whole exercise might well take over a fortnight.[378]

On 8 March, a meeting was held at Gamelin's house. He was asked directly whether he was in a position to drive the Germans back out of the zone. He replied that 'war would be started from the moment that the French entered the zone that would require general mobilisation and it would be necessary to have the guaranteed support of Britain, Italy and Belgium'.[379] Eden told the Belgians, on 10 March, that Britain was not going to go to war over the Rhineland. [380]

In the result, France got no sort of support from the British who had made it abundantly clear that they were only to give moral support and that any sort of action, which might result in war with Germany, was to be avoided at all cost. Maisky's view of the British lack of support was that 'I don't like the British response to Hitler's coup. The mood of the English? They are in the mood to negotiate. It is clearly a national English disease; negotiations, negotiations, negotiations. Therefore, the British Government is prepared to begin exploration (what a lovely word!)'.[381]

---

[377] DDF, Ibid. no 525.

[378] Adamthwaite. A. (1977) *France and the Coming of the Second World War*, London: Frank Cass, p. 39.

[379] DDF series 2 Tom. I, no 334.

[380] DBB, Tom. IV, no 44.

[381] Gorodetsky, G. (Eds.) (2015) The Maisky Diaries. 1932--1943., Yale University Press. 2015

The relations between the two countries could not have been worse. Indeed, nothing much had changed over the years. As early as 6 December 1935, Vansittart had expressed the view that there was a growing lack of confidence in Britain about France and that he was apprehensive about the future of Anglo-French relations.[382] The political crisis and the forthcoming French elections, with the advent of the Popular Front, did not encourage heroic resolutions. The idea of a general mobilisation within six weeks of a general election would have been folly.[383] Further, there was considerable worry about the state of the franc. The French public was against taking any action.

The British view was that neither before, nor after the reoccupation, did the French Government have any sort of policy. They were, it was said, looking for a type of action which would have public support but without risk of war. If the French had been more resolute, could they, in fact, have prevented the reoccupation or once it had occurred, could they not have removed the Germans? We know today that von Fritsch and von Blomberg were frightened by the risk which Hitler was taking and recommended against it.[384]

There are divided views as to whether the Germans would have retreated if French troops had resisted.[385] However, a distinguished historian set out the French position in trenchant terms. "This argument (that the French missed an opportunity to stop Hitler in time) is fallacious, relying only on the fact that the French army, in numbers and fighting power, was still much stronger than the German, but ignoring all those factors of opinion, nerve and determination, which made it a foregone conclusion that the superior French power would not be used in the event."[386]

---

[382] DBFP series 2 Vol. XV. no 324

[383] Néré, Ibid. p 189.

[384] Wheeler-Bennett, Ibid. p 352.

[385] Flandin, P. (1947) *Politique Francaise 1919-1940*, Paris, p. 199. Emmerson, J. (1977) *The Rhineland crisis*, London: Temple Smith Ltd., pp. 98–100. Watt, D. C. (1966) *German plans for the reoccupation of the Rhineland (A note Journal of Contemporary History)*, pp. 193–199. Weinberg, G. (1980) *The Foreign Policy of Hitler's Germany Starting World War II*, Chicago: University of Chicago Press, p. 252. Churchill, S. W. (1948) *The Second World War*, London: Cassell & Co. Ltd., p. 152.

[386] Barnett, C. (1972) *The Collapse of British Power*, New York: William Morrow & Co. Inc., p. 385.

The strategic relationship between the Abyssinian crisis and the occupation of the Rhineland is clear. The French had had to deploy 14 divisions in the Alps and in Tunisia against a possible threat from Italy. Militarily the British were also caught off balance. At the height of the Abyssinian crisis, the British had had similar problems to the French over the deployment of their forces, particularly in the Mediterranean. The Royal Navy, in home waters, was reduced to only three ships capable of fighting the new German 'pocket-battleships'. The Royal Air Force, at home, was so reduced by reinforcements to Egypt that the Air Minister found it difficult to imagine a worse state and the Army was equally weakened by drafts to the Middle East.[387]

There can be no divided view about the consequences. After the Anschluss, the French Military Attaché in Vienna reported: "The prestige of France in Central Europe, already seriously damaged by the events of 7 March 1936, comes out of the Austrian affair…completely destroyed, even among those professing to be our most loyal friends."[388] After Munich, Cadogan wrote, "We ought to have reacted against the occupation when we could have done so effectively."[389] Churchill wrote, "If the French government had mobilised, there is no doubt that Hitler would have been compelled by his own General Staff to withdraw and a check would have been given to his pretension, which might well have proved fatal to his rule."[390] On 6 March, Belgium had renounced the secret Military Convention of September 1920 and returned to the pre-1914 policy of full neutrality. Although unconnected with the Rhineland reoccupation, this decision put an end to the French plans to advance into Belgium in the event of a war with Germany.

Further, the reoccupation of the Rhineland made it almost impossible for the French to come to the assistance of her Eastern Allies, particularly of Czechoslovakia, by direct action on the Western Front against Germany. Naturally, the Eastern Allies viewed the reoccupation with dismay. They asked rhetorically if the French could not defend themselves on this occasion, how were they going to be able to defend their allies in the future.

On 2 March, the French Ambassador in Brussels had spelt out the danger, indicating that the members of the Little Entente were profoundly unhappy at the

---

[387] Barnett, Ibid. p. 383.
[388] DDF series 2, Tom. IX, no 10.
[389] FO 371/21659.
[390] Churchill, Ibid. p. 152.

prospect of reoccupation and that if France did nothing, the members would lose all hope of effective assistance under their Treaties and might seek a change of alliances.[391]

On 12 March, Massigli, the Director of Political Affairs at the Quai D'Orsay, pointed out the dangers which were already being noted with cries of alarm from his foreign agents.[392] Benes warned that the success of German plans in the Rhineland would rapidly lead to the collapse of the security system in the east.[393] In view of all this, it is perhaps not surprising that sometime later, on 6 November, Benes let it be known that he was not averse to the idea of a non-aggression pact with Germany. In December, with France's approval, he actually discussed with the Germans the possibility of a German-Czech settlement.

There were many reports of the demoralisation of the Eastern Allies as a consequence of the Rhineland reoccupation,[394] although the decision on 29 June by the French to send aircraft to the Czechs was some form of palliative.[395] In July 1936, there was a meeting of the French War Council to discuss France's ability to help its Allies in the East, particularly in relation to Czechoslovakia. It was suggested that the rapid arrival of French units in Central Europe, acting in liaison with the armies of the Little Entente and Italy, would provide a coherent allied front and would eventually contribute to the salvation of Czechoslovakia.[396] The idea that Italy would be a major ally of the French (or indeed of the British) after the outbreak of the war in Abyssinia, only shows how far French political thought was removed from reality. Blum's comment that 'his nation could rely on the working class to defeat a German invasion rather than on a politically dangerous elite tank force', [397] speaks volumes about French thinking.

Italy's view of Britain was described by Duff Cooper, then the First Lord of the Admiralty, when he wrote about a railway coach provided by the Italian government to take him from Naples to Calais. "Unfortunately, there was set in the wall of the principal compartment, an engraved tablet containing the names

---

[391] DDF series 2, Tom. I, no 270.

[392] DDF, Ibid. no 407.

[393] DDF, Ibid. no 343.

[394] DDF, Ibid. no 182, 204 & 318.

[395] DDF, Ibid. no 369.

[396] DDF, Ibid. no 419.

[397] Werth, A. (1942) *The Twilight of France. 1938–1940*, New York, p. 44.

of those countries who had applied sanctions against Italy during the Abyssinian war and an intimation that Italy would never forget. High on the list stood the name of Great Britain."[398]

Although the French secured a closer relationship with Britain, by way of a defensive alliance together, in truth, there was not much help to be had from that source.[399] In March and April, Britain renewed its Locarno obligations. It further agreed to hold staff talks (which were extremely limited) and in certain specified circumstances to commit two infantry divisions to Europe. But the British were certainly not going to give an unequivocal declaration of automatic assistance to the French.

Its position was made clear in a speech by Eden on 20 November when he said at Leamington: "Our arms could be, and if circumstances rendered it necessary, would be used to defend France and Belgium against unprovoked aggression in accordance with our present obligations."[400] It was scarcely a clarion call to support France. The reasoning was based on the detestation of Military Pacts, which were seen as the prime cause of the Great War. Britain wanted a rapprochement with Germany and still believed that negotiations could achieve a settlement.

The Spanish Civil War, which began in July 1935, played an important part in the decision-making (or lack of it) of successive French Governments. It affected the attitude of the Soviet authorities towards France and soured relations between the British and French Governments. Because of the possibility of a victory for Franco, the civil war was a constant source of anxiety to the French. Preoccupation with the threat of danger to its colonies in North Africa and with the probability of a hostile Spain on its southern border diverted French attention from the problems in Central Europe. There were a variety of reasons.

A hostile Spain would not only be a danger on the land frontier of the Pyrenees but, it would also be likely to cause a serious problem in preventing the transport of French troops from Morocco. Nearly a third of the French army was stationed there. In April 1938, Daladier told Chamberlain that 'provision was being made in the French budget for important improvements to the port at Dakar with a view to bringing troops from Dakar, by the Atlantic route, in time of

[398] Cooper, D. (1954) *Old Men Forget*, London: Rupert Hart Davis, p. 208.

[399] DDF series 2, Tom. I, no 202.

[400] DDF series 2, Tom. IV, no 4.

war'.[401] In addition, the threat to its Mediterranean position from a combination of Germany, Italy and Spain naturally led the French Government to be inward-looking. Thus, it was French policy to give first consideration to its own defence rather than to the protection of its remote Allies in Central Europe to whom it was bound by a Treaty.

The initial reaction of the French Government to the outbreak of the civil war was to set the tone for the future policy of successive Governments in relation to the conflict. The Republican Prime Minister of Spain, Jose Giral sent a telegram to Blum: "Beg you to help us immediately with arms and aeroplanes."[402] Initially, Blum and the Air Minister supported the Spanish Government's request for help. However, opposition from the Defence Minister and a right-wing press, together with a warning from Eden to be careful, caused Blum, fearful of losing British support, to adopt non-intervention in Spain as official French policy.

There were a number of reasons for the surprising failure of one socialist government to support another. First was the possibility that the civil war in Spain would escalate into a European war. In November 1936, Delbos, the French Foreign Minister, observed: "Europe is on the verge of general war." [403] Secondly, the division between right and left in France was such as to destroy any prospect of national unity in regard to a Spanish policy. The right regarded a Soviet intervention in Spain as a prelude to a European war and the left passionately believed that the fight against fascism had to be won there.

The risk of civil war in France was too serious to be ignored and there was a fear that it might topple Blum's newly elected Popular Front and destroy his reforms.[404] Blum believed that Spain could not have been saved and that intervention would have led France to turn fascist.[405] Generals Gamelin, Duval and Jouart warned that the slightest suggestion of involving the country in the Spanish conflict risked provoking a major storm. [406]

France's position was succinctly set out by the French Ambassador in Moscow when he wrote, on 12 November, that "there were two policies, one of the conflicting ideologies and the other based on the reason of State. The former

---

[401] DBFP series 3, Vol. I, no 164.

[402] Thomas, L. (2003) *The Spanish Civil War*, London: Penguin Books Ltd., p. 324.

[403] FRUS 1936 II, p. 578.

[404] Adamthwaite A. (1995) *Grandeur and Misery*, London: Arnold, p. 206.

[405] Preston, P. (2006) *The Spanish Civil War*, London: Harper Perennial, p. 144.

[406] Beevor, A. (2006) *The Battle of Spain*, London: Weidenfeld and Nicolson, p. 131.

would lead to divisions at home and isolation abroad."[407] Additionally, the French were very dependent on British support. This was particularly important because of the French fear of encirclement by a combination of the Axis powers and Spain. The risk of offending Britain played a significant part in the French Cabinet's decision to reverse its policy of intervention.[408] One result was that they were less likely in the future to make any decision unless they had the clear support of the British Government. In August, there was a meeting between the British Ambassador in Paris and Delbos. Speaking 'without instructions' and on 'a personal note', Sir George Clerk told Delbos, "I felt that in so critical a situation, I must put before him the danger of any action which might definitely commit the French Government to one side of the conflict and make more difficult the close cooperation between our two countries."[409]

At the same time, the failure of the French actively to support the Republican Government in Spain against fascist aggression, alienated the Soviet Union and caused subsequent difficulties in Central Europe. Its inability to give active support to the Republic gave little encouragement to France's Allies. Attempts to consolidate the Eastern Alliance failed and any rapprochement with Germany which Blum desired was doomed to failure because of the German intervention in Spain.

The feeling of 'never again' played a significant part in the making of French policy. The casualties suffered by the French in the Great War and the destruction of its industries and infrastructure were of horrendous proportions. There was scarcely a family which was left untouched, as the war memorials in every little village and town bear witness. Their loss in dead alone was far more, in terms of population than Germany or Britain. Twice in a single generation France had been occupied by German forces with disastrous consequences for the French. The French fear of another Western Front was well justified.

It was against a further occupation of French territory that the Maginot line was designed and with it came the Maginot mentality. Thus, protected by a wall of concrete (except at the Belgium border) along its frontier, France believed it was safe against a further onslaught. The Maginot line would offset the shortage of manpower, which had been caused by the fall in the birth rate between 1914 and 1918. The length of military service was reduced to 18 months in 1923 and

---

[407] DDF series 2. Tom. III, no 472.

[408] Thomas, Ibid. p. 376.

[409] DDF series 2, Tom. III, no 108.

then to 12 months in 1928. Chautemps, who became Prime Minister, was a married man, who had lost three brothers in the War. He was recorded as telling Delbos, a lifelong bachelor that 'they should never appoint bachelors to key positions. They should appoint fathers of families like myself. I tell you that I will not go to war under any circumstances'.[410] In addition, the French anxiety about the effect of yet another war was inexorably linked to the fear that it would bring with it a social revolution.

On 4 March 1938, the Czech Minister in Paris reported to Krofta that 'in Paris, people of diverse professions and walks of life not excluding journalists and Members of Parliament, have begun to give form and expression to their resistance to the thought that France may have to go to war with Germany over Czechoslovakia.' He added that 'Minister Delbos, terribly tired and extremely fearful, what he would most like is not merely to quit his post but simply to run away if he only knew how. He is afraid of any idea that has a definite colouring, all colours hurt his eyes and his feelings'. He further said that Delbos was unwilling to say that France remained faithful to her pledges and would go no further than that France would pursue a policy of national security and European peace.[411] Churchill's phrase 'France was armed to the teeth and pacifist to the core' aptly summarises French attitudes during the 1930s.[412]

In March 1938, Maxim Litvinov, the Soviet Foreign Minister is reported as saying: "France has no confidence in the Soviet Union and the Soviet Union has no confidence in France."[413] It was not only the right-wing parties in France which preferred national socialism to communism. Even a radical socialist like Daladier was reported as saying at a private meeting with the German Ambassador on May 22: "The catastrophic frightfulness of modern war would surpass all that humanity has ever seen into the battle zones. Cossack and Mongol hordes would pour bringing to Europe a new 'culture'."[414]

Later, he told Bullitt, "Germany would be defeated in the war...the only gainers would be the Bolsheviks as there would be a social revolution in every

---

[410] International Affairs 1, 38 April 1962, p. 220.

[411] Documents and Materials, Vol. 1, no 4.

[412] Churchill, W. (1964) *The Second World War 1: The Gathering Storm*, London: Cassell, p. 40.

[413] Davies, J. E. (1941) *Mission to Moscow*, New York: Simon and Schuster, p. 290.

[414] DGFP series D, Vol. II, no 194.

country of Europe... Cossacks will rule Europe".[415] Bonnet is reported as having expressed the view in May 1938, that 'the Franco-Soviet Pact was very vague and the French Government was not at all inclined to rely upon it... Personally, he was no adherent of collaboration with communism'.[416]

He also said that while it was impossible to denounce that pact, the French Government had decided to bury it, 'to put it to sleep' in other words.[417] The electoral victory of the Popular Front not only gave rise to the slogan 'better Hitler than Blum' but led Gamelin to write: "the crisis of May/June 1936, terrorised a great section of the bourgeoisie. It made many of us lose sight of the dangers of Hitlerism and Fascism because behind the Popular Front, one saw the spectre of Bolshevism." [418]

The fear of Bolshevism was one of the reasons why, even though the French and the Soviets entered into a non-aggression pact in 1935, attempts to set up joint military talks ran into the sand. The idea of a coordinated approach to the threat of Germany fell on deaf ears. France and Czechoslovakia had entered into two Treaties in January 1924 and October 1925. It was agreed that there should be cooperation between the two General Staffs, but only one such meeting is thought to have taken place. In the event of Germany invading Czechoslovakia, France was bound by Treaty to go to her help. No doubt in 1938, the picture looked very different from that envisaged in 1924 and 1925. No other country had that primary obligation.

The Czechoslovak-Soviet Treaty of May 1935 only obliged the Soviets to go to the aid of the Czechs if France fulfilled its Treaty obligations to the Czechs. It was also clear that unless Poland and Romania allowed Soviet troops over their territory, the assistance which the Soviets could give would be of little value. In truth, the Soviet Union was regarded by the French with grave suspicion and after Stalin's purge of his Generals, the French regarded the possibility of any effective help from that quarter as non-existent.

The Franco-Soviet Treaty of May 1935, was a pact of mutual assistance. It had the effect of keeping the Soviet Union out of the German camp and of giving support to the Eastern Alliance. In April 1936, the French Ambassador in Moscow wrote: "The main object of the pact of mutual assistance is to confront

---

[415] FRUS 1938 1, pp. 601 and 687.

[416] Documents and Materials, no 11.

[417] DGFP series D, Vol. II, no 147.

[418] Gamelin, G. (1946) *Servir*, Paris, Vol. II, p. 219.

German expansionism with such a bloc as we could hope would prevent an attack" and he envisaged collaboration in a time of war 'as giving support by way of equipment, provisions, raw materials and munitions as seemed necessary'. [419] The Treaty was not only unpopular with the French public but the British reservations, forcibly expressed by Vansittart in April 1937, made clear the total lack of enthusiasm in Whitehall. [420]

By May 1937, the French had, however, come to the conclusion that French security depended on an alliance with Britain and hoped that they could rely on the British, in case of war, which was not the case with the Soviets, who had let them down in the Great War. A military accord with the Soviets, it was said, would endanger the cordial and happy Anglo-French relations.[421] Quite where the idea of 'cordial and happy' relations between Britain and France in 1937 came from is difficult to fathom. In the result, France and the Soviet Union scarcely had meaningful talks until the fruitless negotiations in the summer of 1939.

In truth, there were very serious doubts among the French that Britain would be a staunch ally. The Anglo-German Naval Treaty of June 1935 was much resented by the French. The Abyssinian crisis was again a source of division. The decision by the British Cabinet to repudiate the Hoare/Laval Pact sowed the seeds of distrust between the two Governments. Their respective attitudes towards non-intervention in the Spanish civil war caused differences as did the question of imposing sanctions on Italy. On many occasions, the French and British spoke not only in a different language but also with different voices.

Some hint of this appears in the minutes of the meeting on 28 November 1937 between the French (Chautemps and Delbos) and the British (Chamberlain, Halifax and Eden) when they discussed the problem of Czechoslovakia. Halifax had already told Hitler during his 'hunting visit' that effectively, Britain was not concerned with Austria or Czechoslovakia. [422] Eden had also pointed out that the Sudeten Germans had a legitimate grievance, which needed to be addressed. The French attitude was one of equivocation.

This meeting with the French was preceded by a memorandum from the British Chiefs of Staff. Criticism was made of France's lack of war reserves and

---

[419] DDF series 2. Tom. II, no 35.

[420] DDF, Ibid. Tom. V, no 299.

[421] DDF, Ibid. no 480.

[422] Post no 455.

her failure to expand her arms industry due to financial, economic and social reasons. In particular, the fighting value of the French air force was doubted. France's fixed land defences were regarded as strong, but it was not sufficient consideration to outweigh French determination not to seek war.[423] The British Government was not prepared to make any commitment to Central Europe. Its attitude was summarised by Chamberlain who said: "There was a strong feeling that we ought not to be entangled in a war on account of Czechoslovakia which was a long way off and with which we had not a bit in common... His Majesty's Government could certainly not go so far as to state what their action would be in the event of an attack (ie on Czechoslovakia)." [424] A constant theme of British cabinet discussions throughout 1937/1938 was that Anglo-French friendship did not require automatic involvement in France's Treaty obligations to the Czechs or indeed to any other country.

The state of their armed forces played a very significant part in the French decision making. The appreciation by the French military and their intelligence, which they conveyed to their political masters about the relative strengths of the French and German armed forces, was wildly inaccurate. The threat of aerial bombardment was grossly exaggerated. (British assessments were no more accurate).[425] Murray's conclusion can be summarised. In 1938, France had overwhelming military superiority on Germany's Western Front but by 1939 and even more so by 1940, the German ground forces had overtaken the French. The Luftwaffe was not the force it became in 1940. In 1938, it would have been unable to bomb Britain because Britain was out of range of German airbases. It lacked reserves of men and materials. Germany was economically vulnerable. "In terms of divisions, economic resources, industrial capacity and naval forces, Germany would have faced overwhelming allied superiority in 1938. Whether she faced only Britain and France or an enlarged coalition that included Russia, the war would not have been easy or quickly won. But the results would have been inevitable and led to the collapse of the Nazi regime." [426]

But the perception in the years 1936–1938 was very different. As early as March 1933, Daladier had told the British that the effectiveness of the German

---

[423] DBFP series 2, Vol. XIX, no 316.

[424] DBFP, Ibid. no 354.

[425] Murray, Ibid. pp. 217–263.

[426] Murray, Ibid. pp. 262/263 see also Bouverie, pp. 294–297.

forces was far greater than those of France.[427] In January 1936, the French General Staff had set out, in a memorandum, how they saw the respective balance between the French and German forces. It pointed out that because of the Abyssinian crisis, the defence of the northeast of France was reduced by ten divisions and two brigades of cavalry. Further, there might be problems with bringing troops from North Africa. Having observed that German forces had increased substantially, it went on to point out that 'independently of this increase of manpower, the increase of German military power is expressed by the development of the artillery strength of the units and mechanisation'. It came to the conclusion that 'the intensive rearmament of Germany, artillery which is powerful in quality as well as in quantity, a mass of tanks, which for the armoured divisions alone approaches 2,000 units, is opposed by (our) artillery system based on the equipment in service during the Great War by limited armament and anti-tank defences, especially with regard to the fortified regions and by modern tanks which barely cover a third of our needs'.[428]

While numerically the French army in 1938 outnumbered the Germans, some 20% of their forces were stationed overseas. The army was made up of a limited number of regulars supplemented by reservists drawn from the civilian population. Thus, any action by the army could only be undertaken after a lengthy process of mobilisation which might take anything up to a fortnight to achieve. The Maginot Line, on which all French military thinking was based while appearing to provide a defence against invasion, was something of a white elephant. It did not extend to the Belgian front. Further, after the Germans had occupied the Rhineland, the French were now prevented from making any useful contribution to the defence of Czechoslovakia by an attack on the Western Front.

The state of the Air Force compared unfavourably with the Luftwaffe, both numerically and in the quality of its aircraft. Although some help from the RAF was expected, there was constant anxiety among the General Staff about this problem. There was persistent gloom about the ability of the Air Force to perform a useful offensive role, or even a defensive role, of any sort. Although the French Air Minister had told the French Cabinet in November 1937 that France was much better equipped than the British with modern aircraft in regard to both

---

[427] DDF series 1, Tom. IV, no 392.
[428] DDF series 2, Tom. I, no 82.

fighters and bombers,[429] by 1937/1938 the German air force equalled the combined totals of France and Britain.[430]

Long before, on 10 November 1932, Baldwin, in a speech in the House of Commons, had raised the spectre of aerial bombardment. He said: "I think it as well for the man in the street to realise that there is no power on earth that can protect him from being bombed. Whatever people may tell him, the bomber will always get through."[431] By September 1938, the French were in, what can only be described, as near panic about the German air force.

On September 20, the Head of the Deuxieme Bureau suggested that because of the German air threat there would be no war.[432] He was not alone in his anxieties about the power of the Luftwaffe. General Joseph Vuillemin had been a French ace in the Great War, who had pioneered night flying. He had been appointed Chief of the Air Staff by the Air Minister, Guy la Chambre, in January 1938. From that time, he never ceased to express the view, sometimes in somewhat graphic terms, that the French air force would be no match for the Luftwaffe.

On 15 January and 15 March, he expressed the opinion that, in a war with Germany, the French air force would be wiped out within 15 days.[433] In August 1938, he went to Germany as a guest of General Milch, the inspector general of the Luftwaffe. This trip was condemned by both the French Ambassador and the Air Attaché in Berlin on the ground that it would be an opportunity for the Germans to put on a staged performance and thereby impress Vuillemin. It succeeded beyond their wildest dreams.[434]

He came back convinced of the terrifying air superiority of the Luftwaffe. He concluded that protecting the public or the mobilisation of troops against German bombers could not be assured and that the French Air Force could only bomb Germany at night. There was a marked disparity in the quantity and quality of the French Air Force compared to the Luftwaffe. This disproportion was

---

[429] DDF series 2, Tom. VII, no 213.

[430] Adamthwaite, A. (1977) *France and the Coming of the Second World War*, London: Frank Cass, p. 161.

[431] House of Commons Official Reports, Fifth Series, Vol. 270, col 632, 10 November 1932.

[432] DBFP series 3, Vol. II, no 1012 & 1034.

[433] DDF series 2, Tom. VIII, no 447.

[434] Stehlin, P. (1964) *Temoignage pour l'histoire*, Paris, pp. 86–91.

described as 'extremely acute'. After the first month, the French would have lost some 40% of its capacity and 64% after two months. The effect would be that the French Army would have no information about German troop movements, while the Luftwaffe could attack French troops at will. The Germans could also launch large scale and repetitive attacks on the civilian population without the French having an opportunity to retaliate.[435]

His views received support from an unexpected quarter. Colonel Lindbergh was an American airman who in 1927, became a household name because of flying solo across the Atlantic from the United States to Le Bourget in France. In the summer of 1938, he visited a number of capitals in Europe, including Berlin, before returning to Paris in September, now convinced of German air superiority. The British Military Attaché in Paris recorded that 'the Fuhrer found a most convenient ambassador in Colonel Lindbergh'.[436] One entry in Lindbergh's diaries records: "The French situation is desperate...one is forced to the conclusion that the German air fleet is stronger than that of all other European countries combined." [437]

His reports to the French caused widespread consternation. Their reaction was contained in a series of communications from Phipps to Halifax between 13 and 30 September. Phipps reported that Bonnet 'was very upset and said peace must be preserved at any price... Colonel Lindbergh had returned from his tour, horrified at the overwhelming strength of Germany in the air and terrible weakness of all other powers. He declares that Germany has 800 military aeroplanes and can turn out 100 a month... French and British towns would be wiped out'.[438] How he arrived at his conclusions or from where these figures came is still something of a mystery. Lindbergh denied giving any figures and indeed that he had any access to them.

Bonnet told Phipps with emotion that 'at no price should we allow ourselves to be involved in war without having weighed all the consequences and without having measured, in particular, the state of our military forces'.[439] Phipps reported that the French Air Minister had told the Chamber of Deputies that the

---

[435] DDF series 2, Tom. XI, no 377.

[436] DBFP series 3, Vol. II, no 1012.

[437] Lindbergh, C. (1970) *The Wartime Journals of Charles A. Lindbergh*, New York, p. 70.

[438] DBFP series 3, Vol 11.

[439] DDF series 2, Tom. XI, no 125.

'air threat was quite catastrophic' and General Dentz, Gamelin's deputy, told the British Military Attaché that 'in war, French cities would be laid in ruins and that they had no means of defence'.[440]

Phipps meanwhile continued to paint such a gloomy picture of the French attitude that he was rebuked by the Air Ministry in fairly trenchant terms. They wrote: "It is not within the province of the Air Staff to comment on the significance of the defeatist attitude of certain sections of the French public. But it does appear that the attitude is influenced to an excessive degree by misinformation." [441]

The suggestion has been made that the combined forces of the French and Czechoslovak army were numerically superior to Germany and that the German defences on the Western Front were inadequate to protect Germany against a French invasion.[442] The comparative strength of the French forces (56 divisions) on the Western Front was very substantially greater than those of Germany (8 divisions) because some 37 German divisions were needed to invade Czechoslovakia, which itself had an army of thirty divisions. While this imbalance would seriously and adversely have affected Germany's ability to resist an invasion by French forces, that is totally to ignore the mindset of the French Military Authorities or of the French politicians involved, who seemed to think that after a modest incursion into German territory, the French army should retreat behind the Maginot line and fight the war from there.[443] Nor were the British any more encouraging. They suggested that the French should be dissuaded from taking any action against Germany without having consulted with the British Government.[444] It is clear that the French were unduly concerned about their ability to wage a European war either on land or in the air. Whatever the actual figures involved, it was the perception which was the decisive factor.

Given all these matters, it is not very surprising that France was unwilling to fulfil its obligations. At the meeting with the British on 28/29 April 1938, Gamelin had been asked to express the French view about the help it could give the Czechs. He suggested that France would take steps on its own territory, moving from giving the alert to setting up a state of security, then taking up

---

[440] DBFP, Ibid. no 1034.

[441] FO 37121596.

[442] Murray, Ibid. pp. 240–241. Bouverie, pp. 294–297.

[443] Faber, Ibid. p. 275.

[444] CAB 27/646.

covering positions and lastly, complete mobilisation. "Upon the Government's decision, the French land and air forces can then carry out offensive operations, in the conditions provided for in our operational plans."[445] The discussions which took place thereafter, throw no light on these operational plans or whether they ever existed. Nor was there any suggestion made as to when, how or where help was to be given to the Czechs. Gamelin's views were so much hot air.

The Czechs were much distressed at being abandoned by their Western Allies. Why then, did it seem to have come as some surprise to them that the French Treaty was of little value? It was certainly clear to the British Government that whatever French ministers might say in public, privately they had no intention of going to war on behalf of Czechoslovakia. In May 1937, Delbos is reported as having said on two occasions: "He could think of nothing better than making concessions to Germany piecemeal in order to stave off war and it is clear that France is no longer strong enough to maintain the status quo in central Europe."[446]

Additionally, the views held by the General Staff that the defence of France was of primary importance resulted in a policy of keeping out of a war at all costs. Nothing better illustrates this than a report dated 8 February 1938. In it, Gamelin set out the military priorities in a time of war. "1. Defence of France and her empire. 2. Offensive action against Italy in the Alps and in Africa. 3. 'If possible' and 'at a convenient time' offensive action against Germany in order to divert part of the German forces for the benefit of our central European Allies."[447]

On 29 November 1937, there had been a meeting between French and British Ministers in London. During a wide-ranging discussion, including the visit of Halifax to Germany, the question of the return of the German colonies and the questions of Austria and of Czechoslovakia then dominated the meeting. Delbos expressed the view that the Sudeten Germans were looking for a federal constitution followed by de facto autonomy and then attachment to Germany. When Chamberlain enquired what would bring France's Treaty with Czechoslovakia into effect, Delbos replied that 'if uprisings among the German population occurred and was supported by armed intervention from Germany,

---

[445] Nogueres, Ibid. p. 50.

[446] FRUS 1937 I, p. 89.

[447] DDF series 2, Tom. VIII, no 127.

the Treaty committed France in a manner to be determined according to the gravity of the facts'.

He went on to add that 'there were two courses, to let things slide or, to take an interest in the problem of Central Europe, in a firm and conciliatory spirit. In this latter hypothesis, the situation did not seem really desperate'.[448] Clearly, the French had already decided not to guarantee the existing territorial and political settlement in Czechoslovakia.

When the French sought some commitment by the British Government in support of Czechoslovakia, the idea was rejected. In February 1938, Delbos made a speech in which he said, "I must once again declare that our engagements towards Czechoslovakia will, if necessary, be faithfully fulfilled."[449] It was, to say the least, a pretty anodyne statement but it had the effect of reassuring the Czechs.

In March and April 1938, the new French Government gave categorical declarations of support for the Czechs. The attitude of the British Government was set out in the statement of Chamberlain in the House of Commons on 24 March having observed that 'where legal obligations were not alone involved, the inexorable pressure of facts might well prove more powerful than formal pronouncements'.[450] In other words, there was to be no new commitment by Britain involving any risk of war On 12 May. Chamberlain had told foreign journalists that neither the Soviet Union nor France nor Great Britain would fight for Czechoslovakia and that Britain was in favour of ceding the Sudeten German districts to Germany.[451]

Talks on 29 April 1938 between French and British Ministers were symptomatic of others that followed during the summer. While on the one hand, the French continued publicly to express their commitment to the Treaty obligations to the Czechs because of the national honour involved, at the same time they sought privately to persuade the Czechs to make concessions to the Sudeten Germans and to make conciliatory overtures to Germany. It was not until 20 July that, for the first time, the French Government officially made the Czech aware of their attitude to the Sudeten problem. The Czechs were told, in the clearest possible terms, that neither France nor Britain would go to war over

---

[448] DDF, Ibid. no 287.

[449] Documents and Materials, no 4.

[450] House of Commons Official Reports. Fifth Series, Vol. 333, col 1405, 24 March 1938.

[451] Faber, Ibid. p. 175.

the Sudeten affair and that while publicly they would continue to assert their solidarity with the Czechs, it was up to the Czechs to find a peaceful solution.

Although thereafter there were public expressions of support, the French did everything possible to bring pressure on the Czechs to make concessions so as to avoid war. On 8 September, Daladier told the British Ambassador that if Germany attacked Czechoslovakia, France would march. And after the talks at Bad Godesberg, the French continued to express the view that if the terms were rejected by the Czechs, they would fulfil their Treaty obligations to the Czechs. The matter was never tested and in the light of their pronouncements on 20 July and thereafter, it is scarcely credible that they would have done anything.

And so, we arrive at 29 September, when the French, together with the British and in the absence of any Czech representatives, effectively signed away Czech independence. France's contribution to the discussions at Munich can best be described as marginal. Not that it mattered very much in the light of what Chamberlain had already conceded.

What then of the French conduct? They had freely entered into a Treaty obligation which they could not fulfil and which, by 1935, they knew they could not fulfil. They were repeatedly warned by the British Government that they could expect no support from that source, but they continued to believe, without evidence, that such support would, in the final resort, be forthcoming. They failed to make it clear to the Czechs, at a very early stage, that they were neither willing nor, in fact, were able, to come to the assistance of the Czechs. The failure to react to the occupation of the Rhineland effectively put an end to any influence the French might have had in Europe. It was not that they were unaware of the danger posed by Nazi Germany. They simply lacked the will to face up to the problem. Correlli Barnett wrote: "France now wore the role of a great power like a decrepit old man shrunken inside the uniform; he had worn so bravely long ago." [452]

---

[452] Barnett, Ibid. p. 469.

Part Four
The British Perspective

Chapter Eleven:
Divergent Views

The British and French had wholly divergent attitudes to the problem of Germany. They reflected the very different effect of the World War on each country and also of the consequences of the Versailles Treaty. It was the second time, within the memory of most of the French population, that Germany had invaded France. In the War, France lost a substantial amount of their industry. Vast areas of France were laid to waste. It had suffered a horrendous number of casualties. At the end of the War their priority, apart from securing war reparations, was to ensure that, at whatever the cost, the Germans never again invaded their country.

The effect of the War on Britain was quite different. It was the first time that it had fought a continental war since Waterloo. France had been its traditional enemy. With Germany not only had there been economic competition before the war but British anxiety about Germany had also been directed at the growth of its fleet and the race for colonies, particularly in Africa. Britain was not invaded. It did not suffer the consequences of occupation, although it, too, suffered large casualties. It incurred very substantial debts in order to keep the war machine operating. Its merchant fleet suffered considerably at the hands of the German U boats and its markets overseas were badly damaged.

By comparison with the French, the physical damage to the country was minimal and its infrastructure was scarcely affected. The previous problems of the German navy and the competition to secure colonies were easily resolved by the Versailles Treaty. The German fleet was required to surrender and a large part of it was scuttled at Scapa Flow. So far as the colonies were concerned, Germany was stripped of them all, some simply being acquired by the Allies and others becoming mandated territories. Although, at great cost, Britain had emerged from the War, having removed the two most important threats from

Germany. It did not appear that Germany was now likely to pose any problem for Britain. Thus, while French policy was directed at forming alliances to lessen the threat of further German aggression, Britain, for its part, wanted to be free of any commitment which might again automatically involve them in European affairs.

The onset of the World War had a certain inevitability. It had resulted from pacts between the Soviet Union, Serbia and France on the one hand and Germany and Austro-Hungary on the other. As a result, Britain had been, somewhat, reluctantly drawn in. It was a constant reminder to British politicians to avoid entanglements in Europe.

For Britain, the restoration of a prosperous Europe was essential to its own economy. Thus, peace in Europe and its own prosperity were inextricably linked. It was thought that by skilful diplomacy and well-timed concessions Germany could be appeased. Thus, in 1935, the British, ignoring French anxieties about a resurgent militant Germany, negotiated a bilateral Naval Agreement with Germany. This enabled the Germans to replace, at least in part, the ships scuppered at Scapa Flow. This was done without any consultation with the French and with the knowledge that it was likely to (as it did) antagonise them. It was in total contrast to France's policy of hostility to Germany.

There was one further difference in the respective outlooks of the two countries. While Britain's initial reaction at the end of the war was 'hang the Kaiser' and 'squeeze the pips until they squeak', it was not very long before British politicians began to doubt whether the Versailles Treaty had been entirely fair to Germany. This was not based simply on the view propounded by Keynes in his book '*The Economic Consequences of the Peace*' that this was 'a Carthaginian peace'. It was predicated on the broader and more pragmatic approach that Europe needed a flourishing Germany to ensure prosperity there. A prosperous Europe would also benefit Britain economically. Restoration of Germany was also seen as a buffer against what was then perceived as the dangers of world communism. Having wholly supported the right to self-determination at the Peace Conference, it would have required a considerable volte-face not to have some sympathy with the Austrians and Sudeten Germans.

For the French, the matter was not so easily solved. The War ended with the Germans still occupying large parts of France. Germany itself was never occupied in the war. Apart from the Rhineland being demilitarised and the return of Alsace Lorraine, the Versailles Treaty had done little or nothing to lessen the danger from Germany. Effectively, it still held the same threatening position on the French border. The French had to make provision to protect itself against any further German incursion. There were a number of different courses which they could follow. The first was to enforce the reparations clauses in the Treaty and to take military action when the Germans failed to pay. This they did, with conspicuous lack of success. Secondly, to build up a series of pacts with other powers in Eastern Europe to provide collective security. These pacts bound France but not Britain. Thirdly, to build the Maginot line behind which the French army could safely shelter and thereby hope to protect France from any invasion by Germany.

Thus, while British policy was to encourage Germany to re-emerge as a power in Europe and to give effect, as they saw it, to the policy of self-determination, embodied in Wilson's fourteen points, the French attitude was directed primarily to ensuring its security against any further German aggression. It is not, therefore, very surprising that the two Governments frequently failed to reach a common policy. Because Britain was an island, a maritime power and blessed with an empire, it was much less concerned about the affairs of Eastern Europe than an essentially continental power like France. It is in the light of these circumstances that it is possible to explain (though not necessarily to excuse) the uncritical view of Germany's good faith adopted by British politicians, in particular by Chamberlain and Halifax.

In October 1937, Harvey, then Anthony Eden's private secretary, recorded: "Halifax is idle and pernickety. Most of the colleagues are 'dictator minded' and hate to see us associate with France".[453] Halifax's pronouncements, during his visit to Hitler in November 1937, give some flavour of the British attitude. In his diary, he records that "I said there were, no doubt, other questions arising out of the Versailles settlement, which seemed to us capable of causing trouble if they were mishandled ie Danzig, Austria, Czechoslovakia. On all these matters, we were not necessarily concerned to stand for the status quo as today…there were possible alterations in the European order which might be destined to come about with the passage of time… But he, Hitler, struck me as very sincere and as believing everything he said."

---

[453] Harvey, Ibid. p. 51.

Of Goering, Halifax said, "… His personality, with his reserve, was frankly attractive. Like a great schoolboy, full of life and pride in all he was doing." [454] The summary of the discussion at the cabinet records: "Lord Halifax's general conclusion, therefore, was that the Germans had no policy of immediate adventure."[455] In July 1937, Chamberlain had told Maisky that 'if we could only sit down at a table with the Germans and run through their complaints and their claims with a pencil, this would greatly relieve the tension'.[456]

In March 1938, after the Anschluss had taken place, Chamberlain was still of the view that 'some general and lasting arrangement with both dictators (Hitler and Mussolini) was not only desirable but possible'. [457] "The seizure of the whole of Czechoslovakia," said Chamberlain at a meeting of the Foreign Policy Committee on 18 March 1938, "would not be in accordance with Herr Hitler's policy, which was to include all Germans in the Reich but not to include other nationalities. If Germany could obtain her desiderata by peaceful methods, there was no reason she would reject such a procedure in favour of one based on violence." The Committee decided, unanimously, that Czechoslovakia was not worth the bones of a British grenadier.[458] On 11 April 1938, after the fall of the French Popular Front government, Halifax was able to write to the Embassy in Prague. "Unless the French and Czechoslovak Governments can be brought to face the realities of the present position, it is to be feared that the Czechoslovak Government will not realise the necessity of making drastic concessions to the German minority, but will content themselves with superficial measures, which, though they might have been adequate in the past, will no longer meet the case."[459]

On 19 September, on his return from Berchtesgaden, Chamberlain told his sisters that Wilson had heard that Hitler was impressed by Chamberlain and had said: "I have had a conversation with a man and one with whom I can do business."

---

[454] Hickleton. Papers. A4/410/3/3 (vi) Lord Halifax. 'Diary of Visit' 17–21, November 1937.

[455] CAB 43(47).

[456] Gorodetsky, Ibid. p. 84.

[457] Gladwyn, L. (1972) Memoirs of Lord Gladwyn, Weidenfeld and Nicolson, pp. 74–75.

[458] Cadogan, Ibid. p. 63.

[459] DBFP series 3, Vol. I, no 135.

Chamberlain added: "I have established certain confidence, which was my aim… I got the impression that here was a man who could be relied upon when he had given his word."[460]

His report to the Cabinet on 19 September contained the phrases 'a new understanding between England and Germany', it was impossible not to be impressed with the power of the man and his objectives were strictly limited and…when he had included the Sudeten Germans in the Reich, he would be satisfied. [461]

On 24 September, Chamberlain returned to London from Bad Godesberg. At the meeting, Hitler had increased the demands to which he had agreed at Berchtesgaden and was now preparing to take military measures against Czechoslovakia. Nevertheless, Chamberlain felt able to announce to a sceptical Cabinet that 'Hitler would not deliberately deceive a man whom he respected…and he was sure that Herr Hitler now felt some respect for him. The crucial question was whether Herr Hitler was speaking the truth when he said that he regarded the Sudeten question as a racial question, which must be settled, and that the object of his policy was racial unity and not the domination of Europe…the Prime Minister believed that Herr Hitler was speaking the truth'.[462] Could self-delusion go further?

On 27 September, Chamberlain broadcast to the Nation. He reiterated his belief that the Sudetenland represented Hitler's last territorial claim in Europe and spoke 'of a quarrel in a faraway country between people of whom we know nothing'.[463] After the Munich Agreement, which set up an International Commission, Hitler ignored it and seized large parts of Czechoslovakia, which had not been part of the agreement. Nevertheless, Chamberlain was able to write to his sister on 19 February 1939. "All the information I get seems to point in the direction of peace."[464] In less than a month, German troops had marched into Prague and occupied the whole of Czechoslovakia.

Chamberlain's whole approach can be summed up by what he said in February 1939, at a Jewellers' dinner in Birmingham. He was talking about Munich and the Dictators: "Let us cultivate the friendship of the peoples…let us

---

[460] Chamberlain Papers NC/18/1069.

[461] CAB 23/95/ 39 (38), 17 September.

[462] CAB 93/95 Minutes 92 (38).

[463] Feiling, Ibid. p. 372.

[464] Chamberlain Papers NC 18/1/1086.

make clear to them that we do not regard them as potential foes but rather as human beings as ourselves…peoples who had come so close to a war that they would henceforth resist it, all the more so, because they believed that Mr Chamberlain is a nice kind old gentleman, who would never want to treat Germans roughly and unfairly."[465] Hitler's view of Chamberlain in 1939 was less than flattering. He was reported as being wont to refer to him in private as '*der alter Arschloch*' (The old asshole!).[466]

Leo Amery had had a distinguished political career. He was a Conservative MP. He had been the First Lord of the Admiralty 1922–1924, Secretary of State for the Colonies 1924–1929 and for Dominion Affairs 1925–1929. He is, perhaps, best remembered for his intervention in the famous debate in May 1940 about the war situation. Quoting the words of Cromwell to the Long Parliament, he said to Chamberlain, who had called on his friends to support him, "You have sat here too long for any good that you have been doing…in the name of God, go."[467]

The debate arose from dissatisfaction about the conduct of the war and, in particular, about the occupation of Norway, which had ended in a British defeat. Chamberlain's boast that Hitler had 'missed the bus' sounded pretty hollow in the light of the subsequent German success in Norway. It was yet another example of Chamberlain's lack of judgement.

While no one could describe Amery as a strong champion of Chamberlain, his views recorded in his memoirs accurately paint a picture of the man. "Inflexibly dedicated to his self-imposed mission, at all costs, to avert the risk of a world war, he ignored the warnings of the Foreign Office, dominated his colleagues, overrode wavering French Ministers, brushing aside their moral compunctions, as lacking realism, and to the last moment, refused to acknowledge failure… It was only in that fixed determination that he could persuade himself, in the face of all evidence to the contrary, that Hitler's promises were sincere or shut his eyes to the dishonourable aspects of his treatment of the Czechs…he claimed for himself, as against the illusionists of collective security, that he was a realist…appeasement as he pursued it, was no

---

[465] Feiling, Ibid. p. 394.

[466] Aldrich, R. J. (2010) *GCHQ*, London: Harper Press, p. 3.

[467] House of Commons Official Reports. Fifth Series, Vol. 360, col 1150, 7 May 1940.

less of an illusion and his passionate pursuit of peace and horror of war, in themselves noble, blinded him to the practical realities." [468]

Another view was that 'his correspondence with his sisters offers an extraordinary insight into his mind and emotions and reveals a personality with marked traits of inferiority and hunger for flattery that nourished a growing vanity and self-righteousness. His letters are almost completely devoid of self-criticism or self-doubt and portray a man with an obsessive sense of mission making predictions, which were invariably optimistic and invariably wrong'. He was described as 'self-satisfied' and 'intolerably smug'[469] and 'moved by some vanity over his own ventures with Hitler and Mussolini'. [470]

One Soviet view was that he was a sinister figure: "Sinister for the profound and innate reactionary character of his views… Neville Chamberlain was a man of narrow views and small capabilities…his political horizons, to use Lloyd George's expression, did not rise above that of a provincial manufacturer of iron bedsteads."[471] Litvinov's view in June 1938, was that 'the reactionary circles preferred to sacrifice their National interests and endanger and even lose their State positions for the sake of preserving their social and class positions'.[472]

Whatever warnings he got from the Foreign Office were totally overshadowed by the reports from Berlin of Sir Nevile Henderson, the British ambassador, for whose appointment in 1937, somewhat ironically, Vansittart had been primarily responsible. Henderson had previously been a Minister in Belgrade 1929–1935 and at Buenos Aires 1935–1937. His qualifications, according to Vansittart, were that while in Belgrade, he had got on well with King Alexander and Prince Paul and that he was regarded as a 'good shot'. What finally decided the appointment was Vansittart's view that 'Sir Nevile has done his stint in South America. He shall have his reward'.[473]

---

[468] Amery, L. (1955) *My Political Life: The Unforgiving Years 1929–1940*, Hutchinson, Vol. III, p. 292.

[469] Boyce, R. and Robertson, E. (ed.) (1989) *Paths to War. New Essays on the Origin of the Second World War*, Macmillan, p. 240–241.

[470] Harvey, Ibid. p. 71.

[471] Maisky, I. (Trans. Rothstein, A.) (1964) *Who helped Hitler?* London: Hutchinson, p. 67.

[472] Documents of Soviet Foreign Policy, Vol. III, page 292.

[473] Colvin, Ibid. p. 146.

The appointment was a total disaster. In modern parlance, he went native ie he started to identify himself with, and support the policies of, the country to which he was accredited. As Murray expressed it: "Vansittart could not have made a worse selection. Henderson fell for Nazi propaganda, hook, line and sinker. He pictured the Nazi leaders and, particularly, Hitler as moderates with limited aims. He argued, right to the end, that they were men with whom Britain could achieve a lasting settlement."[474]

His appointment initially found favour with Cadogan, with whom he had been at Eton. Cadogan thought him 'sanguine, a prey to moods and impressionable and liked him privately'. On 30 January 1938, Cadogan dined with him. "... We had quite a useful talk. I think he's very good."[475] But his failure properly to convey his instructions to the Germans, or to report adversely on German policy, was because of his consistent belief in their goodness. In his view, this must, on no account, be disturbed by even the slightest hint of criticism by Britain. When in May 1938, Henderson exceeded his instructions in discussions with the German Chargé d'affaires, Cadogan noted: "Nevile Henderson) really does want a gentle jab in the mouth occasionally." [476]

In February 1939, five months after the Munich Agreement, Henderson had returned to Berlin after some month's absence. His first impression was that 'the Germans are not contemplating any immediate wild adventure and that their compass is pointing to peace'. Within three weeks, the Germans marched into Prague. Cadogan's view of his old school friend had changed. On 24 February 1939, he recorded: "Nevile Henderson is completely bewitched by his German friends. Vansittart, on the contrary, out Cassandras Cassandra, must talk to Halifax about it. He ought either to rebuke Vansittart or recall Nevile. I don't know which is the sillier of the two."[477]

Of Henderson, the historian Lewis Namier wrote: "Conceited, vain, self-opinionated, rigidly adhering to his preconceived ideas, he poured out telegrams, dispatches and letters in unbelievable numbers and of formidable length, repeating a hundred times the same ill-founded views and ideas. Obtuse enough to be a menace and not stupid enough to be innocuous, he proved *un homme*

---

[474] Murray, Ibid. p. 60.
[475] Cadogan, Ibid. p. 43.
[476] Ibid. p. 75.
[477] Ibid. p. 151.

néfaste important because he echoed and reinforced Chamberlain's opinions and policy." [478]

Of him, Sir Orme Sargent also wrote: "He had no preconceived dislike of authoritarian government as such. He was, therefore, ready to believe that Great Britain and Germany could be reconciled, even if this meant tacit acquiescence by Britain in the adoption by Germany of the Nazi philosophy of life and system of government, as well as the aggrandisement of Germany in Central Europe." Henderson believed that his appointment to the British embassy 'could only mean that I had been specially selected by providence for the definite mission of, as I trusted, helping to preserve the peace of the world'. [479] It was he who was responsible for requiring the England FA XI in May 1938 in the Berlin Olympic Stadium humiliatingly to give the Nazi salute in the match against a German XI (see the picture of the cover).

Chamberlain's support of appeasement has to be looked at in the light of a number of conflicting factors. While he wholly misunderstood the nature of the German threat to the rest of Europe, his actions were necessarily circumscribed by three different concerns which, separately and cumulative, forced him to take the approach which he did. The first was the effect of public opinion, not only in Britain but equally in the Dominions. The attitude of the Dominions played a crucial part in Chamberlain's thinking about appeasement. The second was the state of the economy and the third was the inadequacy of the armed forces. The latter two points were inexorably linked.

Two events can be identified as expressing the public point of view of rearmament. In October 1933, there was a by-election at East Fulham. A Conservative majority at the general election of over 23,000 was overturned. Labour won the seat with a majority of 4840. There were, as always, in by-elections, a number of local issues, but both the lobby correspondent of the *Times* and the victorious Labour candidate described the result as a victory based entirely on the pacifist issue and a defeat for a policy of rearmament. [480]

So too did Baldwin, then Prime Minister, in his famous speech in November 1936, when he referred to the general election in 1935. He observed that 'to have asked for a mandate for rearmament from this pacific democracy, would have

---

[478] Namier, L. B. (1952) *In the Nazi Era*, New York, p. 162.

[479] Henderson, S. N. (1940) *Failure of a Mission*, London: Hodder and Stoughton, p. 13.

[480] Cook, C. and Ramsden, J. (1973) *By-elections in British Politics*, London: The Macmillan Press Ltd., pp. 118–137.

made the loss of the election certain'.[481] Nor was East Fulham an isolated result. Between June 1933 and March 1935, there were a whole series of by-elections, where swings against the government varied from 14% to an astonishing 50% at Lambeth North.

The second event was the Peace Ballot organised by the League of Nations Union (LNU). This worthy body had been formed to carry the cause of peace to the country. It had royal patronage and involved all the main political parties. Among its leaders were Gilbert Murray and Lord Robert Cecil. The latter had played a significant role in setting up the League of Nations. In 1935, the LNU conducted their Peace Ballot, effectively asking the general public their views about how to preserve peace between Nations.

The results showed that some 11 million wanted Britain to remain a member of the League. Of these, 10 million agreed that if one Nation were to attack another, the other Nations should take steps to deal with the aggressor by way of economic and (perhaps more importantly) non-military measures. Nor did the Labour party support the idea of rearmament. They consistently voted against the defence estimates. Even in 1939, astonishingly, they voted against the introduction of conscription.

The next factor in Chamberlain's reluctance to support the Czechs was the attitude of the Dominions. In 1914, almost without exception, they had entered the War with enthusiastic support for the mother country. Their exploits on many battlefields are legendary and the extent of their support cannot be exaggerated. Since that time, however, their attitudes had changed materially. A number of them had now become self-governing and their attitude to Britain was no longer that of a child to its mother but rather of a friendly relation.

As early as 1919, when Lloyd George offered Clemenceau, on behalf of Britain and the Empire, a military guarantee against future German aggression, Smuts issued a warning against, including South Africa in the guarantee. As a result, Lloyd George amended the guarantee so that it would not be binding on the Dominions until ratified by them. Thus, the Dominions were no longer bound by Britain's Treaty obligations and were free to make their own choices as independent nations.[482]

---

[481] Middlemas and Barnes, Ibid. p. 746. House of Commons Official Reports Fifth Series, Vol. 317, cols 1144/1145, 12 November 1936.

[482] Lentin, A. (2010) *General Smuts*, London: Hans Publishing Ltd., p. 82.

They no longer believed in being treated as some subservient colony. For a number of countries, memories of what happened in the Great War had not led them to accept that uncritical support of the British government was necessary for their best self-interest. Australia and New Zealand, in particular, had bitter memories of what had happened at Gallipoli and were now determined to exercise their own independent judgement.

On 16 June 1937, Malcolm MacDonald reported that Commonwealth Prime Ministers at the London Imperial Conference had been inclined: "To look rather more critically at British involvement in Europe than His Majesty's Government itself cared to. Even the Australian Government had rather criticised our opposition to the Anschluss." [483]

General Herzog of South Africa put it more bluntly: "I maintain that peace in Europe can be assured today, and should be assured, if Great Britain approached Germany in the same spirit of cooperation that she has shown France since 1919. I sincerely hope that I shall not be accused of unfriendly feelings towards the British government if I say the impression, so far given by Great Britain's attitude towards Germany is far too much of cold, repelling, indifference compared with the warm welcome given to France... If war did come because England continued to associate with France in policy in respect of Central and Eastern Europe, calculated to threaten Germany's existence, through unwillingness to set right the injustices flowing from the Treaty of Versailles, South Africa cannot be expected to take part in the war."[484]

"Mackenzie King intended to play the Canadian role of intermediary in situations of international tension...he would visit Hitler and express sympathy with his constructive work, but he intended to add that if Germany ever turned to destructive efforts against the United Kingdom, all the Dominions would come to United Kingdom's aid."[485]

But none of the Prime Ministers, except Mr Savage of New Zealand, was prepared to back Britain to the hilt in every circumstance, even that of war in

[483] Colvin, I. (1971) *The Chamberlain Cabinet*, London: Camelot Press Ltd., p. 43.

[484] Ovendale, R. (1975) *Appeasement and the English Speaking World*, Cardiff: University of Wales Press, pp. 42–43.

[485] Ovendale, Ibid. see also Watt, D. C. (1965) *Personalities and Politics Part 3*, pp. 159–174.

Europe, in a cause that did not appear to raise a direct threat to the existence of Britain and the Commonwealth. [486]

Thus, there were no more fervent supporters of Chamberlain's policy of appeasement than those who directed National Affairs in Ottawa, Canberra and Pretoria. On 7 September, the position of the Dominions was summed up by Halifax: "Furthermore, it was becoming clear that the Dominions were isolationist and there would be no sense in fighting a war, which would break up the British Empire, while trying to secure the safety of the United Kingdom." [487]

The South Africans still believed that they could remain neutral in a war but would allow the Royal Navy to use its port facilities at Simonstown. But it was not thought that a world war over Czechoslovakia was justified. Eventually, both Australia and Canada indicated that they were prepared to fight.[488] Thus, at the last hour all the Dominions, except perhaps Eire and South Africa, seemed to indicate their strong support for Britain, in the event of war. But, according to Malcolm MacDonald, when he met the Dominion High Commissioners on 26 September 1938, they had all said in the strongest possible terms that 'if there was any possible chance of peace by negotiation, the opportunity should not be lost. In their view, acceptance of Hitler's proposals was better than war'.[489]

This lack of support from the Commonwealth confirmed Chamberlain in his view that his policy of preserving peace was the right one. Chamberlain saw the reluctance of the Dominions to fight and the consequent break-up of the Commonwealth as very important. The views of the High Commissioners had considerable, though not decisive, influence on ministers' thinking.[490]

Finally, on the subject of Dominion support, Chamberlain said that 'it would have been difficult to convince them that we should have been justified in giving such an assurance (ie to support Czechoslovakia)'. South Africa was determined to remain neutral in such a quarrel, the Australian Labour Party was against intervention and it was most doubtful whether, in such a cause, MacKenzie King could rally Canadian opinion as a whole'.[491]

---

[486] Colvin, Ibid. p. 44.

[487] DBFP series 3, Vol. II, no 252.

[488] Murray, Ibid. p 213.

[489] CAB 23/95/256 Cabinet 45 (38), 26 September 1938. Ovendale, Ibid. pp, 165–171.

[490] Ovendale, Ibid. p. 319–320.

[491] Feiling, Ibid. p. 362.

In November 1940, the Editor of *The Times* wrote a letter. "No one who sat in this place, as I did during the autumn of 1938, with almost daily visitations from eminent Canadians and Australians, could fail to realise that war with Germany, at that time, would have been misunderstood and resented from end to end of the Empire." [492]

In April 1938, the Dominions had also been asked for their view about an Anglo-Soviet Pact. The South African government replied that they firmly opposed any irrevocable commitment to the Soviet Union and described such a pact as the ingredient that would probably decide Hitler in favour of war.

The third factor affecting the policy of successive British Governments was the state of the armed forces. On 28 January 1937, the Chiefs of Staff reported in '*A Summary of Conclusions by Chief of Staff Sub Committee*' at para 38 (v). It reads: "We assume that any idea of leaving to our Continental Allies the exclusive burden of providing these land forces…is out of the question for political reasons. (vi) It is therefore impossible to discount altogether the contingency of having to send military forces to the continent at some stage of the war and, perhaps, at the outset." What was therefore envisaged was that Britain would be able to land four divisions of the regular army on the continent within two weeks of zero days.

That would be followed up by a force of eight territorial divisions within four months (conscription was not in force at this time). The report concluded by saying (at xviii): "In view of the importance of the time factor, we wish to emphasise the serious effect that the delay in reaching a decision on the role of the British Army is causing. This delay gives us great cause for concern."[493]

Vansittart had been pointing out the urgency of the problem since March 1934. He now repeated his anxieties to Eden by observing that 'this is a dreadful record of all-round improvidence'.[494] In 1936, the Defence Requirements Committee observed that "any additional strain might put our present programme in jeopardy…the rearmament programme must not be allowed to interfere with home production or export trade. Any interference would adversely affect the general prosperity of the country."[495]

---

[492] Times Newspaper, November 1940.

[493] Colvin, Ibid. pp. 24–25.

[494] Ibid.

[495] CAB 23/87 Cab 5 (37) p155A. 3.2.37 CAB 24/259 CP (36)12.2.36.

In October 1936, Chamberlain, then Chancellor of the Exchequer, had observed: "In my view, apart from any other consideration, we had not the manpower to produce the necessary munitions for ourselves…to man the enlarged Navy, the new Air Force and a million men Army…if we were now to follow Winston's advice and sacrifice our commerce to the manufacture of arms, we should inflict a certain injury on our trade from which it would take generations to recover. We should destroy the confidence, which now happily exists and we should cripple the revenue."[496] This fairly represents the view of British Governments for this period.

Chamberlain had been responsible for some modest expansion of the Air Force in 1934 and had wished to fight the 1935 general election on defence. In 1935, the British Government issued a white paper on defence, announcing a cautious programme of rearmament. It was not until February 1936 that the decision for major rearmament was taken and the programme was only underway in 1937. The reasons for the delay were varied. The Treasury, under Neville Chamberlain, opposed great schemes for rearmament on the ground that the economy could not afford it for which there was indeed a credible argument. There were divided views about the extent of German rearmament and there was always the public desire for peace, supporting a policy of general disarmament. Committees charged with reporting on the need for rearmament proceeded at a leisurely pace and their reports were frequently ignored.

The figures for military expenditure during the 1930s paint their own picture. In 1932, the figure was £102 million; in 1935, £137 million; in 1936, £186 million; in 1937, £256 million and £397 million in 1938. The British expenditure in 1935 and 1936 was less than a quarter of Germany's in 1937. In 1938, it amounted to less than a third of Germany's.

The attitude of the Chiefs of Staff was equally subject to complaint. In February 1938, it was described as most disturbing. "Whenever any action is proposed, they produce nothing but criticism… The Chiefs of Staff persist in regarding the problem as though we had three enemies—Germany, Italy and Japan—who might all attack together and we should have no one to help us. They are terrified of any cooperation with the French." [497]

What then were the financial constraints? They were threefold. Firstly, the State of the economy was such that expenditure on armaments would have a

---

[496] Chamberlain Papers NC 18/1/982.
[497] Harvey, Ibid. p. 87 & 89.

serious effect on trade, particularly having regard to the adverse trade balances in the 1930s. The British population in 1936 was only two thirds that of Germany so that the comparative expenditure on armaments needs to be looked at in context. The cost of rearmament without the flow of exports could well have caused an adverse effect on the balance of payments, triggering a financial crisis similar to that which occurred at the start of the Korean War in 1951.

The second was that the manpower required for the munitions programme not only had to be trained, but they would be taken away from producing goods urgently needed for the export market. There had to be created new industrial facilities in the form of shadow aircraft and munitions factories as well as shipyards. Mass production had been part of American and German industrial practice for decades, but Britain still relied on high-quality individual production, the result of which was that output was comparatively slow. Nor did Chamberlain believe that, in time of peace, it was possible to introduce industrial conscription.[498] Further, any expenditure had to be paid for by borrowing and not by an increase in taxation.[499]

What had caused the economic crisis which had such a fundamental effect on the attitude of successive British Governments to the question of rearmament? Like all other countries, the collapse of the banking system in 1929–1931 had had a profound and adverse effect on the ability of Britain to maintain her balance of payments or to defend the strength of its currency. Britain was essentially a trading nation, which depended on its ability to produce enough exports to pay for the imports of raw materials. These were vital not only for the production of goods for the home market but to provide the finished materials for goods destined for the export market.

The balance of trade showed that between 1931 and 1938, there was only a year in which there was a favourable balance which was in 1935. A trade depression in 1938, had seen a serious falling off in tax revenues, income tax and interest rates were at their highest since 1914, defence spending resulted in large deficits and defence loans weakened the pound. They also increased borrowing very substantially. The outlook for the balance of payments was very serious. The effect on the economy was twofold. Imports had to be paid for out of

---

[498] House of Commons Official Reports Fifth Series, Vol. 336, col 1265–1266, 25 May 1938.
[499] CAB24/270.

decreasing revenue and exports were uncompetitive because spending on rearmament caused inflation and adversely affected the export market.

The effect of these financial restraints and the belief in a policy of peace at all costs was reflected in the inability of the armed forces to contribute in any meaningful way to the defence of the country. In March 1938, the Chiefs of Staff produced a devastating report on the State of the armed forces.[500] "The Army could contribute only two divisions to support France and there was a serious deficiency of modern equipment for them. The Air Force was nearly a year short of its expansion programme. Not all the planes could bomb Germany except from French bases and there was no arrangement with the French about using their bases. A lot of the fighters were obsolete and slower than the majority of the German bombers." The report went on: "The net result of these deficiencies is that the air force cannot, at the present time, be said to be in any way fit to undertake operations on a major war scale."

So far as the Air Defence of the country was concerned, 'there was a lack of modern anti-aircraft guns, radar was in its infancy and only one-third of the necessary searchlights were available. There were no air-raid shelters' and it was concluded that 'we cannot ignore the fact that our air raid precautions organisation has not yet reached a stage when air attacks could be faced with any confidence.' Unsurprisingly, the politicians found this report wholly supportive of their policy of peace at all cost.

---

[500] CAB 27/627 FP (36) 57. COS 698.

Chapter Twelve:
Negotiations

Sir Alexander Cadogan had joined the diplomatic service in 1908 and was successively posted to Constantinople and Vienna. During the war, he served in the Foreign Office and attended the Peace Conference. In 1923, he became Head of the League of Nations section. In 1933, he was the British Minister in China. In 1936, he was recalled to London by Eden to become Deputy Undersecretary for Foreign Affairs. Robert Vansittart was the Permanent Undersecretary until 1938 when he was appointed as the Government's Chief Diplomatic Adviser. In the official communiqué, on 31 December 1937, this was described as a promotion for Vansittart. In truth, it was no more than a way for Chamberlain to remove a tiresome critic of his policies. The job was, in effect, something of a sinecure. Chamberlain wrote to his sister, Ida on 12 December saying: "After all the months that S. (Stanley Baldwin) wasted in futile attempts to push Van out of the Foreign Office, it is amusing to record that I have done it in three days… Van has accepted my proposal. Indeed, I did not give him any alternative! When Anthony Eden can work out his ideas with a slow, sane man as Alick Cadogan, he will be much steadier".[501]

Thus, Cadogan became Permanent Undersecretary. Eden described him in 1933 as 'carrying out his thankless task with a rare blend of intelligence, sensibility and patience'.[502] Elsewhere, he was said to be 'in negotiation resourceful, straightforward and emollient…receptive and a good listener'.[503]

He kept a diary from the time of his appointment, covering the period leading up to and including the events of Munich. It is, therefore, possible by reference

---

[501] Chamberlain Papers NC/18/1031.

[502] Avon, L. (1962) *Facing the Dictators: The Eden Memoirs*, Cassell, p. 62.

[503] Cadogan, Ibid. p. 19.

to his diaries to get a bird's eye view, from a perceptive and neutral observer, of the discussions and political events during that time. It provides a valuable snapshot of how and why decisions came to taken (or not, as the case may be). In particular, it sheds considerable light on the attitude of the British Government towards the French.

At the meeting on 29 November 1937, between French and British Ministers, the question of Czechoslovakia dominated the meeting. The French made it very clear that they could not guarantee the existing territorial and political settlement in Czechoslovakia. When they sought a commitment from Britain in support of the Czechs, the idea was firmly rejected. The French issued a communiqué about the talks. Cadogan's view was: "I was asked what I thought of it…said I feared reaction in Germany. We make an advance to Germany, then rush into a huddle with the French and issue a communiqué talking about our 'interest' in Central Europe. I should say it blew the Halifax visit out of the water. (Halifax had visited Germany in November 1937) …maybe wrong. If it doesn't produce a violent reaction in Germany, that may show the Germans are more anxious to be friendly than Hitler professes to be."[504]

On 12 March 1938, Germany occupied Austria. After Vojtech Mastny, the Czechoslovak Minister in Berlin had received assurances from Germany about the future of Czechoslovakia. Masaryk asked Halifax for the British Government to make some positive demonstration in favour of Czechoslovakia. It was agreed that Chamberlain would make a statement in the House of Commons acknowledging, publicly, the good intentions of Germany towards Czechoslovakia. On 14 March, during the debate, Chamberlain simply expressed the view that the British Government were always interested in Central Europe, because what happened there largely affected security elsewhere.[505] On 13 March 1938, Cadogan had recorded: "We are helpless as regards Austria…we may be helpless as regards Czechoslovakia… Must we have a death struggle with Germany again? Or can we stand aside? Former does no one any good. Will latter be fatal? I'm inclined to think not."[506]

On 17 March, Litvinoff, the Soviet Foreign Minister, repeated to the Czech Minister in Moscow, the assurances which President Kalinin, titular Head of State, on 13 March 1938, had given to a deputation of Czech trade unionists. He

[504] Cadogan Papers, 29 November 1937.
[505] House of Commons Official Reports Fifth Series, Vol. 333, col 49, 14 March 1938.
[506] Cadogan, Ibid. p. 62.

expressed the willingness of the Soviet Government to honour its obligations to Czechoslovakia. As a result, on 18 March, Litvinov proposed to the British, French and United States Governments that there should be a four-power conference to discuss how to deal with further aggression.

On 20 March, Chamberlain wrote: "… With France winning in Spain by the aid of German guns and Italian planes with a French Government in which one cannot have the slightest confidence and which I suspect to be in close-ish touch with our opposition, with the Russians, stealthily and cunningly, pulling strings behind the scenes to get us involved in war with Germany…and finally with a Germany flushed with triumph and all too conscious of her power…it ('a grand alliance') is a very attractive idea; indeed there is almost everything to be said for it until you come to examine its practicability. From that moment, its attraction vanishes."

"You have only to look at the map to see that nothing, that France or we could do, could possibly save Czechoslovakia from being overrun by the Germans, if they wanted to do it. The Austrian frontier is practically open. The great Skoda munition works are within easy bombing distance of the German aerodromes, the railways all pass through German territory and Russia is 100 miles away. Therefore, we could not help Czechoslovakia, she would simply be a pretext for going to war with Germany. That, we could not think of unless we had a reasonable prospect of being able to beat her to her knees in a reasonable time. Of that, I see no sign. I have therefore abandoned any idea of giving guarantees to Czechoslovakia or to the French in connection with her obligations to that country."[507]

On 22 March, the Cabinet rejected the Soviet proposal for a four-power conference. On 24 March, in the course of a debate in the House of Commons, Chamberlain said: "It had been suggested that Great Britain should give, forthwith, an assurance that she would immediately come, with all her power to the support of France, in the event of France being called upon as a result of German aggression, to implement her obligations to Czechoslovakia. It had also been suggested that Britain should, at once, declare her own readiness to defend Czechoslovakia against unprovoked aggression and should take the lead in inviting other nations to associate themselves with such a declaration."

---

[507] Chamberlain Papers NC/18/1042.

He went on to say: "His Majesty's Government is not prepared to agree to either of these proposals or to any others which might result in Britain finding herself in a position where the decision to go to war should be automatically removed from the discretion of the Government."[508] And he went on to urge the Czechs to meet the reasonable wishes of the Germans minority.

This speech followed a meeting of the Cabinet on 24 March, which effectively ratified the decision on 18 March of the Foreign Policy Committee. That decision was based on a memorandum by Halifax entitled 'Possible Measures to Avert German Action to Czechoslovakia'. This became known as 'The Guessing Position'. Halifax defined that policy at the Cabinet meeting on 24 March when he said: "It cannot be in our interests to see France overrun…but we have entered into no kind of definite and automatic commitment (to Czechoslovakia) … This has the great advantage that we are able to keep both France and Germany guessing as to what our attitude in any particular crisis would be". Thomas Inskip, the Minister for Coordination of Defence, had pointed out that the only way Britain could exercise any pressure on Germany would be a naval blockade. This would take two or three years to bring Germany to its knees.[509] Churchill's idea of a grand alliance had already been rejected on the basis that it would give Germany an excuse, opportunity and provocation for an attack on Czechoslovakia.

On 5, April Cadogan recorded: "Masaryk came at 11:50 to tell me what his people are doing (little enough, I suspect)."[510] Pressure on the Czechs continued. On 20 April, Cadogan sent a memo to Halifax in which he wrote: "I don't think we should go further than impress Benes in general terms with the need for making a considerable effort. I don't even see why we should express an opinion on the 'reasonableness' of any proposals…it is not the reasonableness of his plans that matters, but its settlement value and on the latter, we can hardly express an opinion."[511]

The British and French met again for two days on 28/29 April. Cadogan subsequently told Halifax on 28 September: "… The French come over here for

---

[508] House of Commons Official Reports Fifth Series, Vol 333, Cols 1405–6, 24 March 1938.

[509] CAB 27/623 26(38), 18 March 1938.

[510] Cadogan, Ibid. p. 67.

[511] Ibid. p. 69.

two reasons. 1. To boost resolutions. 2. To tighten our leading string".[512] Of the events on 29 April, he wrote: "At 10, Czechoslovakia, the wholetime. Impassioned appeals by Daladier, putting the whole of Van's case about German 'Hegemony'. Very beautiful but awful rubbish…broke off for lunch with everyone looking rather blue…meeting 2:45 and Halifax put our point… German demands like mushrooms grow in the dark. French seized on this… Agreed we should both urge Benes to do his utmost and that we should ask Berlin what they want!"[513]

What the French wanted was a joint declaration, to the Germans, that is the independence of Czechoslovakia should be threatened, then both Britain and France would take the appropriate steps to maintain it. The best that the British Government could offer was to instruct Henderson to issue a statement that if France in the discharge of her obligation was forced to intervene, Britain could not guarantee that she would not do the same. Meanwhile, it was agreed that the Czech Government should be encouraged to meet the demands of the Sudeten Germans 'within the framework of the constitution'. This was duly done, as Henderson informed the German Foreign Ministry, on 7 May.[514]

On the previous day, Cadogan had seen Masaryk and told him what instructions had been sent to Prague. Masaryk's reaction was to complain that the British were doing the dirty on the Czechs. With this view, Cadogan expressed some sympathy, but asked rhetorically: "…how in Hell were we to help them?"[515]

As for the French, their attitude was well summed up by Lord Strang (Head of the Central Department of the Foreign Office, 1937–1939) when he wrote: "While the declared policy of France was to stand by her obligations, a very different impression was given by what French Ministers said behind the scenes, whether in social gatherings or to foreign representatives."[516]

British policy was scarcely different. Newton, in Prague, had written on 15 March: "If I am right in thinking that having regard to her geographical situation, her history and the racial divisions of her population, Czechoslovakia's present position is not permanently tenable, it will be no kindness, in the long run, to try

---

[512] Ibid. p. 70.
[513] Ibid. p. 73.
[514] DBFP series 3, Vol, I, no 187.
[515] Cadogan, Ibid. p. 75.
[516] Strang, L. W. Ibid. p. 134.

to maintain her in it. We should rather make it as easy for her, as possible, to adjust her position to the circumstances of post-war Europe, while she can still do so in more favourable conditions than will obtain later."[517]

The British view of Czechoslovakia at this time is well illustrated by an article written in his *Daily Mail* on 5 May by the hapless Lord Rothermere, who owned the paper. A copy was signed by the editor and sent to the German Ambassador in London. Rothermere wrote under the caption 'Czechs Not Our Business': "Czechoslovakia is not of the slightest concern to us. If France likes to burn her fingers there, that is a matter for France. The State of Czechoslovakia, which was created by those short-sighted Treaties of eighteen years ago, has behaved from the first not only oppressively towards her minorities but eccentrically." [518].

Rothermere's attitude to the Peace Treaty may not be unconnected to the humiliation of his brother, Lord Northcliffe, by Lloyd George in the House of Commons, in 1919. Northcliffe, a somewhat egocentric press baron, had given Lloyd George an ultimatum about the terms of the Peace Treaty and the part that, he, Northcliffe, should play in the negotiations. Lloyd George had rejected the idea that Northcliffe should play any part. In a remarkable put down in a debate in the House of Commons, Lloyd George gestured with his hand to his head, indicating that Northcliffe had 'lost his marbles'.[519] In the 1930s, Rothermere had not only hosted a dinner for Hitler in Germany with Ribbentrop, Goering and Goebbels among the guests but also regularly corresponded with Hitler and sent him gifts.[520]

---

[517] DBFP series 3, Vol. I, no 86.

[518] Documents and Materials, Ibid. Vol. 2, no 1.

[519] House of Commons Official Reports Fifth Series, Vol. 114, cols 2952–2953,16 April 1919.

[520] Faber, Ibid. p. 191.

Chapter Thirteen:
Weighed in the Balance

On 10 May 1938, Ivone Kirkpatrick (then Undersecretary at the British Embassy in Berlin) told Prince Bismarck, the German minister in London that "if the German Government would advise the British Government confidentially what solution of the Sudeten German question they were striving after...the British Government would bring such pressure to bear in Prague that the Czechoslovak Government would be compelled to accede to German wishes."[521]

On 14 May, the *New York Times* and the *New York Herald Tribune* published articles from their correspondents, who were resident in London, reporting 'off the record' statements made by Chamberlain. This was at a luncheon party given by Lady Astor for American and Canadian newspaper correspondents on 10 May. His remarks were to the effect that neither France nor the Soviet Union nor, indeed, Britain would come to the aid of Czechoslovakia in the event of a German invasion of Czechoslovakia and that Czechoslovakia could not continue to exist in its present form. He left the impression that the way to solve the Sudeten problem was to give Germany the Sudeten areas and thereafter to enter into a four-power agreement between Great Britain, France, Italy and Germany to keep the peace in Europe. When tackled about these articles in the House of Commons on 20, 21, and 27 June by two MPs, Mander and Sinclair, Chamberlain gave evasive replies. [522]

It is quite clear that by this time, the British Government had decided not only that Czechoslovakia was not a cause worth fighting for, but also that any assistance from the French was absolutely worthless. Thereafter, the whole

---

[521] DGFP series D. II, no 151.

[522] House of Commons Official Reports Fifth Series, Vol. 337, cols 851–858, 953–959, 2539, 20, 21 & 27 June 1938.

situation had the makings of a Greek tragedy with the British Government giving the public appearance of support for Czechoslovakia (though pretty anaemic in its language), while in private, telling the Germans and the Czechs the opposite.

The events of 19/22 May 1938 (the phantom invasion of Czechoslovakia) have been the subject of acute controversy not only over what actually took place but also over the conclusions which the various protagonists drew. The reaction of the British and French on the one hand and the Germans on the other to these events could not have been more different. Hitler decided that enough was enough and brought forward his plans for an invasion to 2 October.

The French and British took a different approach. It might have been thought that the lesson to be drawn from the events of 21 May was that a strong show of force would present a very potent weapon against the German aggression. The Western Allies did not seek to discuss arrangements among themselves or with the Czechs or with the Soviets to present a united front against the threat from Germany. Quite the contrary. The Allies complained, somewhat petulantly, that they had not been consulted by the Czechs about their mobilisation. The Czechs were instructed that they must not, thereafter, repeat the exercise, without the permission of the Allies. The French went so far as to suggest that by mobilising as they had, the Czechs were in breach of their Treaty with France.[523]

It took no time for the effect of these events to be realised. The pressure was piled on the Czechs by the Allies. On 24 May, Cadogan recorded: "Halifax wants to sever French-Czech and Czech-Soviet connection. I tell him this can only be done by some form of 'neutralisation'."[524] Further entries in the diary are to the same effect. "We are putting pressure on the Czechs. Afraid this is the wrong thing to do". Halifax decides to wield a big stick on Benes. On 17 June he recorded: "Got off a telegram to Paris about 'neutrality' of Czechoslovakia. In it, it was suggested that on the ground that the root of the German-Czechoslovak difficulty lay in the undertakings of France and Russia towards Czechoslovakia, they might be remodelled."[525]

On 3 June, the *Times*, then widely regarded as the official organ of the British Government, published a leader in which it advocated a plebiscite for the German population in Czechoslovakia so that they could decide their own future, even if it meant their secession from Czechoslovakia to the Reich. It went on: "It

---

[523] SC, pp. 67–69 supra.

[524] Cadogan, Ibid. p. 80.

[525] Cadogan, Ibid. pp. 80–83. DBFP series 3., Vol. I, no 421.

is easily intelligible that the Czech Government might not willingly agree to a plebiscite, which was likely to result in a demand for a transfer of the Sudetens and the loss of their territory for the republic. Nevertheless, if they could see their way to it, they might, in the long run, be the gainers, having a homogeneous and contented people." [526]

The *Times* followed this up with another article on 14 June, when it observed that 'it really will be the bankruptcy of European statesmanship if this question of the future of something over 3 million German Czech subjects were allowed to plunge a continent into a devastating war'.[527]

Notwithstanding denials that this represented British Government policy (which it clearly did), the Germans immediately recognised that the articles were supporting a plebiscite, which accorded with their own policy. On 9 June, the German Ambassador in London informed his Foreign Ministry that 'the German Press Attaché took the view that the leading article in the Times is based on Chamberlain's interview with representatives of the British press…and that in all probability this article reflects a point of view which agrees with Chamberlain's line of thought.' [528]

The *Times* was at least consistent in its views. On 7 September it published another leader. "If the Sudetens now ask for more than the Czech Government are apparently ready to give in their latest set of proposals, it can only be inferred that the Germans are going beyond the mere removal of disabilities and do not find themselves at ease within the Czechoslovak Republic. It might be worthwhile for the Czechoslovak Government to consider whether they should exclude altogether the project, which has found favour in some quarters…making Czechoslovakia a more homogeneous state by the secession of that fringe of alien populations, who are contiguous to the Nation by which they are united in race (ie Germany)…the advantages to Czechoslovakia of becoming a homogeneous State might conceivably outweigh the obvious disadvantages of losing the Sudeten German districts of the borderland."[529]

This article and, in particular, the phrase 'which has found favour in some quarters' was taken as representing the views of the British Government. It caused consternation among the Czechs and their friends. Meanwhile, on 16

---

[526] The Times, 3 June 1938, p. 15.

[527] The Times, 14 June 1938, p. 17.

[528] DGFP series D, Vol. I, no 247.

[529] The Times, 7 September 1938, p. 13.

July, Runciman had accepted his mission as 'mediator' in Czechoslovakia. On 18 July, Wiederman (Hitler's representative) had a meeting with Halifax. 'He gave most binding assurances that barring major incidents, Germany was determined not to resort to force'.[530]

In the same month, Chamberlain spoke at the centenary of Birmingham as a city: "The Government of which I am, at present, the head, intends to hold on its course, which is set for the appeasement of the world."[531] Throughout 1937–1938, the British had continued to receive, almost daily, intelligence from numerous influential sources about Hitler's intentions towards Czechoslovakia and making pleas to support those who opposed Hitler and, above all, to make it crystal clear that Britain would act in defence of Czechoslovakia.

Even Henderson, the arch supporter of Hitler's ambitions, was moved to write a private letter to Halifax on 12 August. "I doubt if Germany would actually go to war this year with Czechoslovakia if she was certain it meant British intervention" and he followed this up by another letter in which he wrote: "… He (Hitler) may threaten the Czechs with worse in the future if they cannot see sense now. I cannot believe he will do more if we tell him that we shall certainly fight him if he does move."

But Chamberlain was determined to stick by his previously expressed view of Canning's bon mot. He was not going to take a chance on his bluff being called but, instead, was going to take the route of forcing concessions out of the Czechs. The best the British Government could manage was to get Simon, then Chancellor of the Exchequer, to make a speech at the summer fete of Lord Dunglass's Lanark Unionist Association. In it, he said: "… In the modern world, there is no limit to the reactions of war. This very case of Czechoslovakia may be so critical for the future of Europe that it would be impossible to assume a limit to the disturbance that a conflict might involve and every country, which considers the consequences, should bear that in mind."[532] It was scarcely a clarion call to protect a little country from being bullied into submission.

Cadogan's opinion was that "Simon's speech seemed to me all right and to have been received fairly well except of course in Berlin…but we mustn't dare (sic) Hitler to be humiliated too much."[533] The German view of Simon was that

---

[530] Cadogan, Ibid. pp. 87–88.

[531] Feiling, Ibid. p. 354.

[532] Cadogan, Ibid. p. 90.

[533] Cadogan, Ibid. p. 91.

"he was one of the most prominent representatives of that typically British mentality, which prefers a bad compromise to a straight solution if that solution involves the assumption of any responsibility."[534] The attitude of the British Government towards the Czechoslovak problem was reflected in the words of Wilson when he told the Germans that "if we two, Great Britain and Germany, come to an agreement regarding the settlement of the Czech problem, we shall simply brush aside the resistance that France or Czechoslovakia herself, may offer in the decision."[535]

The next step taken by the British Government to deal with the ever-growing crisis, which was gathering pace in advance of Hitler's speech at Nuremberg on 12 September (and which was regarded as something of a watershed in the affairs of Czechoslovakia), was to recall Henderson. He let it be known that this was to consult about the serious position in connection with Czechoslovakia.[536]

On 30 August, there was a meeting of Ministers. While it included Henderson, a number of members of the Cabinet were absent. Chamberlain expressed the view which echoed what Halifax had already said that "…no State, certainly no democratic State, ought to make a threat of war unless he was both ready to carry it out and prepared to do so. This was a sound maxim…war in present conditions was not a prospect which the Defence Ministers would view with great confidence… The policy of an immediate declaration or threat might result in disunity in this country and the Empire."[537] A suggestion that the date of the Fleet Manoeuvres might be brought forward was rejected on the grounds that it might be provocative, as was the idea of any sort of warning to Germany.

The conclusion of the meeting was that the policy on Czechoslovakia would remain unchanged and that "Britain should try to keep Germany guessing as to our ultimate attitude." It was at this time that the British Government first seemed to become aware of the importance of the Sudeten areas to Czech security because the Czech fortifications lay within the Sudeten areas. Chamberlain never seems to have understood the strategic importance of Czechoslovakia in the European context, nor did he see international relations from a strategic point of view.

---

[534] Documents and Materials, Ibid. no 6.
[535] Documents and Materials, Ibid. Vol. II, no 7.
[536] DBFP series 3, Vol. II, Appendix IV, p. 686.
[537] CAB 23/94/289–96.

No mention was made at this meeting that Chamberlain had conceived the idea of a visit to see Hitler. It was apparently discussed on 29/30 August between Chamberlain, Henderson, Halifax, and Wilson. Neither Vansittart nor Cadogan, who was at Le Touquet on a golfing holiday, were party to the conversation. Chamberlain's view about the visit appears in a letter which he wrote on 3 September, to his sisters. "Is it not positively horrible to think that the fate of hundreds of millions depends on one man and he is half-mad. I keep racking my brains to try and devise some means of averting a catastrophe if it should seem to be upon us. I thought of one so unconventional and daring that it rather took Halifax's breath away. But since Henderson thought it might save the situation at the 11th hour, I haven't abandoned it, though I hope all the time that it won't be necessary to try it."[538]

Cadogan, having been recalled from his holiday, started his diary again. On 4 September, he wrote: "I gave some support to the idea of a private warning to Hitler that we should have to come in to protect France". On 5 September, his diary reads: "Discussing advisability of giving Hitler another serious and private warning." The British Government were still getting information from German sources about Hitler's intentions.

On 6 September, Wilson told Cadogan that he had been called on by Herr X. "He had put conscience before loyalty". Herr X was, in fact, Theodore Kort, who was then the Chargé d'affaires, at the German embassy in London. He said, "Hitler had taken his decision to 'march in' on 19 or 20."[539]

The rest of the week was taken up with fruitless discussions about whether to warn Hitler and if so, in what terms and how. The idea was to prevent Hitler from committing himself, irretrievably, at Nuremberg on 12 September. Henderson's contribution to solving the problem of Czechoslovakia was contained in a despatch he sent on 6 September. It read in part: "I do wish it might be possible to get the press to write up Hitler as the apostle of peace…it will be a mistake to flatter Benes too much. But give Hitler as much credit as possible… Let it [the press] abuse his evil advisors, but give him a chance of being a good boy."[540] Perhaps it is not surprising that the politicians at home floundered in the wake of this expert's advice.

---

[538] Chamberlain Papers NC 18/1/1069.

[539] Cadogan, Ibid. pp. 94–95.

[540] DBFP series 3, Vol. II, no 793.

Halifax's view, at this time, is admirably summed up in a despatch he sent to Phipps in Paris on 7 September. In it he said: "Although Great Britain might feel obliged to support France in a conflict, if only because it would recognise that British interests were involved in any threat to French security, it did not mean that we should be willing, automatically, to find ourselves at war with Germany because France might be involved in discharge of obligations which Great Britain did not share and, which a large section of British opinion had always disliked."[541]

However, on 9 September, Halifax did authorise Henderson's deputy in Berlin (Henderson having gone incommunicado to Nuremberg) to communicate a warning to Hitler. On 10 September, Henderson vetoed the idea of any warning saying: "It is likely to be fatal to the prospects of peace," although some warning was eventually given to Ribbentrop. Meanwhile, Ministers decided to hold their hand.[542] However, they did announce naval moves which 'impressed the German Naval Attaché'.[543]

After Hitler's speech on 12 September, the French seem to have completely lost their nerve. Phipps in a despatch thought: "This had been caused by the realisation of the imminent danger, Litvinov's evasions at Geneva and Lindbergh's hair-raising account of the overwhelming superiority of the German air force."[544] Phipps described his interview with Bonnet in these terms: "M. Bonnet's collapse seems to me so sudden and so extraordinary that I am asking for an interview with M. Daladier. According to Cadogan, 'telegrams had come in from Paris showing that Bonnet was completely deflated'… When Daladier's message came through, it was not quite as limp as Bonnet but had very little backbone… Bonnet's messages showed that he, at least, was panicking."[545]

Chamberlain now decided to put Plan Z ('The visit to Hitler') into effect. He did not consult the French nor invite Daladier. The French only learnt of the idea just before it was announced in the press. On 14 September, Henderson reported to the Foreign Office that all was ready for Chamberlain to fly to see Hitler at Berchtesgaden. This he did on 15 September. Chamberlain had already effectively conceded the principle of a plebiscite because his Press Secretary

---

[541] BDFP, Ibid. no 798.

[542] Cadogan, Ibid. p. 97.

[543] Ibid. p. 96.

[544] DBFP series 3, Vol. II, no 855.

[545] Cadogan, Ibid. pp. 97–98.

briefed German correspondents in London, that Chamberlain was prepared to consider one.[546]

At the meeting at Berchtesgaden, Paul Schmidt was Hitler's interpreter. For some reason, Chamberlain did not take his own interpreter. Thus, we are mainly dependent on Schmidt's notes as the record of what took place. (Chamberlain, own notes are much less full.)[547] They were supplemented by Chamberlain's explanation to his colleagues and the French.[548] To his sisters, he wrote: "Personally, I don't care two hoots, whether the Sudetens are in the Reich or out of it".[549] Schmidt's notes of the conversation were, for some reason, deliberately withheld from the British Government. It required a protest for them to be provided, which eventually they were on 21 September.

Although his visit to Hitler had already been agreed on 13 September, the majority of the Cabinet were not informed of the proposal until September 14. The French had not been informed of the visit until late afternoon of 14 September. They had not been asked for their approval. Nor were they invited to enter into any discussion as to what they might like Chamberlain to say. The British attitude towards the French is perhaps best summed up in Cadogan's entry for 17 September. "Got leave from Halifax and P.M. to see Corbin (the French Ambassador) and tell him something, not too much!"[550]

On 13 September, French public opinion was thought to be becoming more and more ready, in order to avoid war, to accept even the solution of a plebiscite, for autonomy, outside the Reich.[551] The Minister for Foreign Affairs was reported on 13 September 'as having completely lost his nerve and as being ready to accept any solution to avoid war'.[552] This included a plebiscite on the general question whether Sudetens should remain inside or should be allowed to join the Reich.[553] As for the Czechs, they, too, were kept ignorant of the proposed visit until late on 14 September. Nor were their views about the fate of their own country ever canvassed. On 18 September, they set out their position, which was

---

[546] DGFP series D, Vol. II, no 470.

[547] DBFP series 3, Vol. II, no 487, 895 & 896.

[548] DBFP, Ibid. no 928.

[549] Chamberlain Papers NC 18/1/1069.

[550] Cadogan, Ibid. p. 99.

[551] DBFP, Ibid. no 847.

[552] DBFP, Ibid. no 852.

[553] DBFP, Ibid. no 874.

that they took it for granted that no decision would be taken without their being previously consulted. They could not, they said, take any responsibility for decisions made without them.[554] Alas for the Czechs, the pass had been sold.

At Berchtesgaden, Chamberlain announced that he had the greatest respect for Hitler, who had observed that "at all costs, he would make possible the return to the Reich of the 3 million Germans in Czechoslovakia and that he would face any war and, even, the risk of a world war for this. The rest of the world might do what it liked, but he would not yield a single step."

During further conversations, Chamberlain expressed, as his personal view, that "he recognised the principle of the detachment of the Sudeten areas. Britain was prepared to acknowledge certain principles and was only concerned with the implementing of these principles in practice."[555]

Having thus conceded the principle of self-determination, Chamberlain was now to return home and consult his colleagues. The only remaining issue left was what was to be the basis of any transfer of the population and what the timetable for it was to be. In the meantime, Hitler promised to take no immediate action against Czechoslovakia. On 15 September Henlein told Hitler that he had informed the British that the Karlsbad programme was no longer a basis for negotiation. He proposed immediate union with the Reich where more than 50% of the population was German. Cadogan's entry for 16 September reads: "PM (on arrival back in England) gave his impressions. Thinks he has held Hitler for the moment. Quite clear that nothing but 'self-determination' will work."[556]

On 18 September, Chamberlain and members of the Cabinet met their French opposite numbers for Chamberlain to explain what had happened at Berchtesgaden and to discuss the way forward. There were three separate meetings. The first began at 11 am and finished at 1:05 pm. The next started at 3 pm and lasted until 7:05 pm and the third started at 10 pm and concluded at 12:05 am. Chamberlain reported that it was agreed that the question of Czechoslovakia was now more urgent and critical; Hitler did not want anything more in Central or South-Eastern Europe save the return of the Sudetens.

Chamberlain wanted the French view on the question of self-determination. Initially, they were reluctant to express an opinion and wanted the British views. Chamberlain quoted Runciman's opinion that any sacrifice of Czech interest

---

[554] DBFP, Ibid. no 929.

[555] DBFP series 3, Vol. II, no 895 & 896.

[556] Cadogan, Ibid. p. 99.

could only be laid at Dr Benes' door and said the only issue left was that of self-determination. Daladier's reaction was to reject the idea. He put the issue back into the British Court, citing French Treaty obligations. He was searching for some alternative to the idea of a plebiscite. It was agreed that they should all adjourn for lunch to enable the French to consult.

After lunch, the French repeated their objection to a plebiscite but agreed to consult the Czechs on the cession of some territory. They further argued that they could not bring pressure to bear on the Czechs to cede territory unless there was some sort of guarantee about the remaining territory. Initially, the British were unenthusiastic about a guarantee, but, by late evening, had agreed. It was concluded that there had to be some transfer of territory, either directly or by plebiscite in those the areas with over a 50% German population. In exchange, the British and French would join in an international guarantee of the new boundaries. This guarantee would be in substitution for the existing Treaties.[557] Thus, at a stroke and without consultation, the French unilaterally tore up their Treaties with the Soviet Union and Czechoslovakia.

The Czechs were to be consulted (some might describe it as 'dictated to') but they were required to give an answer before Chamberlain returned to Germany on 21 September. The proposals were sent to Prague overnight to be handed to Benes after the French Cabinet had approved them. This was even before Chamberlain had sought the approval of his own Cabinet. On 19 September, after a heated discussion, the British Cabinet finally agreed. Cadogan's Diary gives a flavour of the meeting. "18 September Daladier and Bonnet and their circus arrived... PM described his talk with Hitler. We had to listen to Daladier, with voice trembling with carefully modulated emotion, talking of French honour and obligation. We brought him back to earth before lunch. He suggested the question was (a) how to avoid war, (b) maintain independence (not integrity!) of Czechoslovakia. Report on French air force coming in too frightful. Drafting message to Benes. Pretty stiff telling him to surrender! PM decided that we must offer a guarantee. Dominions don't even know of the suggestion!"[558]

On 18 September also, the Czechs had been persuaded by both the British and French to delay any plans for mobilisation, while further negotiations took place at Bad Godesberg. Pressure on the Czechs, however, still continued. On 20 September, Cadogan noted: "Reports began coming in of unfavourable Czech

---

[557] BDFP, Ibid. no 928.
[558] Cadogan, Ibid. p. 100.

reply…bad telegram in from Prague…drafted reply driving the screw home on poor Czechs."[559]

The Czech reaction was, unsurprisingly, one of shock. The French added their weight to the British by informing Benes on 21 September that the only possible course was to accept the Franco-British plan, saying in effect that if they continued obdurate, France would stand aside.[560] But in the evening, the Czechs turned down the idea and asked the British and French Governments to reconsider. They pointed out, with some prescience, that "at this decisive time, it is not only the fate of Czechoslovakia which is in the balance but, also, that of other countries and particularly, of France."[561] On 21 September, Phipps in Paris telephoned London to say: "I have consulted Minister for Foreign Affairs and suggested that he should give Czech Minister in Paris a piece of his mind."[562]

The pressure on the Czechs had its effect. On 21 September, they finally accepted the Franco-British terms. Newton reported to London: "Dr Krofta handed a note of which following is a summary: 'Under pressure of urgent insistence, Czechoslovak Government sadly accept French and British proposals on supposition that the two Governments will do everything…to safeguard vital interests of Czechoslovakia… They are of opinion that details of the execution of proposals will be settled in agreement with Czechoslovak Government."[563] Nothing was further from the minds of the British and French Governments. Even today, over 80 years after these events, it is impossible to comprehend how the Czechs came to be excluded from important decisions about the future of their own country.

The stage was now set for Chamberlain to go to see Hitler again. This time the meeting was at Bad Godesberg. The purpose was to discuss the details, which had been left open for discussion at Berchtesgaden. They were an orderly transfer of territory, under international supervision, with safeguards for the exchange of populations. The criterion for transfer was to be based on a majority of over 50% of the population being German. This time Chamberlain took his own interpreter, but he was in for a very rude shock. Hitler had completely changed his stance.

---

[559] Ibid. p. 102.
[560] DDF series 2, Tom. XI, no 249.
[561] BDFP series 3, Vol. II, no 986 & 987.
[562] Ibid. no 1001.
[563] Ibid. no 1002, 1004 & 1005.

He now demanded the immediate occupation of German-speaking areas by German troops and this was to be completed by 1 October. He added one other new condition, namely that the territorial demands of Hungary and Poland were to be met. Hitler went on to draw up a map. He declared that a frontier line must be drawn at once, that the Czechs must withdraw the army, police and all state organs, from that area which would be immediately occupied by Germany. The border would be determined on the basis of language. The plebiscite, in the occupied territories, would be based on the 1918 census. Thus, while the Czechs who had been planted there after the war would not have a vote, those Germans who had lived there in 1918 and emigrated would. Hitler was totally unwilling to give any guarantee about the rest of Czechoslovakia. Chamberlain managed to persuade Hitler to do nothing while negotiations continued, but as the invasion was not to begin until 1 October, this was little more than a placebo.

A further meeting was arranged for 11 am on 23 September. Chamberlain's view of the previous meeting was that it had been unsatisfactory. He might have to return home on the following day. Wilson's view was the same. The Czechs were not yet to be allowed to mobilise, without the consent of the Western Allies, for fear of upsetting the ongoing negotiations.[564] Before the meeting arranged for the morning of 23 September, Chamberlain wrote to Hitler. In his letter, he pointed out that public opinion in England, France and the rest of the world could not possibly agree to Hitler's proposals and that if the Germans entered the Sudetenland, it was his view that the Czechs would order their forces to resist.

The meeting with Chamberlain was postponed but at 3 pm, a letter from Hitler was handed to Chamberlain. It repeated German complaints about Versailles and the ill treatment of the Sudeten Germans. It ended: "If, as now appeared to be the case, Germany found it impossible to have the clear rights of Germans in Czechoslovakia accepted by way of negotiation, then she would be determined to exhaust other possibilities, which then alone remain open to her."[565]

Chamberlain wrote another letter to Hitler at 6 pm. In it, he asked Hitler to set out in a memorandum his proposals, together with a map, which he could forward to the Czechs, for whom he was now acting as an intermediary. At 11 pm, Chamberlain returned to see Hitler and to receive his memorandum. Its main proposals were "1. Withdrawal of the whole of the Czech armed forces, the

---

[564] Ibid. no 1031.
[565] DGFP series D, Vol. II, no 573.

police, the gendarmerie, the customs officials and the frontier guards from the area to be evacuated as designated on the attached map, this area to be handed over to Germany on October 1st (changed from the original proposal of 26 September). 2. No private property or capital assets were to be evacuated by Czechs departing from the territory in dispute, including food products and livestock, and no compensation would be paid for property forsaken. 3. Sudeten citizens were to be discharged from the Czechoslovak armed forces. 4. All 'political prisoners of German race' were to be released from detention... 5. A plebiscite was to take place in those areas which would be more definitely defined before 25 November under the control of an international commission. All persons residing in the areas in question on the 28 October 1918, or who were born in those areas prior to this date, would be eligible to vote. 6. Military installations, public utilities and transport facilities in the Sudeten territories were to be handed over intact. 7. All further details were to be handled by a German-Czechoslovak or international commission."[566] It was, as Chamberlain described it, nothing less than an ultimatum.

While these negotiations were taking place in Germany, reports of their progress were causing considerable disquiet in London and Prague. In London, the Foreign Office had received some information on the tone of the talks.[567] Chamberlain had described the first meeting to Halifax as 'most unsatisfactory'. Wilson told the Foreign Office that "the conversations had been pretty difficult." The effect of these reports was to persuade Halifax to convene informal meetings of his fellow Ministers in his office on 22 and 23 September.[568] One decision, which was agreed upon at the meetings, was that "it would be very difficult for us to defend the action taken in urging the Czechoslovak army not to mobilise if an immediate German attack was launched against the country". The resignation of the Hodza government on 22 September, replaced by that of General Syvovy (the iconic commander of the Czech Legion in the Soviet Union) caused a change in outlook in Prague. Talk of any capitulation by the Czechs ceased.

The British and French now finally agreed that they could no longer advise the Czechs not to mobilise. Instructions were, therefore, sent at 8 pm to tell Newton in Prague to deliver that message, but, at the same time, to postpone the delivery until 9 pm. It was feared, by Chamberlain, that such an announcement

---

[566] DBFP Ibid. no 1068 & 1073.

[567] DBFP, Ibid. no 1035, 1040, 1048, 1058 and 1068.

[568] CAB 27/646/65–89.

might seriously compromise his efforts at negotiation. Newton was instructed to postpone further delivery of the message.[569] However, Halifax's Ministers had had enough. At 3 pm, on 23 September, the Czechs were given the go-ahead to mobilise if they so wished. This was despite a further caution by Chamberlain against such action. Halifax not only ignored this advice but pointed out to Chamberlain that "we had gone to the limit of our concessions."[570]

The Czechs duly mobilised. The news reached Hitler in the early hours of 24 September when he was in discussion with Chamberlain. Hitler made no further demands but again promised that 1 October was the deadline for transfer. Cadogan records: "September 24. Hitler's memo now in. It's awful...we salved our conscience by stipulating that it must be an 'orderly' cession...now Hitler says he must march in AT ONCE to keep order and the safeguards and plebiscites can be held AFTER! ...this is throwing away every last safeguard that we had."

"Meeting of Inner Cabinet at 3 pm. PM made his report to us. I was completely horrified; he was quite calmly for total surrender. More horrified still to find that Hitler has evidently hypnotised him to a point. Still more horrified to find PM has hypnotised Halifax who capitulates totally...there was practically no discussion...Halifax got back at 8, completely and quite happily defeatist-pacifist, about 10, drove him home and gave him a bit of my mind, but didn't shake him. I've never before known him make up his mind so quickly and firmly on anything."

There was a further problem, as Cadogan recorded: "I know there is a shattering telegram from Phipps about position in France". It set out the State of French public opinion. "...war would now be most unpopular in France...all that is best in France is against war almost at any price...to embark upon what will, presumably, be the biggest conflict in history with our ally, who will fight, if she must, without eyes (air force) and without real heart, must surely give us furiously to think."[571] What is somewhat surprising is that the French, who had Treaty obligations with the Czechs, had taken no part in any negotiations and seemed indifferent to being excluded.

Chamberlain told the informal meeting of Ministers that he believed Hitler was speaking the truth when he said that the Sudetenland represented the limit of his territorial ambitions, that he had won important concessions from the

---

[569] DBFP, Ibid. no 1027.

[570] DBFP, Ibid. no 1068.

[571] DBFP, Ibid. no 1076.

Fuhrer and that "Hitler would not go back on his word once he had given it to me."[572] When he spoke to the full Cabinet, later in the afternoon, he told them that the terms of Hitler's memorandum should be accepted and that the Czechs should be so advised. He went on: "He believed that Herr Hitler had certain standards…he would not deliberately deceive a man, whom he respected and with whom he had been in negotiation…he was sure that Herr Hitler now felt some respect for him. He was convinced that Hitler was speaking the truth and that he thought that he had now established an influence over Herr Hitler and that the latter trusted him and was willing to work with him."[573] It is difficult to think of a more monumental misjudgement of character than Chamberlain's views about Hitler.

By the Cabinet meeting, the next morning, Halifax had changed his mind. Cadogan's entry for 25 September summarises what happened overnight. "Cabinet up about 6. Halifax sent for me. He said, 'Alec, I'm very angry with you. You gave me a sleepless night. I woke at 1 am and never got to sleep again. But I came to the conclusion that you were right and at the Cabinet when PM asked me to lead off, I plumped for refusal of Hitler's terms… Seems Cabinet anyhow wouldn't allow PM to make any further concessions (and I'm sure country wouldn't).' Halifax said, 'He now felt a moral obligation rested upon us, in consequence of the concessions which Czechoslovakia, on British advice, had agreed to make.' He pointed out that there was a world of difference between an orderly and disorderly transfer, with all that the latter implied, for the minorities in the transferred territories… He could not rid his mind of the fact that Herr Hitler had given us nothing and that he was dictating terms, just as if he had won a war without having to fight…and he thought it right to expose his own hesitations with complete frankness."[574]

The suggestion that this Damascene conversion of Halifax was due to his 'letting personal political calculations enter into his reasoning' [575] can be readily discounted. It is far more likely to have been a combination of circumstances. According to Harvey, on 4 October, Halifax said: "There had been only one night when he did not sleep and that was when the question had arisen of putting further pressure on the Czech Government to accept the memo… Halifax had

---

[572] CAB 27/646/91–92.

[573] CAB 23/95/179–180.

[574] CAB 23/95/178? 43 (38), 25 September 1938.

[575] Roberts, A. (1997) *The Holy Fox*, London: Phoenix Press, p. 116.

woken at one a.m. and did not sleep again. He said once he had made his decision, he did not worry again."[576] The informal meeting of Ministers had been disturbed by the news coming out of Bad Godesberg. They viewed the new terms with something akin to horror. Unlike Chamberlain, they had not been hypnotised by Hitler. Lastly, as is clear from Cadogan's diary, Halifax's conscience and judgement finally persuaded him, that "while he had worked most closely with the Prime Minister throughout the long crisis…he was not quite sure that their minds were still together as one."[577]

For the Czechs, having finally and with much reluctance accepted the Berchtesgaden proposals, the new terms were quite unacceptable. This, they made clear, not only by their representations to London but also by their decision to mobilise. On 24 September, Masaryk told Halifax that the "Czechs would rather go down fighting than accept Hitler's proposals." He followed this up on 25 September, with a powerful polemic.[578] Having decided to reject the Bad Godesberg terms, the time had come (somewhat belatedly it may be thought), for the British Government, to seek the views of their French Allies.

Accordingly, on the evening of 25 September, Daladier and Bonnet met Chamberlain and his colleagues in London when a full and frank exchange of views took place. The French, as Daladier explained, had already decided to reject the Bad Godesberg demands. Chamberlain sought to paint a picture of the events at Bad Godesberg, of himself, bravely, standing up to Hitler. He demanded of the French what they intended to do next. When Daladier sought to return to the terms of the original Anglo-French plan, Chamberlain asked him what was to happen if, as was inevitable, Hitler would not agree. Daladier's reply was that "each of them would have to do his duty". Chamberlain was having none of these generalities and observed that they "could no longer fence about this question and that they had to get down to the stern realities."[579]

It was then the turn of Simon, using his well-honed skills as an advocate, to press the French, in a searching cross-examination, about what they were actually going to do if war came. There were a number of questions which he put to the hapless French. "Were they going to sit behind the Maginot line or would they invade Germany? Were they only going to employ ground forces or would

[576] Harvey, Ibid. p. 208.

[577] CAB, Ibid.

[578] Sc paras 173 & 174 supra.

[579] DBFP series 3, Vol. II, no 1093.

the Air Force be used over Germany? Was the Air Force in fact non-existent? And if the Germans retaliated by bombing France, were the French public mentally prepared? What support did they expect from Russia?" Like all witnesses who have not thought through their evidence, Daladier simply floundered.[580] Cadogan described the effect of the cross-examination as 'awful'.[581]

At the end of the meeting, Chamberlain announced that he was sending Wilson with a letter to Hitler, suggesting an international commission to settle the transfer of territory. If Hitler declined, it meant war. The letter read: "The French Government have informed us that if the Czechs reject the memorandum and Germany attacks Czechoslovakia, they will fulfil their obligations to Czechoslovakia. Should the forces of France, in consequence, become engaged in active hostilities against Germany, we shall feel obliged to support them."[582] When Wilson delivered the letter to Hitler on 27 September, Hitler told him that "he would smash Czechoslovakia if his memorandum were not accepted. He had prepared for all emergencies. Not for nothing had he spent 4 ½ billion marks on fortifications in the West."[583]

Hitler's speech in the Sortsplatz on 26 September did nothing to lower the temperature. On the same day, there was a private meeting between Daladier, Gamelin, Corbin and Chamberlain. It appears that Gamelin was more positive than the politicians. He said that France would attack Germany, both on land and in the air, within five days of a German invasion of Czechoslovakia. This view was repeated by Daladier later in the morning.[584] Cadogan described this meeting in his diary. "September 27. Gamelin seems to have put heart into the PM, so we declared solidarity with France in the event of her being engaged in 'active hostilities'."

"Cross-examination of Gamelin showed that 'active hostilities' probably meant a squib offensive (to bring us in) and then retirement to the Maginot line to wait (six months) for our 'Kitchener armies!'... This didn't suit at all, so John S[imon] took up his pen and drafted a telegram to Paris, emphasising that we

---

[580] Ibid. no 1093.

[581] Cadogan, Ibid. p. 105.

[582] CAB 23/95/247 Cabinet 45(38), 26 September. DBFP, Ibid. no 1129.

[583] DBFP, Ibid. no 1129.

[584] CAB 23/95/249 Cabinet 45 (38), 26 September. DDF series 2, Tom. XI, no 405. Gamelin, Ibid. Vol. II, p. 351 seq.

must 'fully concert' beforehand any offensive… Ministers frightened out of their wits by Gamelin's conversation by a telegram from Phipps about French feeling and by Malcolm Macdonald (and Bruce) on the subject of Dominions… Horace (Wilson) had drafted telegram of complete capitulation, telling Czechs to accept Hitler's memo." [585]

When Chamberlain broadcast to the nation that evening, he said: "How, horrible, how fantastic, incredible it is that we should be digging trenches and trying on gas masks because of a quarrel in a faraway country between people of whom we know nothing." It was a phrase which was to come back to haunt him. He went on: "It is still more impossible that a quarrel that has already been settled in principle, should be the subject of war…however much we may sympathise with a small Nation confronted by a big powerful neighbour, we cannot in all circumstances undertake to involve the whole British Empire in war simply on her account…"[586]

On the evening of 27 September, Hitler sent Chamberlain a letter indicating that German troops would not move beyond the territory which the Czechs had already agreed to cede, that the plebiscite would be carried out by a free vote and that Germany would join an international guarantee of Czechoslovakia. Chamberlain offered to visit for the third time.

The dramatic events in the House of Commons leading up to Chamberlain and Daladier's visit to Munich are graphically recorded in Cadogan's entry on 28 September. "PM sent telephone messages to Hitler and Mussolini saying he was ready to go to Germany again… Mussolini had got 24-hour postponement of German mobilisation. 3 Henderson rang me to say Hitler invited PM Mussolini (accepted) and Daladier to Munich tomorrow (due 2 pm today) … Dictated message and ran with it to House. Fished H[alifax] out of Peers' Gallery and we went along to behind Speaker's Chair and sent it in to PM who was still speaking. He used it for his peroration with tremendous effect and House adjourned. Thank God!"[587] Next day, Chamberlain and Daladier set off for Munich. There appears to have been no sort of discussions between them as to the tactics to be employed, what part each was to play in the negotiations or what they were prepared to accept as the final terms.

---

[585] Cadogan, Ibid. p. 107.

[586] Chamberlain, N. (1939) *The Struggle for Peace*, London: Hutchinson, pp. 274–276.

[587] Cadogan, Ibid. p. 109.

Chamberlain was anxious for the Czechs to be present but no meaningful discussions with them appear to have taken place before the Czechs were presented with the Four Power Agreement, as a fait accompli. The nearest they got to any agreement between them was, on 27 September, when a draft document agreed by the British and French Governments was sent to Newton to be relayed to the Czechs. It envisaged immediate occupation of Eger and Ach on 1 October, followed by an international boundary commission and a phased transfer of other Sudeten territories between 3 and 10 October.[588] To make sure the Czechs understood their position, the draft continued: "The only alternative to this plan would be the invasion and dismemberment of their country by forcible means and though that might result in general conflict entailing an incalculable loss of life, there is no possibility that at the end of that conflict, whatever the result, Czechoslovakia could be restored to her frontiers today."[589] It could scarcely be described as a friendly message by an Ally.

Nor were the Soviet Union, who had Treaties both with the Czechs and the Frenchs, consulted or invited to take part in the discussions at Munich. The terms of the Munich Agreement were substantially based on a five-point agreement drawn up by Mussolini. "1. Evacuation will begin on 1 October... 2. It shall be completed by 10 October... 3. Sets out a timetable for the occupation of the various zones delineated on an attached map. 4. An international commission will determine the territories in which a plebiscite is to be held. 5. The final determination of the frontier will be carried out by the international commission." [590]

Chamberlain continued thereafter to insist that the negotiations at Munich had been successful and that they had resulted in an improvement on what was on offer at Bad Godesberg. This was not a universal view. In the House of Commons debate, Churchill said: "We really must not waste time...upon the difference between the positions reached at Berchtesgaden, at Godesberg and at Munich. They can be very simply epitomised... £1 was demanded at the pistol's point. When it was given, £2 were demanded at the pistol's point. Finally, the dictator consented to take £1.7s. 6d and the rest in promises of goodwill for the

---

[588] DBFP, Ibid. no 1138 & 1140.

[589] Ibid. no 1138.

[590] Ibid. no 1224.

future."[591] Even Simon was moved to agree that "Herr Hitler has again achieved the substance of his immediate and declared aim without war."[592]

In the euphoria surrounding his return, Chamberlain may perhaps be excused for expressing his view of the effect of the agreement when speaking from the first floor of Downing Street in this way: "This is the second time in our history that there has come back from Germany to Downing Street peace with honour. It is peace in our time."[593]

More mature thought did not cause him to change his mind. He told the House of Commons in winding up the debate on 6 October: "What we did was to...give her (Czechoslovakia) a chance of new life as a new state, which involves the loss of territory and fortifications but may, perhaps, enable her to enjoy, in the future, and develop a national existence under neutrality and security; comparable to that which we see in Switzerland today."[594] That this was his genuine belief can be confirmed by a letter he had written to the Archbishop of Canterbury on 2 October. After observing how prayers had sustained him in his efforts, he added: "I am sure that someday the Czechs will see that what we did was to save them for a happier future."[595]

Halifax was no less optimistic. On 9 August 1939, the German Ambassador in London recorded a conversation with Halifax in which the latter said: "he would now like to give me an exact picture of his ideas and views as they had stood after Munich... After Munich, he had been persuaded that fifty years of world peace was now assured."[596] After Munich, peace for Britain and France lasted less than a year and for the Czechs, it was no more than a few months. They lost their independence and were not allowed to exist as a free democratic country for some 50 years. For them, Munich was a disaster on a grand scale.

That Chamberlain was dedicated to the cause of peace is not in doubt and it must be accepted that he was sincere in his beliefs. Explanations for the conduct of British policy for which he had assumed almost total responsibility are manifold. Neither militarily nor economically was Britain in any sort of position

---

[591] House of Commons Official Reports Fifth Series, Vol. 339, col 361 and 375, 5 October 1938.

[592] Ibid. col 339.

[593] Feiling, Ibid. p. 381.

[594] House of Common, Ibid. col 547.

[595] Feiling Ibid. p. 375.

[596] Materials and Documents, Vol. II, p. 128.

to engage in a war. Britain had no Treaty obligation to the Czechs and only a moral obligation to the French. The principle of self-determination which Britain had supported lay at the heart of the Versailles Treaty. Appeasement of Germany would secure two particular benefits for Britain. It would leave it free to deal with any threat from either Japan or Italy (or both) and it would have the further advantage that it would remove the burden of competitive rearmament with Germany. Germany was perceived by many, particularly those with political and social influence in Britain, to have been unfairly treated at Versailles. The country had had enough of war. There were still too many families whose lives had suffered for them to want any repetition. There was always the communist threat to distract attention from Eastern Europe. Conflicts in Spain and Abyssinia were ever-present in the minds of politicians, while the rise of Japanese power in the Far East gradually gave rise to concern. Nor did the Dominions, now much more independent than in the past, show any enthusiasm for involvement in European affairs. The French, who had been our natural enemy throughout the nineteenth century, were not regarded as a very reliable ally. The Soviet Union was treated with the deepest suspicion. All these factors provide an explanation for what can, fairly, be described as a betrayal of the Czechs. But do they provide an excuse?

We need to look at Chamberlain's character to begin to understand how Munich happened. Much has already been said about his personality. Three questions remain to be answered. How could Chamberlain have suffered from such misjudgement that he still believed in Hitler's good faith in March 1939, shortly before the invasion of Prague? Secondly, why did he treat the French with such disdain and fail to involve them seriously in any of the negotiations with Hitler and finally, why did he take on the role of spokesman for the Czechs? Britain had no Treaty obligations to the Czechs, but it had no compunction, first in bullying them and then in leaving them in the lurch.

That Chamberlain wholly misjudged Hitler's personality or the threat that Nazi Germany posed cannot be seriously questioned. His self-confidence in his ability, virtually singlehanded, to deal with the negotiations and his belief that Hitler respected him would have been laughable, if it were not so serious. This confidence was breath-taking. He was impervious to any suggestion that even for one moment, he could be wrong in his views. Self-confidence can be an admirable trait in a politician but arrogance cannot. These defects were combined with a total lack of judgement and woeful ignorance of Foreign Affairs.

It is not surprising, therefore, that he found himself out of his depth when dealing with Hitler. He was not much helped by the despatches he received from Henderson in Berlin, who was more native than the natives. Harold Nicolson famously described Chamberlain's approach in this way: "Chamberlain and his advisor, Sir Horace Wilson, stepped into diplomacy with the bright faithfulness of two curates entering a pub for the first time. They did not observe the difference between a social gathering and a rough house, nor did they realise that the tough guys assembled did not speak or understand their language. They imagined that they were as decent and honourable as themselves."[597] Another view was that "English statesmen were like elderly Victorian cavalry generals trying to conduct a great tank battle."[598]

The second problem was the French. They were meant to be an ally. It might be thought, if Britain were ever going to support France, that serious and urgent practical steps would have been taken to agree on a common policy and then to give effect to it. Instead, while giving the impression of supporting the French, at moments of crisis, the British retreated into the explanation that they were not prepared to commit the country to be tied to French obligations. They regarded French politicians with faint derision. They did not have any trust in their reliability or in the capability of their Governments to provide a cohesive policy. Nor did the Popular Front find much in common with a British Conservative Government.

The treatment of the Czechs was nothing less than shameful. Britain had been partly responsible for setting up the new state and encouraging its formation. While it had no Treaty obligations as such, it undoubtedly had a moral obligation to support it. The whole of its involvement in Czechoslovakian affairs in 1937 and 1938 was due to the perception, by Britain, that the Czechs, as a rather backward nation, needed a spokesman to guide their affairs. It was a noble idea but from the practical point of view, quite untenable. Britain gave the impression to the Czechs that they could shelter behind the might of England but that, on no account, were they to make any independent decisions, which might conceivably upset the Germans.

While the Czechs sincerely believed, even up to the last moment, that Britain would protect them, it is clear that by the end of 1937, whatever they may have told the Czechs, Britain had decided that there was no way in which it wished to

---

[597] Nicolson, H. (1939) *Why Britain is at War*, London: Penguin, p. 106.
[598] Barnett, Ibid. p. 451.

be involved in this 'far away country'. Chamberlain took on the self-appointed role of spokesman for the Czechs. This was done without any consultation with the Czechs. He negotiated on their behalf without clear instructions as to what they wanted. Finally, he readily made concessions to Hitler, contrary to such instructions as he did receive.

Two examples suffice. Without any prior consultation or agreement, Lord Runciman, a total stranger, was sent to seek to negotiate away the fate of an independent Nation. No one asked the Czechs if they wanted someone to carry out these negotiations before it was announced or whether they approved of Lord Runciman to act in this capacity. It might be thought that before he was sent on his mission, someone would have sought Czech approval or even enquired what the Czechs considered the bottom line in negotiations about the fate of their country.

The same criticism applies to the various negotiations by Chamberlain himself. To them, the Czechs were not invited nor consulted, in spite of their making it abundantly clear that no decisions ought to be made which did not have their approval. And then to be bullied into accepting the unfavourable terms, which Chamberlain had accepted on their behalf, merely added salt to the wound. The British failed fully to understand that, as a result of the negotiations, the Czechs would lose vital areas of their defence system. This was coupled with the diktat that on no account were the Czechs to mobilise without the express consent of Britain and France and that if they did, the Western Allies would wash their hands of them.

What is perhaps surprising is that the Czechs allowed themselves to be bullied and to accept the highly unsatisfactory efforts by Chamberlain. It is, of course, impossible to decide what would have happened if Chamberlain had not gratuitously involved himself in Czech affairs, but one thing is clear, namely, that his belief in the integrity of Hitler and his reluctance to deal transparently with the Czechs led to their ultimate destruction. If at any time the Czechs had decided to go alone, they could not possibly have been any worse off. That was certainly Churchill's view. In the debate in October 1938, he said: "I believe the Czechs left to themselves and told they were going to get no help from the western powers would have been able to make better terms than they have got, they could hardly have worse."[599] Harvey's view on 10 September, which turned

---

[599] House of Commons Official Reports Fifth Series Vol. 339 col 361, 5 October 1938.

out to be prescient, was that "I do not believe they (ie the Government) realise that the independence of Czechoslovakia if allowed to be overthrown, without any counteraction by the Western Powers, would spell the end of British prestige for a very long time. We would suffer for it in every quarter of the globe."[600] The verdict on Chamberlain's interference in the affairs of Czechoslovakia sadly must be 'found wanting'.

---

[600] Harvey, Ibid. p. 175.

Part Five
Soviet Union Perspective

Chapter Fourteen:
The Ghost at the Feast

The Soviets took no part in the Munich Agreements. They were not invited to participate, nor were they even invited to be present. They had not been informed about the negotiations, let alone been consulted. Thus, one of the most powerful Nations in Europe, bound by Treaty to France and Czechoslovakia and regarded as an important figure in the affairs of the Little Entente, was totally ignored as if it had no contribution to make towards the solution of the Czechoslovak problem. That it was also a member of the League of Nations did not appear to have any influence on the decision of the Western Allies to exclude the Soviet Union from the negotiating table. Nor did the Soviet Treaties with France and Czechoslovakia encourage the Western Allies to persuade the Soviets, as a matter of collective security, that together they should face up to the threat posed by Germany. The reasons are not far to seek. Both France and Britain had a deep suspicion of communism. They regarded the Soviets as unreliable allies (shades of the Great War). They also thought that the Soviets were in no position, after the great military purges, to make any useful contribution to the defence of Czechoslovakia.

More particularly, given that the Soviet Union did not have a common frontier with either Germany or Czechoslovakia, the idea of the Soviets making any sensible contribution to the defence of Czechoslovakia was regarded as completely unrealistic. Even given the will, the logistics of troop movements were insuperable. It was unclear whether the Soviets would have been allowed to transport troops across Romania or Poland and it is doubtful that the transport facilities would have enabled their troops to be moved in any useful quantity. Not only there was an almost total absence of diplomatic consultation with the Western Allies, but military collaboration, particularly with the French, was practically non-existent. While the Czechs, themselves, had made an effort to agree on military exchanges, the fear of communism and the effect of the great military purges (in particular the execution of Marshal Tukachevsky) caused the French military to decline any sort of collaboration with their Soviet counterparts. Without some form of joint planning, any intervention in support of Czechoslovakia was likely to be fraught with difficulty. But the most important question is whether if France had followed its Treaty obligations towards the Czechs, would the Soviets have done the same?

Czechoslovakia had had economic and political contacts with the Soviet Union ever since 1922 in what had amounted to the de facto recognition of the Soviet Government. The decision to extend de jure recognition to the Soviet Union was taken in June 1934 by Czechoslovakia and Romania after a meeting of the Council of the Little Entente. Discussions had been delayed, pending a Soviet decision to enter the League of Nations. Given that the Czechs had fought against the Bolsheviks in 1918/1920 with great success, it is a little surprising that the Soviets were willing to ally themselves with the Little Entente. The Entente had been formed in 1920/21 by three countries which, by the Treaty of Trianon, had benefited from the breakup of the Austro-Hungarian Empire. Czechoslovakia was formed by Bohemia, Moravia and Slovakia, Yugoslavia was formed by joining Serbia (on whose behalf Russia had gone to war in 1914), and Montenegro with Slovenia and Croatia. Romania acquired Transylvania from Hungary, Bukovina from Austria, Dobrudja from Bulgaria and Bessarabia from the Soviet Union. The Soviets refused to recognise this latter annexation.

During the many discussions between the Soviets and the Romanians about the right of passage, it was agreed not to enter any discussion about the judicial status of Bessarabia. The Little Entente was designed to protect the three countries against Hungary. There were further Treaties in the 1920s. The Treaties which the French, the Czechs and the Soviets entered into in May 1935 were two bilateral pacts and not as the Soviets would have liked; a single Soviet-Franco-Czechoslovak Pact.

The Soviet Union was not a member of the League of Nations until September 1934. Nor was it a party to the Locarno Treaty. By 1934, the Soviet economy had vastly improved in part due to its five-year plan. It revised its policy of seeking to impose its outworn Comintern tactics on the world and now sought to advocate a policy of collective security. One particular failure of its previous policies had been to advise the German communists to vote for Hitler in his election. In 1930, the Social Democrats in Germany were the dominant political force. It was decided by the 11th Plenum of the Comintern that the Social Democrats, who were the most active in preparing an attack on the Soviet Union, must be opposed at all costs.

To that end, the communists joined with the Nazis in April 1931 when the latter had sought a referendum to overthrow the Socialist-led Government of Prussia. This alliance was repeated in the Presidential Election of March 1932. Again, in July and November, in the elections to the Reichstag, the Communists allied themselves with the Nazis. In 1933, when Hitler was now Chancellor, the Praesidium of the Comintern Executive of the Communist International was still able to take the view that the German Communist support for Hitler was the correct policy.[601] In that year, Germany had left the League of Nations and announced its intention of rearming. In January 1934, Germany signed a non-aggression pact with Poland. Conscription was introduced. Now, albeit somewhat belatedly, Germany was perceived to be a threat to the central European powers as well as to France and, in particular, to the Soviet Union.

The Franco-Soviet Pact in May 1935 was the result of protracted negotiations. It was not an idea which had universal approval in France. It appears that it was the views of the Army, in the persons of Petain, Gamelin and Weygand, early advocates of closer relations with the Soviets, which proved decisive.[602] There was no Military Convention attached. The reason for that was the reluctance of France, in particular of the Prime Minister, Laval and his Minister of War, Fabry, to enter into a Military Agreement because "it gave too many opportunities for war and because the French Government was sincerely attached to peace and any risk of war made it attentive and suspicious."[603]

There were some contacts between the Soviet Military Attaché and a member of Weygand's staff, the main purpose of which was not so much to acquire the Soviet Army as a fighting ally but to prevent any relationship between the Germans and the Soviets. From the Soviet point of view, it was the increasing military strength of Germany and its claim to rearm, together with the reintroduction of conscription, by Germany in March 1935, which persuaded

---

[601] Beloff, M. (1947) *The Foreign Policy of Soviet Russia*, Oxford University Press, Vol.1, p. 68.

[602] Ibid. p. 139.

[603] Beloff, Ibid. Vol. 2, p. 400.

Stalin that Germany was now bent on a policy of aggression. In April, Litvinoff made special reference to this problem at the League of Nations.[604]

It did not stop the Soviets from signing a commercial agreement with Germany on 29 April 1936. In December 1937, Litvinov gave an interview to a French journalist in which he heavily criticised French policy in general and its attitude to the Soviet Union, in particular. When asked how he reacted to the unsatisfactory relationship with France, Litvinov expressed the view that "other arrangements were possible." By this, he meant with Germany. He went on to add that "a German-Soviet rapprochement is possible. In acceding to power, Hitler renewed the Treaty of 1926 with us. He wanted to remain on good terms with us. He changed his attitude when he realised that we were opposed to German expansion in Central Europe and that we wanted to maintain the territorial status quo. He realised also, that by our policy of collective security, we formed an obstacle to his projects...the security of France depended on defending the system of Versailles for which Russia was not responsible."[605]

Coulondre, the French Ambassador in Moscow, pointed out that "if the Russians were abandoned by the French, they would consent to serious sacrifices in order to obtain from Germany, at least a truce that would assure them the several years of respite that they need...if USSR is not with us, it will be against us."[606] The Soviets were no more enamoured of Britain. On 21 September 1938, Pravda published an article in which it set out the Soviet view of British policy. "The Soviet Union examines with composure the question, which particular robber stretches out his hand, for this or that colony or vassal state, for it sees no difference between German and English robbers." [607]

Churchill once famously described Soviet Foreign Policy as 'a riddle, wrapped up in a mystery, inside an enigma'.[608] Britain's view of the Soviet Union had been well summarised in a minute written by Eden after a conversation between Vansittart and Maisky, the Soviet ambassador in London, as early as November 1935. "I have no sympathy to spare for M. Maisky... I hope that the next time M. Maisky comes with complaints, he will be told that our goodwill

---

[604] LONJ pp. 556 ff.

[605] Ragsdale, H. (2004) *The Soviets, the Munich Crisis and the Coming of World War II*, Cambridge University Press, p. 30. DDF series 2, Tom. VII, no 390 (annexe).

[606] Ibid. no 390.

[607] Pravda, 21 September 1938.

[608] BBC Radio Broadcast, 1 October 1939.

depends on his Government's good behaviour ie to keep their noses and fingers out of our domestic politics. I have had some taste of this lately and M. Maisky will get no sympathy from me. I am through with Muscovites of this hue."[609] Nor was he alone in his views. In March 1938, Halifax was described as "being very suspicious of Russia."[610] The German Ambassador reported in June 1938, after an interview with Chamberlain that "his dislike of the Soviet Union is unmistakable."[611]

The Soviet Union had sought other Allies. As far back as May 1934, together with the French, they had tried to set up an Eastern Pact involving Poland, the Little Entente and the Baltic States. It had not been successful. In June, there was a draft of a new agreement, now to include Germany, Poland and Czechoslovakia. Initially, it provided for consultation and mutual assistance in accordance with the Covenant of the League of Nations.

Britain, for its part, now saw the solution to the problems of Europe, not in the narrow confines of little groups but within a general settlement of the various problems, with Germany playing a full part. Germany's participation would afford the best ground for the resumption of negotiations to be directed towards the application of the principle of German equality of rights in armaments within a regime of security for all Nations.[612] Germany and Poland could not agree and in their absence, the French and the Soviets continued their efforts. In February 1935, Germany proposed a new multilateral non-aggression pact, but it contained no reference to any mutual assistance.[613] In the absence of a general agreement, on 2 May 1935, France and the Soviet Union proceeded to enter the Franco-Soviet Pact.

The immediate negotiations leading up to the signing had been conducted between Laval and Litvinoff.[614] Although consultation is mentioned in Article 1, the obligation arose in the context of a threat of aggression against either party. There was no obligation, in the absence of such threat, for any consultation to take place at all. Also, the consultation envisaged only related to the procedure at the League of Nations. The pact imposed no other obligation of consultation

---

[609] DBFP series 2, Vol. XV, no 238 (n).

[610] Harvey, Ibid. p. 121.

[611] DGFP series D, Vol. II, no 266.

[612] CMD 5143, pp. 7–8.

[613] Ibid. pp. 17–19.

[614] Ibid. p. 21 seq.

between the parties, of which there was precious little, either on the Diplomatic Front or more particularly in Military Circles. The Franco-Soviet Pact of May 1935 was one of mutual assistance. It had the effect of keeping the Soviet Union out of the German camp and of giving support to the Eastern Alliance.

In April 1936, the French Ambassador in Moscow wrote: "The main object of the pact of mutual assistance is to confront German expansionism with such a bloc as we could hope would prevent an attack" and he envisaged collaboration in a time of war as giving support by way of providing equipment, provisions, raw materials and munitions as seemed necessary.[615] It was not, therefore, a proper Military Alliance.

The French reticence was due partly to the unpopularity of the Treaty with the public but also because of British reservations, forcibly expressed by Vansittart in April 1937.[616] Long before this, in March 1933, Military Attaches had been exchanged but progress to the pact had been slow. In October 1936, Daladier, then Minister of Defence, took the view that the exchange of staff talks with the Soviets would give the Germans an excuse to categorise them as an attempt at their encirclement. Indeed, the recent reoccupation of the Rhineland had been excused by the Germans as a natural consequence of the ratification of the Franco-Soviet Pact.

For their part, the Soviets wanted to know what help France could actually give them.[617] In the autumn of 1936, General Schweisguth, who was Head of the French Military Mission in the Soviet Union, attended their manoeuvres. He reported that the object of Soviet policy was to thrust back to the West, a storm which it felt was mounting towards the East. Tukhachevsky had issued an invitation to one of the officers of the mission to encourage contact between the French and Soviets. However, Schweisguth spoke to Benes and suggested that it would be more sensible before entering into talks with the Soviets for the Czechs and French to decide on a common policy of cooperation with the Soviets. Benes agreed that it was essential to do so.[618]

On 17 February 1937, Blum and the Soviet Ambassador in Paris, Potemkin discussed how the Soviets could help France and Czechoslovakia in event of war. It was agreed that there were two possibilities. Either troop could cross

---

[615] DDF series 2, Tom. II, no 35.
[616] DDF, Ibid. Tom. V, no. 299.
[617] DDF, Ibid. Tom. IV, no 457.
[618] Ibid. Tom. III, no 343.

Poland or Romania or troops could be sent by sea to France.[619] Neither was a real possibility. Poland and Romania were unwilling and the transport facilities were woefully inadequate. Although in July 1936, a large quantity of arms had been sent from France to the Soviet Union. France could not now supply armaments which it needed for itself. Nevertheless, on 15 April 1937, the French General Staff were finally authorised to go ahead with full Staff Talks. [620] There were still further objections that a German-Polish combination might result from the talks.[621]

In May 1937, the French General Staff now gave serious consideration to the advantages and disadvantages of the proposals for Staff Talks. The advantages were summarised as placing the power of Russia more securely in the French camp and strengthening the security of Poland and Romania against Germany in the unlikely condition that they accepted assistance from the Soviet Union. The disadvantages were more numerous. It would provoke a vehement reaction in Germany. It would risk the disruption of the Franco-Polish alliance and the formation of a German-Polish alliance. It would risk the break-up of the Little Entente and it would offend British opinion. The gravest danger for France would be the provocation of Germany into a declaration of war, coupled with the abandonment of France, by Britain.

In the result, the French decided that their security depended, above all, on a close understanding with Britain, whose strength in the event of conflict was regarded as worth more to France than Soviet strength, as the experience of the Great War had demonstrated. A closer Soviet alliance was only possible if the British agreed. In the event, the arrest of Tukhachevsky on 26 May and the military trials in Moscow, which followed, put an end to immediate talks, which were not resumed until 1939.

A further review in June 1937, led the French to the conclusion that "the internal situation of Soviet Russia and especially the complete instability of the Military High Command considerably diminished the authority of the Soviet officers who would, at present, be designated to establish liaison with the representatives of the French General Staff... It seems then that before engaging

---

[619] Ibid. Tom. IV, no 457.

[620] Ibid. Tom. V, no 285.

[621] Ibid. Tom. VI, no 35, Tom. V, no 480.

in military conversations, it would be prudent to wait for the appearance of certain domestic stability in the USSR."[622]

Although the Soviet-Czech Pact imposed no primary obligation on the Soviets to assist the Czechs in the event of a German invasion, the Soviets have always contended that they would assist the Czechs, irrespective of French involvement. How this unilateral agreement between the Soviet Union and Czechoslovakia came about is something of a mystery. It would have been easy to have had one single Soviet-Franco-Czechoslovak Pact instead of two unilateral pacts with different provisions. One view is that the Soviets introduced the proviso, at Litvinov's insistence, so that the Soviet Union would not be committed to a war with Germany from which France might hold aloof. Another view was that it was introduced by Benes to prevent internal and external enemies of his Government from branding Czechoslovakia as a tool of the Soviets.[623]

It was certainly Litvinov's view that it was inserted by the Czechs. On 23 September 1938, he spoke to the Political Committee of the League Assembly and explained the background "… The Franco-Soviet and Soviet-Czechoslovak Pacts of mutual assistance were the result of action undertaken for the creation of a regional pact of mutual assistance, with the participation of Germany and Poland, based on the principle of collective assistance."

"In consequence of the refusal of those two countries (ie Germany and Poland), France and Czechoslovakia had preferred, instead of a single Soviet-Franco-Czechoslovak Pact, the conclusion of two bilateral pacts. Moreover, it was the Czechoslovak Government that had, at the time, insisted that Soviet-Czechoslovak mutual assistance should be conditional upon assistance by France that was reflected in the Treaty in question."[624]

Further, one of the protocols, which referred to the genesis of the Franco-Soviet Pact, had made it clear that the pact would apply only in the case of aggression by Germany. This gave Germany the pretext to abrogate the provisions of the Locarno Treaty and was further used as an excuse for the decision to invade the Rhineland.

The Soviet view about the question of French troops seeking to remove the German troops from the Rhineland was expressed by Litvinov when he said,

---

[622] Ibid. series 2, Tom. VI, no 35.

[623] Beloff, Ibid. Vol. 1, p. 156.

[624] L.O.N.J. Spec. Suppl. 189, pp. 34–35.

rather surprisingly, that he hoped they would not do it as 'that would mean immediate war'.[625]

[625] FRUS 1936, Vol. 1 212-213.

Chapter Fifteen:
Mixed Messages

Historically, the Soviets have always maintained that in the event of an invasion of Czechoslovakia, even if the French did not fulfil their own treaty obligations, they would have come to the rescue of Czechoslovakia. But subject to what conditions is not clear. On 19 September 1938, Benes summoned the Soviet Minister and asked him to put two questions to Moscow. 1. In the event of a German invasion, would the Soviets render military assistance to the Czechs, if the French did? 2. Would they do so, even if the French did not, but with the approval of the League of Nations under Article 16?

The answer to both questions was 'yes'. The answer to the first question was determined by the terms of the Russo-Czech Pact, but the answer to the second question also involved seeking the approval of the League of Nations.[626] While the French and the Soviets had been suspicious of military cooperation, Soviet-Czech talks were more fruitful. After the signing of the Soviet-Czech alliance, military missions had been exchanged, but no formal staff talks had been held. Exchange of military intelligence, however, was agreed. On 23 April 1938, formal military assistance was offered by Moscow.[627]

In June, Marshal Voroshilov said that the Red Army would not hesitate to cross foreign territory, whether an agreement to that effect existed or not and Benes and Litvinov agreed to proceed gradually in the field of military cooperation. The arrangements for staff talks between the Czechs and the Soviets were, from the Czech point of view, fruitful. Benes thought that cooperation with the Soviet Union after the conclusion of the Treaty of 1935 had, in general, been normal, lasting and consistent.

---

[626] Beloff, Ibid. Vol. 11, p. 151.

[627] New Documents on History of Munich (ed.) Various. (Orbis, Prague 1958). no. 7

In 1935, the Chief of the Czech Air Force paid a visit to the Soviet Union and a Soviet Army Delegation took part in Czech army manoeuvres, saw the Czech armament industry and prepared the way for arms delivery to the Soviets, who also visited Czech airfields. This was followed by a visit by the Czech Chief of Staff to Soviet manoeuvres. During 1936 and 1937, there was cooperation in the sphere of aviation, armaments and the mutual exchange of political and military information. Military Missions were exchanged to examine joint preparations for defence. Agreements were reached about Soviet air assistance to the Czechs in case of German aggression and further exchange of military and intelligence information.

There was also an agreement for the Soviets to supply the Czechs with aircraft. Coulondre in Moscow reported in the spring of 1938, that "his colleague, Fierlinger, head of the Czech Diplomatic Mission, had obtained the immediate delivery of sixty bombers. Twenty have already landed at the airfield of Uggorod in Slovakia. It is thus proved that Russian planes can land in the less immediately threatened part of the country. On their side, the Russians have laid out a great airfield at Vinnitza, considerably nearer the frontier west of Kiev. The Uggorod airfield where the work had to be held up because of a German press campaign is not yet finished and it still has to be supplied with the spare parts and petrol storage needed for the Soviet planes." [628]

The value of any Soviet assistance has been much debated. There is no doubt that the Soviets publicly expressed support for the Czechs and that they constantly affirmed their intention of honouring their Treaty obligations towards the Czechs. The Soviet Representative in Prague, while charged with publicly advising the Czech government to proceed with prudence and moderation towards Germany, was also encouraging them to make concrete proposals for military aid from the Soviets. The Soviets frequently expressed their resolve to participate in the defence of Czechoslovakia. Doubts, however, have arisen as to the reality of such participation because of the difficulties involved in transporting troops to Czechoslovakia. Not only was there the problem of them travelling across either neutral Poland or Romania but also because the rail and road transport systems were, in any event, inadequate for that purpose.

At all times, the Poles were vehemently opposed to the idea of Soviet troops on their soil, even in transit and the Romanians, while less determined to object,

---

[628] Coulondre, Ibid. pp. 136–137.

never formally agreed. When challenged in March 1938 about the difficulties involved in helping the Czechs, the Soviets simply expressed the view that "a way would or had already been found."[629] Thus all Soviet claims that they and they alone were willing to help the Czechs need to be evaluated in the light of the practical difficulties of giving effective military assistance. It has also to be borne in mind that the Soviet obligation was a secondary and not a primary obligation. It is important, therefore, to look at Soviet pronouncements in the light of the foregoing.

The Soviet attitude was perhaps best expressed in a despatch from the French Chargé d'affaires in Moscow when in April 1938, he wrote: "The Soviet Government maintains the principles, which it has not ceased to defend in the course of these last years, of the necessity for the peaceful powers to form a front for peace and to organise themselves to bar the route to the aggressors. The Muscovite Cassandra continues to preach the urgency of action for which there is not, according to it, a moment to lose, but seeing that no one is listening and feeling that it is mistrusted, its voice grows little by little more distant, its accents more embittered."[630]

Shortly after the Anschluss, on 15 March 1938, Litvinov had repeated to the Czech Minister in Moscow and the press what President Kalinin had told a deputation of Czech trade unionists a few days earlier, namely that the Soviet Union would honour its obligations to the Czechs to the full. Litvinov said: "I am therefore able to state on its behalf, (the Soviet government) it is ready as before."[631] On 18 March, he suggested a four-power conference involving Britain, France, the United States and the Soviet Union to agree on measures to deter aggression. The suggestion fell on deaf ears.

It was not a new idea. In March 1935, Stalin had said that "the only way to meet the present situation was by some scheme of pacts. Germany must be made to realise that if she attacked any other nation, she would have Europe against her. As an illustration, he said while chuckling: 'Take those of us present in this room (Stalin, Molotov, Eden and Maisky). Suppose we concluded a mutual assistance pact and suppose Comrade Maisky wanted to attack one of us, what would happen? With our combined strength, we would give Comrade Maisky a hiding.' Com MOLOTOV (humorously) 'That is why Comrade Maisky is

---

[629] Ragsdale, Ibid. p. 82.

[630] DDF series 2, Tom. IX, no 115.

[631] DBFP series 3, Vol. I, no 92.

behaving so humbly'."[632] Maisky did not appreciate Stalin's rather sardonic humour and grinned somewhat nervously.[633]

In the spring of 1938, the Soviet Ambassador in Prague who had been recalled for consultation was instructed to tell Benes that the Soviet Union in conjunction with France was ready to take all necessary steps relating to the security of Czechoslovakia. On 26 April, Kalinin hinted that the USSR might aid Czechoslovakia even if France did not. But nowhere did the Soviets give an unqualified undertaking that they would support the Czechs. Even when war was imminent, they required the approval of the League before being willing to help. Obtaining permission from the Romanians either to overfly or transport troops across their country by road or rail was of vital importance in any consideration of Soviet ability to provide assistance.

By 15 September, the Romanian Government was now allowing Soviet planes to overfly their territory. As a result, at the time of Munich, there were said to be some 200 Soviet planes in Czechoslovakia. Earlier in September, Litvinov had urged Bonnet to approach the Romanians for their cooperation. He also suggested to Payart, the French Chargé d'affaires in Moscow, that steps should be taken to alert the Council of the League so that the procedure of Geneva might be ready to be activated from the moment when aggression occurred.[634] Litvinov got no support from the French in his approach to the League which simply accepted a proposal to abrogate the provisions of the covenant. Again, the League looked powerless. "Covenants, without the sword, are but words and of no strength to secure a man at all." Thomas Hobbes wrote rather bleakly in the seventeenth century.[635]

When Litvinov had spoken at the League of Nations on 21 September, he said: "When, a few days before I left for Geneva, the French Government for the first time (my emphasis) enquired as to our attitude in the event of an attack on Czechoslovakia. I gave in the name of my Government the following perfectly clear and unambiguous reply. 'We intend to fulfil our obligations under the pact and, together with France, to afford assistance to Czechoslovakia by the ways open to us. Our War Department is ready immediately to participate in a conference with representatives of the French and Czechoslovak war

[632] Gorodetsky, Ibid. p. 45.

[633] Avon, Ibid. p. 173.

[634] DDF series 2, Tom. X, no 534.

[635] Thomas Hobbes, Leviathan, Chapter 17; Barnett, Ibid. p. 243.

departments, in order to discuss the measures appropriate to the moment."[636] Nothing occurred. On 23 September, he enquired, rhetorically whether the Soviets should not announce, at least, a partial mobilisation.

On 26 September, Gamelin gave an account of the respective strengths and weaknesses of the various armed forces. During the conference, he received a telephone call from his Chief of Staff, General Jeannel, in Paris, who had just seen the Soviet Military Attaché. Speaking for Voroshilov, the Attaché told General Jeannel that the Soviets had at their disposal 30 divisions of infantry, mass of cavalry, many tank formations and the greater part of their Air Force ready to intervene in the West.[637]

On the same day, a communiqué was issued by the British Foreign Office in which it was stated: "If a German attack is made upon Czechoslovakia, the immediate result must be that France will be bound to come to her assistance and Great Britain and Russia will certainly stand by France." This official communiqué was treated by the Quai d'Orsay and Bonnet as if it were a forgery and thus lost any impact it might have had.[638] But its importance is in Halifax associating the Soviets with assistance to the Czechs. Transport of troops to the Czechs was not the only help which the Soviets could have given them. East Prussia was a short distance from the Soviet border and within easy flying range of Soviet bombers.

What else they could have done was set out in answer to a conversation which Litvinov had had with the German Ambassador, Schulenberg on 26 August. Schulenberg had repeatedly asked Litvinov what the Soviet Union could do in the event of war. Litvinov said that the Soviet Union had promised its support to Czechoslovakia and would keep her word but was cagey about how that was to be achieved. Schulenberg thereupon consulted his own military and Naval Attachés. He received the following advice. "1. The Soviet Union is attempting to force Britain and France to take the initiative, while it, itself, will hold back... 2. It will not attack Germany not having a common frontier but will mobilise the Western Military districts. 3. It can attack Germany from the air. 4. By employing U-boats, light naval forces and naval aircraft and also by laying mines, the Soviet Union could considerably disrupt German shipments of ore from Sweden and Northern Norway. 5. The Soviet Union can attack East Prussia

---

[636] SDFP Vol 3, p. 303. DDF, Ibid. Tom. II, no 253.

[637] Gamelin, Ibid. Servir 2. p. 348.

[638] Werth, Ibid. p. 243.

across the Baltic by naval and land aircraft and can also interrupt sea communication between the Reich and East Prussia."

That this threat of bombing would not have been an empty threat is well illustrated by the German reaction in the summer of 1940 to a few bombs falling on Berlin. Hitler immediately ordered the Luftwaffe to stop bombing British airfields and to bomb London instead. It was a move which some historians believe was decisive in the Battle of Britain. 6. The Soviet Union would supply massive war materials but not troops.[639]

It is not entirely clear whether the Romanians would have continued to object to the transport of Soviet troops across their territory. Article 123 of the Romanian Constitution was the main obstacle. It read: "No foreign armed force may be admitted into the service of the State, nor enter or cross the territory of Romania except by virtue of a specific law." The other problem was the question of Bessarabia. It had been annexed by the Romanians in 1918 after the Soviet revolution but the Soviets had refused to recognise its legitimacy. For a while, Litvinov and Titulescu, the Romanian Foreign Minister, entered into a gentleman's agreement to put the question of Bessarabia on the back burner.

The Soviets had made it clear at an early stage that as a result of their Treaty with the Czechs, they intended, if war came, to come to the assistance of the Czechs across Romania with or without the consent of the Bucharest Government. The Romanian General Staff had drawn up plans in 1936 to permit Soviet troops so to do and were ordered to draw up an appropriate itinerary. In 1937, King Carol had assured Gamelin that he would allow the Soviets to cross Romanian territory but that it must remain a secret.[640]

It was also thought that Article 16 of the Covenant obliged Romania, as a member State, to permit the passage of Soviet troops in the event of aggression. However, the dismissal of Titulescu and a change of Government in Bucharest resulted in a reconsideration of the idea. A scandal involving the disappearance of the Soviet Chargé d'affaires, Feder Butenko, in February 1938, exacerbated relations between Moscow and Bucharest. In March 1938, after the Anschluss, the Romanians had made it clear now that there would be no formal agreement to support the French and that they would make no irreversible decision in advance.

---

[639] DGFP series D, Vol. II, no 601 & 629–631. Ragsdale, Ibid. pp. 129–130
[640] Gamelin, Ibid. Servir 2, p. 279.

Apart from the constitutional problems, there were other objections to the passage of Soviet troops across Romania. It would interfere with their Polish alliance and the public was, in any event, against the idea. The Czechs understood the problem. Krofta wrote: "From the Czechoslovak point of view, it would be sufficient, in the immediate future, to keep the question open right up to the moment when its actual settlement became necessary or until Soviet-Romanian relations are generally improved and harmonised."[641]

In July, the French had tried again but were unsuccessful. Indeed, on 25 July, Comnen, the Romanian Foreign Minister, told Bonnet that Romania would never tolerate the passage of Soviet troops through her territory. A new constitution repeated the previous ban on foreign troops. Thierry, the French Ambassador, in May and Bonnet in September, got the same answers. It is clear that the Romanians were determined to keep their options open, a view reiterated by King Carol in July.[642] However, in September, Krofta told the American Minister that "all was prepared for the passage of Soviet troops over Romania."[643] Romania eventually agreed to the passage of Soviet troops on 24/25 September. The difficulty was that the agreement was so hedged by various provisos that it was near unworkable. The Soviets were to be allowed the passage of no more than 100,000 men and the arrangements had to be completed in six days.

The question of whether Soviet troops would have been allowed to cross Romania and whether they could have done so in effective numbers, therefore, remains something of a mystery today. It was never put to the test. All one can surmise is that if France had fulfilled her obligations under its Treaty with the Czechs and the Soviets had become involved, it is very likely that the Romanians, faced with that scenario, would have given way. This view is confirmed by a conversation which Churchill had with Maisky on 2 September. Maisky told Churchill that Litvinov had told the French that the Soviets would fulfil their obligations and that the Romanian problem could probably be overcome.[644] On 24 September, Maisky asked Litvinov, "Poland and Romania-will they let us through?" to which Litvinov replied: "We have information that

---

[641] New Documents, no 16.

[642] DDF, Ibid. Tom. X, no 194.

[643] FRUS 1938, Vol. I, p. 615.

[644] Churchill, Ibid. pp. 294–295.

Romania will, particularly if the League of Nations pronounces Czechoslovakia, a victim of aggression."[645]

It is highly improbable, however, that the Soviet Union would have been willing to go to war, on behalf of the Czechs, on its own, (or to give any sort of undertaking to that effect). What is much clearer is that the Soviets did supply the Czechs with military equipment and that before Munich, the Soviets had carried out some mobilisation on its Western Borders against the possibility of being involved.

What was the extent of Soviet assistance? The Romanians did not object to Soviet aircraft overflying their territory. Krofta admitted as much to the Poles in June, telling them that there was an agreement with Romania for these overflights. Reports from various Polish and Romanian sources confirmed that in 1938, regular flights were made. Ever since April 1937, the Czechs had been purchasing 61 SB-2 bombers, coupled with a licence to produce 161 more in Czechoslovak industries.

From the middle of September, the Polish Consul in Kishinev made a number of reports of Soviet military aid being sent through Romania to the Czechs. A report from the French Military Attaché in Bucharest, at the same time, described a conversation he had with the Romanian Chief of Staff in which the latter said that the Soviets were gathering a special force on their Western border which would give them an opportunity to intervene.[646]

But the question of Romanian permission was not the only problem. Even if permission were granted, how were the troops to be transported? Criticisms of the transport facilities in both the Soviet Union and Romania appear in a number of contemporary documents. Neither the roads nor the railways were capable of carrying numbers of soldiers or their equipment without very substantial delay.[647]

Had the Soviets taken any and, if so, what, steps to mobilise their troops or even to put them on a war footing? The Soviets had always believed that if all the Great Powers stood up to Hitler, he would back down. Although such an approach might involve the risk of war with Germany, it was a risk that the Soviet Union claimed it was prepared to take. But the Soviet approach to the problem

---

[645] Maisky, I. (1966) *The Munich Drama*, New Times, p. 28.

[646] DDF, Ibid. Tom. XI, no 457.

[647] DGFP series D, Vol. II, no 434. DBFP series 3, Vol. I, no 411 (enclosure), Vol. II. no 898. DDF, Ibid. Tom. XI, no 96. DDF, Ibid. Tom. VIII, no 445/446.

of Czechoslovakia, as in all its political decision, is full of contradiction and something of an enigma. It was never consistent. On 26 August, Litvinov told the German Ambassador that "the Soviet Union regarded the Sudeten German question as an internal affair of Czechoslovakia; the Soviet Union had not interfered in any way and had not given the Czech Government any advice either in one direction or the other… The Soviets had always been in favour of the right of self-determination of peoples."[648]

On 21 September, after the Czechs had accepted the Anglo-French terms, Litvinov once again spoke at Geneva. He said that the Czech acceptance gave the Soviets the moral right to be relieved of any obligation to the Czechs, but he continued that "the Russians were not looking for any such pretext and that Russia regarded the original terms of the Treaty as still valid and that Russia was prepared to defend Czechoslovakia, provided the French did the same."[649] On 23 September, Litvinov had proposed bringing the question of the Sudeten issue before the League of Nations, relying on Article 16 of the Covenant.

This article was designed to apply military sanctions to an aggressor. This followed a speech by Butler, then the British Undersecretary of State for Foreign Affairs, when he said: "The circumstances in which occasion for international action under Article 16 may arise, the possibility of taking such action and the nature of the action to be taken, cannot be determined in advance; each case must be considered on its merits. In consequence, while the right of any member of the League to take any measures of the kind contemplated by Article 16 remains intact, no unconditional obligation exists to take such measures."[650] With other countries subscribing to this view, the political committee reported to the assembly that "there is a general agreement that the military measures contemplated by Article 16 are not compulsory." Butler could not have made it clearer that Britain was determined to take no steps to support the Czechs. On 30 September, on the British initiative, it was resolved to abrogate Article 16.[651]

On 23 September, Litvinov had also observed that "the Soviet Government had no obligation to Czechoslovakia in the event of French indifference to an attack on her. In that event, the Soviet Government might come to the aid of Czechoslovakia in virtue of a voluntary decision on its part or in virtue of a

---

[648] DGFP, Ibid. Vol. II, no 396.

[649] DDF series 2, Tom. II, no 253 & 367.

[650] L.O.N.J. 1938, no 183, pp. 42–45. Ragsdale, Ibid. pp. 130–131.

[651] L.O.N.J., Ibid. 189, p. 103. Ragsdale, Ibid.

decision by the League of Nations."[652] In view of the foregoing, the claim that they would have supported the Czechs unilaterally, much touted by the Soviets subsequently, has a rather hollow ring.

Apart from the transport problems, there was another difficulty facing the Soviets if they were to go to war to help the Czechs. This was the purge of the military in 1937 and 1938. The effect was to remove 51 out of 57 corps commanders and 140 of 186 divisional commanders. While there was general agreement in military circles that the Czechs would give a good account of themselves, there was equally general agreement among the Military Attachés in Moscow that the Red Army was quite incapable of any form of offensive action which was amply borne out by their disastrous showing in their subsequent invasion of Finland in 1939 and 1940.

Did the Soviets, in fact, take any practical steps to support the Czechs? On 24 September, France had declared a partial mobilisation. The Soviets had done the same but only announced it publicly after the French followed suit. According to Maisky, when he met Litvinov on 24 September, he said to him, "What you proposed to the British just now means war... Has it been seriously considered in Moscow and decided in earnest?" "Yes", said Litvinov, "it has been decided in earnest. When I was leaving for Geneva, we had started concentrating troops on the Romanian and Polish border. It is nearly a fortnight since then and I would say we have at least 25 to 30 divisions there now."[653]

The Soviets reported to the French that they were ready to mobilise 30 divisions. However, a report from the German Counsellor, at the Embassy in Moscow, casts some serious doubt about the accuracy of the reports of the extent of Soviet mobilisation. On 3 and 10 October, he reported that Moscow had failed to take even preliminary measures of mobilisation. The Soviets disagree. Zakharov, for instance, Assistant to the Chiefs of the General Staff, claimed that 60 infantry divisions, 16 cavalry divisions, tank corps, tank brigades and air brigades were mobilised.[654] It is not easy to ascertain where the truth lies.

What is quite clear from all the various documents and speeches is that the Soviets were only going to help Czechoslovakia if the French did the same or Germany were branded an aggressor by members of the League of Nations. Even if the Soviets did, in fact, mobilise and put themselves on a war footing, nowhere

---

[652] L. O. N. J., Ibid. 189, pp. 34-35.
[653] Maisky, Ibid. p. 28.
[654] Ragsdale, Ibid. pp. 140–148.

do we find any hard evidence that, absent French support, or that of members of the League of Nations, the Soviets ever gave unqualified support to the Czechs. Given their Treaty obligations, they had no duty so to do. That is not, however, a good reason to claim, as they did frequently, that they would have been willing, unilaterally, to assist the Czechs.[655]

In 1948, Vansittart writing about Soviet policy at the time of Munich said: "... I have changed my mind since 1938. I was an advocate of Anglo-Russian cooperation to prevent war. In the light of all subsequent Soviet conduct, I have long been convinced that we should have been double-crossed as indeed we were in 1939. Stalin's infamous deal with Hitler whereby he got the Baltic States and half of Poland—and plotted to divide the world with his fellow dictator—made plain his real motive, which was to precipitate the war and get the maximum profit from it." [656]

On 21 September, Czech radio reported: "... Since the Soviet Union could afford us military help, only in company with France or alternatively if France would not act until Germany had been declared an aggressor by the League, we found ourselves faced with the threat of war..." [657] The Czechs clearly realised the parameters of Soviet assistance. Soviet Foreign policy has always been dictated by something akin to paranoia. This is, perhaps, unsurprising given the history of the Communist revolution.

The military purges necessarily had their effect on the Soviet approach to the threat of war, but the diplomatic purges at the Narkomindel (the People's Commissariat for Foreign Affairs) were equally devastating, making it almost impossible to pursue level headed policies. There were three waves. The first was at the end of 1937. The second gathered momentum after the Munich Conference and the third occurred in May 1939. Stalin was determined to break up the old cliques formed from a cosmopolitan, polyglot and independent-minded retinue, in many cases, members of the intelligentsia from the Tsarist days.

They were replaced by a new generation, owing their promotion to Stalin personally. At least 62% of top-level diplomats and officials among the old guard were wiped out, 16% only remaining in a post and the Office was infiltrated by

---

[655] Maisky, Ibid. pp. 79, 83 & 84. Beloff, Ibid. Vol. 2, p. 163. Wheeler-Bennett, Ibid. p. 179.

[656] Vansittart, L. (1948) *The Listener November*, pp. 676–677.

[657] Beloff, Ibid. Vol. 2, p. 155.

NKVD[658] officials. Circumspection became the order of the day, as illustrated by Maisky's diaries.

Between August and December 1937, there were no more than three entries. Litvinoff's deputy was shot in 1938 and Litvinoff was dismissed in 1939.[659] Stalin's approach to purges is reflected in this passage from Maisky. "One should never forget the words of Mirabeau (a figure from the French Revolution) who said, some 140 years ago, that 'revolution cannot be made with lavender oil."[660]

The events of 1938 were no different. The Soviet Union did express a desire to enter into a diplomatic, as well as military, dialogue with the Western Allies and Czechoslovakia. The Western Allies exhibited very little interest in Soviet diplomacy. Although the Czechs were more forthcoming, the Soviets can scarcely be blamed for how the Czechs came to find themselves deserted by the Allies.

The Soviet Union was not a party to the events at Versailles. It was not consulted about the Runciman mission. It was not consulted about the visits to Berchtesgaden, Bad Godesberg or Munich itself. It was not privy to the views of Chamberlain about any of the negotiations, nor invited, at any time, to give advice or to discuss how best the problem of Czechoslovakia could be resolved. For the Western Allies, the Soviet Union might simply not have existed.

The Soviet Union, of course, had its own problems, both internally and externally. Externally, it was suspicious that the Western Allies would be only too happy for Germany to turn East. This would involve the Soviet Union in a war with Germany, which the former might be required to fight alone. The Allies could then sit back in peaceful contemplation of the Nazis and the Communists destroying each other. The behaviour of the Soviets in the Second World War echoes these suspicions (shades of 1942 'Second Front Now'). Of all the countries involved, the Soviet Union, after Czechoslovakia, has the least reason to be criticised save, perhaps, for the former's attempts to rewrite history.

---

[658] The People's Commissariat for Internal Affairs, abbreviated NKVD, was responsible at this time for both public law enforcement and secret police activities.

[659] Gorodetsky, Ibid. P. 90.

[660] Gorodetsky, Ibid. p. 26.

Chapter Sixteen:
Conclusion

Why?

Czechoslovakia: For the Czechs, there are three questions. 1. Why did they agree at Versailles to include in their territories a very substantial number of minorities? 2. Why did they allow themselves to be bullied by the Western Allies? and 3. Why did they not refuse to accept the terms negotiated on their behalf, thus compelling France and the Soviet Union to fulfil their Treaty obligations? It is clear that at Versailles, Benes was conscious of the problem of minorities and was willing to make some adjustments but believed that the country could become, in modern terminology, multi-ethnic. Further, it is clear that the invasion by the Germans was quite unrelated to the Sudeten problem. As for being bullied, they had placed their faith in the Western Allies and believed until late on that they and the Soviets would fulfil their obligations. The Czechs could not contemplate fighting Germany alone. Once they realised that they would get no support from the Western Allies, sadly, they had no alternative but to give in. If they had fought alone, they could hardly have been worse off.

Germany: At the heart of Germany's behaviour lay its long-held desire for lebensraum and *grossraumwirtschaft*, the sphere of economic domination of Europe. German history from 1870 until June 1941 bears eloquent testimony to this overwhelming ambition. Its humiliation at Versailles, involving the loss of its colonies and Alsace and Lorraine, together with the occupation of the Ruhr and the Saar, did nothing to diminish this determination. The problems of the Sudeten Germans proved the ideal excuse for the long-planned invasion of Czechoslovakia. The feebleness of the Western Allies did nothing to discourage the Germans in their pursuit of power. The reason why the Generals failed to thwart Hitler's plans were twofold. They had sworn an oath of allegiance to Hitler personally and Prussian standards still obtained in the army. Secondly,

Hitler's successes in the Rhineland and the Anschluss had enabled him to emasculate the power of the Generals. What of the resistance? Given the constant threat from the secret police, it is difficult to believe that a disparate band of resisters, however brave, but all with different agenda, were, after Hitler's successes, ever going to unseat him.

France: The French are also the villains of Munich. On their behaviour depended the actions of Britain, the Soviet Union and Czechoslovakia. They were the lynchpin on which everything else depended. Why, then, were they so feeble in support of a country which they had created and whose inception they had supported? No doubt, things looked very different in 1936–1938 from the heady days of 1918. But that fails to explain the almost total indifference shown to the plight of the Czechs or the resistance to Soviet overtures. Even more surprising, given that within the memory of two generations, France had twice been invaded, it failed to face up to the problems created by a renascent Germany. Internally, France was riven by factions. The Military seemed to lack courage while the Politicians lacked quality. Neither had any backbone. The constant changes of Government failed to produce any coherent or settled policies. Abroad, there were very real problems with Spain and Italy. The French hope, that by handing over the problem of Czechoslovakia to Britain, France could avoid its own responsibility, was doomed to failure from the outset. The best description of France's treatment of the Czechs in 1938, is that "France behaved with consummate infamy".[661]

Great Britain: A desire for peace in Europe was a noble sentiment. But to pursue it at all cost (those costs being borne by others) suggests incompetence. It was Chamberlain who decided, personally, to take charge of the problem of peace in Central Europe and to take on himself the role of spokesman for the Czechs. This, he did, without any meaningful consultation with the French, the Soviets or particularly with the Czechs. It was his personal failure to appreciate the nature of German ambitions while putting unfailing trust in Hitler's word. These were two major factors in Britain's contribution to the events of 1938. While Chamberlain was, no doubt, entitled to treat the German resisters with some scepticism, it does not explain why the information they brought was totally ignored. And to go to three meetings with Hitler, without ever seeking advice, from the French, the Czechs or even from the Embassy in Prague has all

---

[661] Seton-Watson. R.W. (1943) *A History of the Czechs and Slovaks*, London: Hutchinson and Co. Ltd., p. 364.

the hallmarks of arrogance (intellectual or otherwise) and an inflated sense of self-importance. That Britain had no legal obligations to the Czechs is beside the point. Having appointed himself as their sole protagonist, Chamberlain owed a clear moral duty to protect them. Sadly, his personal defects prevented him from doing so.

The Soviet Union: The Soviet obligations depended either on the French or on the League of Nations. In the event, they were not required to do more than they did. This amounted to encouraging the Czechs and providing some military equipment without actually going to war on their behalf. The Soviets were entitled to be very suspicious that, absent France's involvement, they might well be left as the only support for the Czechs. They considered that there was a plot by the Western Allies to ensure that the two Great Powers, Germany and the Soviet Union, fought it out alone while the Allies sat back and looked on.[662] Nor indeed did the behaviour of the Allies do anything to disabuse them of that suspicion. Failure to agree to any sort of collaboration with the Soviets was one element in that suspicion. It was repeated in the summer of 1939. It was that fear coupled with the difficulties of actually providing any assistance, which explains why the Soviet Union never gave the Czechs an unqualified message of support.

---

[662] Maisky, I. (Trans. Rothstein, A.) (1964) *Who helped Hitler?* London: Hutchinson, p. 77–91.

Bibliography Munich

Manuscript Collections

Sir Alexander Cadogan	Churchill College Cambridge
Neville Chamberlain	Birmingham University Library
Lord Halifax	Borthwick Institute, University of York (The Hickleton Papers)
Jan Smuts	Smuts Papers, South African Archives, Pretoria.
Viscount Cecil	British Museum
Sir Eric Phipps	Churchill College, Cambridge
Cabinet Papers	National Archives
Foreign Office Papers	National Archives
Dominion Office Papers	National Archives

Newspapers

The Listener

The Daily Mail

Published Official Documents

British Documents on Foreign Affairs Volumes 3 and 10, Universal Publications of America. CMD 5143, 5847 and 5848. Czech Territorial Claims.

Dictionary of National Biography.

Documents and Materials relating to the eve of the Second World War. Dirksen (ed.). Foreign Language Publishing House, 1947.

Documents Diplomatique Francais 1932–1939, Series 1 and 2, Imprimerie Nationale, 1964–1986.

Documents on British Foreign Policy 1919–1939 Third Series, Volume I, Woodward, E. and Butler, R. (eds.) His Majesty's Stationery Office, 1949.

Documents on British Foreign Policy 1919–1939 Second Series, Volume XIX, Medlicott, W. and Dakin, D. (eds.). Her Majesty's Stationery Office, 1982.

Documents on British Foreign Policy 1919–1939 Third Series, Volume IV, Woodward, E. and Butler, R. (eds.) His Majesty's Stationery Office, 1951.

Documents on British Foreign Policy 1919–1939 First Series, Volume VI, Woodward, E. and Butler, R. (eds.) Her Majesty's Stationery Office, 1956.

Documents on British Foreign Policy 1919–1939 Third Series, Volume II, Woodward, E. and Butler, R. (eds.) His Majesty's Stationery Office, 1949.

Documents on German Foreign Policy 1918–1939 Series C, Volume IV, Her Majesty's Stationery Office, 1962.

Documents on German Foreign Policy 1918–1945 Series D, Volume I, His Majesty's Stationery Office, 1949.

Documents on German Foreign Policy 1918–1945 Series D, Volume II, His Majesty's Stationery Office, 1950.

Documents on German Foreign Policy 1918–1945 Series D, Volume IV, His Majesty's Stationery Office, 1951.

Foreign Relations of the United States 1918 Supplement WWI. Government Printing Office, Washington, D.C., 1933.

Foreign Relations of the United States 1937, Volume I. Government Printing Office, Washington, D.C., 1954.

Foreign Relations of the United States 1938, Volume I and II. Government Printing Office, Washington. D. C., 1956.

Foreign Relations of the United States 1918, Lansing Papers, Government Printing Office, Washington, D.C., 1939–1940.

Foreign Relations of the United States 1936 Volume I and II, Government Printing Office, Washington, D. C., 1953.

Foreign Relations of the United States. Peace Conference, Government Printing Office, Washington, D.C., 1942–1947.

French Parliamentary Commission of Enquiry, 1948.

League of Nations' Journal

New Documents on History of Munich (ed.) Various. Prague: Orbis, 1958.

Parliamentary Debates, House of Commons, Fifth Series.

Soviet Documents on Foreign Policy Degrassi (ed.) Volume III, Oxford University Press, 1953.

Trial of the Major War Criminals Before the International Military Tribunal, Nuremberg, 1946.

Published Sources

Adamthwaite, A. (1977) *France and the Coming of the Second World War*, London: Frank Cass.

Adamthwaite, A. (1995) *Grandeur and Misery*, London: Arnold.

Aldrich, R. J. (2010) *GCHQ*, London: Harper Press.

Alexander, M. S. (1963) *The Republic in Danger*, Cambridge: Cambridge University Press.

Amery. L. (1955) *My Political Life: The Unforgiving Years 1929–1940*, Hutchinson, Vol. III.

Andrew, C. (1985) *Secret Service: The Making of the British Intelligence Community*, London: Heinemann.

Avon, L. (1962) *Facing the Dictators: The Eden Memoirs*, Cassell.

Barnett, C. (1972) *The Collapse of British Power*, New York: William Morrow & Co. Inc.

Beevor, A. (2006) *The Battle of Spain*, London: Weidenfeld and Nicolson.

Beloff, M. (1947) *The Foreign Policy of Soviet Russia*, Oxford University Press, Vol 1 and 2.

Benes, E. (1954) *Memoirs of Dr Eduard Benes*, London: George Allen and Unwin Ltd.

Benes, E. (1928) *War Memoirs*, London: George Allen and Unwin Ltd.

Bouverie, T. (2019) *Appeasing Hitler*, Bodley Head.

Boyce, R. and Robertson. E. (eds.). (1989) *Paths to War. New Essays on the Origin of the Second World War*, Macmillan.

Brownell, W. and Billings, R. (1987) *So Close to Greatness: A Biography of William C. Bullitt*, New York: Macmillan.

Bruce, L. R. (1938) *Guns and Butter*, Putnam.

Bruegel, J. W. (1973) *Czechoslovakia before Munich*, Cambridge University Press.

Bullitt, W. (1973) *For the President, Personal and Secret*, London: Deutch.

Chamberlain, N. (1939) *The Struggle for Peace*, London: Hutchinson.

Churchill, S. W. (1948) *The Second World War*, London: Cassell & Co. Ltd., Vol. I.

Colvin, I. (1971) *The Chamberlain Cabinet*, London: Camelot Press Ltd.

Colvin, I. (1951) *Chief of Intelligence*, Victor Gollancz.

Colvin, I. (1965) *Vansittart in Office*, London: Victor Gollancz.

Cook, C. and Ramsden, J. (1973) *By-elections in British Politics*, London: The Macmillan Press Ltd.

Cooper, D. (1954) *Old Men Forget*, London: Rupert Hart Davis.

Coulondre, R. (1950) *De Staline à Hitler*, Paris: Hachette.

Czernin, O. (1919) *Im Weltkriege*, Berlin: Verlege bei Ullstein.

Daladier, E. (1939) *Defence du Pays*, Paris.

Davies, J. E. (1941) *Mission to Moscow*, New York: Simon and Schuster.

Dilkes, D. (ed.) (1971) *The Diaries of Sir Alexander Cadogan 1938–1945*, Cassel and Co.

Duroselle, J-B. (1979) *La Decadence 1932–1939*, Paris: Imprimerie Nationale.

Dutourd, J. (1957) *Three Taxis of the Marne*, Secker and Warburg.

Emmerson, (1977) *The Rhineland crisis*, London: Temple Smith Ltd.

Eubank, K. (1963) *Munich*, Oklahoma: Norman: University of Oklahoma Press.

Faber, D. (2008) *Munich: The 1938 Appeasement Crisis*, London: Simon and Schuster.

Feiling, S. K. (1946) *Life of Neville Chamberlain*, London: Macmillan and Co. Ltd.

Fenby, J. (2010) *The General*, London: Simon and Schuster.

Flandin, P. (1947) *Politique Francaise 1919-1940*, Paris.

Foerster, W. (1953) *Generaloberst Ludwig Beck*, Munich: Isar Verlag.

Fry, M. L. I. and Goldstein, E. (eds.) (1999) *The Munich Crisis 1938*, Frank Cass.

Gagan, K. and Kvacek, R. (1965) *Germany and Czechoslovakia 1918–1945* Prague: Orbis.

Gamelin, M. (1946) *Servir*, Paris, Vol II.

Gedye, G. (1939) *Betrayal in Central Europe*, New York.

Gedye, G. (1939) *Fallen Bastions*, London: Victor Gollancz.

Gilbert, M. and Gott, R. (1967) *The Roots of Appeasement*, New York.

Gorodetsky, G. (ed.) (2015) *The Maisky Diaries 1932–1943*, Yale University Press.

Harvey, J. (ed.) (1970) *The Diplomatic Diaries of Oliver Harvey 1937–1940*, London: Collins.

Hauser, H. (1915) *Methodes Allemands d'expansion economique*, Paris.

Heineman, J. (1979) *Hitler's First Foreign Minister, Constantin Freiherr von Neurath*, Los Angeles: University of California Press.

Henderson, S. N. (1940) *Failure of a Mission*, London: Hodder and Stoughton.

Hitchcock, E. B. (1940) *"I Built a Temple for Peace": The Life of Edward Benes*, New York: Harper Bros.

Hitler, A. (1969) *Mein Kampf. (Trans. Manheim, R.)*, Hutchinson.

Hoffman, P. (1988) *German Resistance to Hitler*, Mass: Harvard University Press.

Kalvoda, J. (1986) *The Genesis of Czechoslovakia*, New York: Columbia University.

Laffan, R. D. G. (1950) *Survey of International Affairs*, Oxford: University Press, Vol. II.

Lentin, A. (2010) *General Smuts*, London: Hans Publishing Ltd.

Lias, G. (1940) *Benes of Czechoslovakia*, Allen and Unwin.

Lindbergh, C. (1970) *The Wartime Journals of Charles A. Lindbergh*, New York.

Gladwyn, L. (1972) *Memoirs of Lord Gladwyn*, Weidenfeld and Nicolson.

Livingstone, D. A. (1935) *The Peace Ballot*, Victor Gollancz.

George, D. L. (1932) *The Truth about the Peace Treaties*, London: Victor Gollancz, Vol. II.

Mackenzie, C. (1946) *Dr Benes*, London: George Harrap and Co. Ltd.

Maisky, I. (1966) *The Munich Drama*, New Times.

Maisky, I. (Trans. Rothstein, A.) (1964) *Who helped Hitler?* London: Hutchinson.

Masaryk, T. G. (1927) *The Making of a State*, London: George Allen and Unwin Ltd.

Masaryk, T. G. (1918) *The New Europe (The Slav Standpoint)*, London: Eyre and Spottiswode.

Masaryk, T. G. (1933) *The Path of Democracy*, Vol. 1, Prague.

McMeekin, S. (2010) *The Berlin-Baghdad Express: The Ottoman Empire and Germany's Bid for World Power* London: Allen Lane.

Middlemas, K. and Barnes, J. (1969) *Baldwin*, London: Weidenfeld and Nicolson.

Murray, W. (1984) *The Change in the European Balance of Power*, New Jersey: Princeton University Press.

Namier, L. B. (1952) *In the Nazi Era*, New York.

Néré, J. (1975) the *Foreign Policy of France 1914 to 1945 (Trans)* Routledge & Keegan Paul Ltd.

Nicolson, H. (1939) *Why Britain is at War*, London: Penguin.

Nicolson, N. (ed) (1966) *Harold Nicolson: Diaries and Letters 1930–1939*, Collins.

Nicosia, F. and Stokes. L. (ed.) (1990) *Germans Against Nazism*, Oxford, Berg Publishers.

Nogueres, H. (Trans. O'Brian, P.O.) (1965) *Munich or the Phony Peace*, Weidenfeld and Nicolson.

Olivova, V. (1972) *The Doomed Democracy*, Sidgwick and Jackson.

Ovendale, R. (1975) *Appeasement and the English Speaking World*, Cardiff: University of Wales Press.

Perman, D. (1962) *The Shaping of the Czechoslovak State*, Leiden: EJ Brill.

Preston, P. (2006) *The Spanish Civil War*, London: Harper Perennial.

Ragsdale, H. (2004) *The Soviets, the Munich Crisis and the Coming of World War II*, Cambridge University Press.

Rauschning, H. (1939) *Hitler Speaks (Trans)*, London: Thornton Butterworth Ltd.

Ripka, H. (1939) *Munich: Before and After*, London: Victor Gollancz.

Roberts, A. (1997) *The Holy Fox*, London: Phoenix Press.

Sargent, S. O. *Dictionary of National Biography*.

Sauvy, A. (1972) *Histoire Economique de la France entre les deux guerres*, Paris.

Seton-Watson. R.W. (1943) *A History of the Czechs and Slovaks*, London: Hutchinson and Co. Ltd.

Seton-Watson, R. W. (1943) *Masaryk in England*, Cambridge: The University Press.

Seymour, C. (1938) *Czechoslovak Frontiers*, Yale Review.

Smelser, R. (1975) *The Sudeten Problem 1933–1938*, Folkestone: Dawson.

Sowerwine, C. (2001) *France since 1970*, Basingstoke, Hampshire: Palgrave.

Steed, H. W. (1913) *The Hapsburg Monarchy*, London: Constable and Company Ltd.

Stehlin, P. (1964) *Temoignage pour l'histoire*, Paris.

Strang, L. W. (1956) *Home and Abroad*, London: Andre Deutsch.

Streseman, G. Vermachtnis. Berlin 1932

Temperley, H. W. V. (1921) *A history of the Peace Conference of Paris*, London: Forgotten Books.

Temperley, H. W. V. (1966) *The Foreign Policy of Canning*, London: Frank Cass & Co. Ltd.

Thomas, L. (2003) *The Spanish Civil War*, London: Penguin Books Ltd.

Tomas–Symonds, N. (2010) *Attlee: A Life in Politics*, London: I. B. Tauris.

von Hassell, U. (1947) *The von Hassell Diaries 1938–1944*, New York: Garden City.

von Klemperer, K. (1933) *German Resistance Against Hitler*, Oxford: Clarendon Press.

Wandycz, P. (1962) *France and Her Eastern Allies 1919–1925*, Minnesota Press.

Wandycz, P. (1968) *The Twilight of French Eastern Alliances 1926-1936*, New Jersey: Princeton University Press.

Watt, D. C. (1966) 'German plans for the reoccupation of the Rhineland', *Journal of Contemporary History*.

Watt, D. C. (ed. Fry, M.) (1965) *Personalities and Politics Part 3*, University of Southern California, Frank Cass.

Weinberg, G. (1980) *The Foreign Policy of Hitler's Germany Starting World War II*, Chicago: University of Chicago Press.

Werth, A. (1942) *The Twilight of France. 1938–1940*, New York.

Wheeler Bennett, J. (1953) *The Nemesis of Power*, Macmillan and Co.

Zeman, Z. and Klimeek, A. (1997) *The Life of Edvard Benes 1884–1948,* Oxford: Clarendon Press.